Library of
Davidson College

BURT FRANKLIN: RESEARCH & SOURCE WORKS SERIES 869
Philososphy Monograph Series 84

VOLTAIRE'S MARGINALIA
ON ROUSSEAU

DISCOURS.

SECONDE PARTIE.

LE premier qui ayant enclos un terrain, s'avisa de dire, *ceci est à moi*, & trouva des gens assés simples pour le croire, fut le vrai fondateur de la société civile. Que de crimes, de guerres, de meurtres, que de miséres & d'horreurs n'eût point épargnés au Genre-humain celui qui arrachant les pieux ou comblant le fossé, eût crié à ses semblables. / Gardez-vous d'écouter cet imposteur ; Vous êtes perdus, si vous oubliez que les fruits sont à tous, & que la Terre n'est à personne :) Mais il y a grande apparence, qu'alors les choses en étoient déjà venües au point de ne pouvoir plus durer comme elles étoient ; car cette idée de propriété, dependant de beaucoup d'idées antérieures qui n'ont

[Voltaire's marginal annotations:]

quoy celui qui a planté semé, et enclos n'a pas droit au fruit de ses peines

quoy cet homme injuste, ce voleur auroit-été le bienfaiteur du genre humain ! voylà la philosophie d'un gueux qui voudroit que les riches fussent volez par les pauvres.

Voltaire's Annotations at the Beginning of the Second Part of Rousseau's *Discours sur l'inégalité*. (See below, p. 15.)

VOLTAIRE'S MARGINALIA ON THE PAGES OF ROUSSEAU

A Comparative Study of Ideas

GEORGE R. HAVENS

BURT FRANKLIN
NEW YORK

Published by LENOX HILL Pub. & Dist. Co. (Burt Franklin)
235 East 44th St., New York, N.Y. 10017
Originally Published: 1933
Reprinted: 1971
Printed in the U.S.A.

S.B.N.: 8337-41675
Library of Congress Card Catalog No.: 73-171515
Burt Franklin: Research and Source Works Series 869
Philosophy Monograph Series 84

Reprinted from the original edition in the Wesleyan Univ. Library.

To
M. GUSTAVE LANSON
[Voltaire et Rousseau]
"Il n'est pas nécessaire que leur guerre se continue dans nos esprits." *(Hist. de la litt. française,* p. 792, n.)

PREFACE

This study represents part of the material collected during two trips to Leningrad, one in 1927, the other in 1930. There Voltaire's books are to be found carefully housed in the great Public Library of the city. It was a real privilege to be able to work in this interesting collection, so long neglected previously, and I am especially glad to express my deep appreciation of the fine cooperation and the never-failing courtesy of the members of the library staff, who gave me every facility for my work and unlimited access to the books I wanted. My warm thanks are due also to the Leningrad office of Voks (The Society for Cultural Relations with Foreign Countries) for numerous courtesies and assistance in new and strange surroundings. I am especially grateful to governmental authorities for according me the privilege of living at the Dom Uchenich (Home for Scholars), beautifully situated on the banks of the Neva instead of at a banal hotel as falls to the lot of most foreigners.

For my second trip to Russia, I am largely indebted to a fellowship of the Guggenheim Memorial Foundation, which thus enabled me to supplement and to complete studies I had undertaken previously. At the same time I was able to spend some weeks consulting Voltaire and Rousseau documents in the libraries of Geneva and deepening my comprehension of these two men of the eighteenth century by contact with scenes so closely associated with them both. By its freedom from rigidity and fixed rule and by its complete spirit of cordial cooperation, the Guggenheim Foundation renders its assistance doubly valuable, and I am glad to take this opportunity of expressing to its Secretary, Mr. Henry Allen Moe, my appreciation of the manner, as well as the nature, of their help.

Professor Norman L. Torrey of Yale University, who was with me at Leningrad in 1927 and with whom I have been closely associated in some general studies of the Voltaire collection, very kindly assisted me, when I was pressed for time, by copying out the marginalia on the pages of Rousseau's *Contrat social*. My wife,

Louise Curtiss Havens, accompanied me on both trips to Russia and by her indefatigable work in the Voltaire library doubled the amount of material I was able to transcribe to my notes. My friend and colleague, Professor Don L. Demorest, in the midst of numerous other demands on his time, very kindly read this study in proof and aided me with many a helpful suggestion. Another colleague, Mr. Irwin A. Johnson, assisted me in proofreading and by his careful work has contributed much to correctness of detail. The staff of the Ohio State University Press has cooperated throughout in the task of printing accurately material which, through its eccentric spelling and unusual arrangement, presented special difficulties. To all who have aided me in various ways I am deeply grateful. Special thanks are due Dean William McPherson of the Graduate School of this university for making possible the printing of this monograph during difficult times and for including it in the Graduate School's monograph series. Finally, I wish to express my appreciation to M. Gustave Lanson for allowing me to dedicate to him a small study in the field of French literature to which he has contributed so much.

G. R. H.

February 15, 1933.

TABLE OF CONTENTS

	PAGE
Table of Abbreviations	x
Introduction	1
Chapter I: Voltaire's Comments on the *Discours sur l'inégalité*	4
Chapter II: Voltaire's Comments on the *Extrait du Projet de Paix perpétuelle de M. l'Abbé de Saint-Pierre*	29
Chapter III: Voltaire's Comments on the *Contrat social*	39
Chapter IV: Voltaire's Comments on Rousseau's *Emile*	72
I. The Part of *Emile* before the *Vicaire savoyard*	72
II. *Le Vicaire savoyard*	92
III. *Emile* after the *Vicaire savoyard*	122
IV. Summary of Voltaire's Attitude toward *Emile*	126
Chapter V: Voltaire's Comments on Rousseau's *Lettre à M. de Beaumont*	129
Conclusion	187
Appendix	191
Bibliography	197

TABLE OF ABBREVIATIONS

H., The Hachette edition of Rousseau's *Œuvres complètes*.

M., The critical edition of Rousseau's *Vicaire savoyard* by Pierre-Maurice Masson.

Moland, The Moland edition of Voltaire's *Œuvres complètes*.

PMLA., *The Publications of the Modern Language Association of America*.

R., The Rey edition of Rousseau's *Discours sur l'inégalité*, Amsterdam, 1755.

RHL., *La Revue d'Histoire littéraire de la France*.

INTRODUCTION

If it is true that "all roads lead to Rome," we might add that most eighteenth-century roads led to Les Délices or Ferney. Pattu, Gibbon, Bettinelli, Marmontel, the Prince de Ligne, Chabanon, Mme Suard, Sherlock, John Moore,[1] Boswell,[2] are but a few of the visitors of various nationalities who sought out eagerly "le roi Voltaire" and enjoyed his picturesque, if often violent, sallies. "Ils viennent me voir comme un monument, après la cathédrale,"[3] was the half-humorous plaint regarding his visitors of that later Voltairean, Anatole France, a plaint that Voltaire himself might have used, perhaps without the slight qualification. Was it not he who complained whimsically that the Abbé Coyer, just the reverse of Don Quijote, took *castles* for *inns*, and sought to stay too long at Ferney?[4] Not only Voltaire's fame, but the magnet of his conversation, drew the men and women of the eighteenth century to his remote home near the Swiss border.

We of today can no longer come into the very presence of Voltaire. We cannot hear him talk with his customary verve, freedom, and even violence about the ideas of his great enemy, Jean-Jacques Rousseau. We cannot emulate Boswell and note down for ourselves and for posterity the piquant and striking sayings of the great man as they were uttered in the privacy of his own luxurious home. Impossible as such an experience now is, it is astonishing how near one comes to it when given the opportunity of reading, in the Public Library at Leningrad, the marginal notes jotted down in ink by Voltaire himself on the very pages of his own copies of Rousseau. By an odd turn of fate, these two unique personalities of the eighteenth century are preserved for us, as it were, face to face.

It was Catherine the Great who was the instrument of this strange destiny. Some six months after Voltaire's death, she purchased his entire private library. She even engaged Wagnière, the secretary of the former owner of these books, to take them from the

---

[1] See Voltaire, *Œuvres complètes* (Moland), Vol. I, Table des matières.
[2] Cf. Boswell's recently published letter to Temple of December 28, 1764, describing his interview with Voltaire at Ferney. R. H. Isham, *Private Papers of James Boswell*, IV (N. Y., 1929), pp. 1 ff.
[3] Marcel Le Goff, *Anatole France à La Béchellerie*, Paris, 1924, p. 109.
[4] Moland, I, 410.

shelves of Ferney and to install them in similar order in her most
un-Rousseauistic Hermitage at Saint Petersburg. There Voltaire's
books stayed until about 1862, when they were transferred to what
was then the Imperial Library and is now the Public Library of that
city. In this great library they are to be found now. The locked
glass doors of their special cases preserve them carefully from dust
and from unauthorized handling.[5]

Voltaire's vivid personality vibrated passionately at opposing viewpoints, even when such hated or despised opinions were expressed,
not to his face, but in the seemingly peaceful pages of a book. Since
there was no man of equal genius among his contemporaries so apt to
rouse his scorn or ire as Jean-Jacques Rousseau, it will not surprise
the reader to learn that Voltaire's marginal comments, rarely, if
ever, colorless, are here peculiarly lively, illuminating, often violently
personal, and at the same time most revealing of the points on
which these two outstanding writers of the eighteenth century agreed
and disagreed,—for it is worthy of note that the master of Ferney
did occasionally express frank approval as well as hostility. His comments therefore are by no means a record of mere personal spleen.

Of all the Voltaire marginalia at Leningrad, these on Rousseau
are naturally the most important and the most deserving of complete
presentation and study. They offer an opportunity for an objective
discussion of these two divergent men of genius which may well call
into play all the calm and the fairness at one's command. These
marginal notes require, and most of them deserve, explanatory comment. Sooner or later they force one to touch upon nearly all of the
most important phases of Rousseau's thought and of many of those
of Voltaire. If the discussion is somewhat disconnected, that is
unavoidable in this case, the order of sequence being imposed by the
order of the marginalia themselves. For the sake of clarity, these
comments are reproduced in juxtaposition with the passages in
Rousseau to which they refer.

Voltaire made marginal notes in his copies of Rousseau's *Discours
sur l'inégalité* (1755), *Extrait du Projet de Paix perpétuelle de*

---

[5] See G. R. Havens and N. L. Torrey, "The Private Library of Voltaire at Leningrad," *Pub. Mod. Lang. Assoc. of America*, XLIII (Dec. 1928), pp. 990-1009, and, by
the same authors, "Voltaire's Library," *The Fortnightly Review*, Sept. 2, 1929, pp.
397-405.

INTRODUCTION

M. l'abbé de Saint-Pierre (1761), *Contrat social* (1762), *Emile* (1762), and *Lettre à Christophe de Beaumont* (1763). Since no separate edition of the *Nouvelle Héloïse* (1761) is now to be found in the Voltaire library, the piquant notes that one would expect in it appear to be no longer extant, at least in Leningrad, nearly complete as the collection evidently is. Perhaps Voltaire did not bother to annotate a mere work of fiction. In any case he must have owned the original edition, or one of the same year, which has since disappeared. A few other works of Rousseau in the Voltaire library, with minor traces of a reader's interest, are noted in the Appendix at the end of the present study.

The notes on the *Discours sur l'inégalité* and on the *Contrat social* have been published previously, but unfortunately with inaccuracies and omissions, by Edouard Gardet in 1860. They were reprinted by Louis Moland in Volume XXXII[6] of his standard edition of Voltaire's *Œuvres complètes*. Some other marginal notes of Voltaire on Rousseau, which do not come from the Leningrad library, were published by M. Bernard Bouvier in the *Annales Jean-Jacques Rousseau* of 1905.[7] These notes also are undeniably in Voltaire's hand and are now to be found in a volume owned by the Archives Jean-Jacques Rousseau in the Bibliothèque publique at Geneva. They deal with that part of Book IV of *Emile* which is called *La Profession de foi du Vicaire savoyard*, and concern therefore the religious ideas both of Rousseau and of Voltaire. They coincide in some respects with the comments on *Emile* in the Leningrad library and are the only marginal notes of Voltaire on Rousseau which have been made the subject of special study, the others in the Moland edition of Voltaire having been merely reproduced without commentary. In publishing here with suitable explanatory material the Voltaire comments on Rousseau found in the library at Leningrad, we shall discuss the annotated works in the order of their mention above, that is, in the chronological order of their first appearance. We turn therefore first to the *Discours sur l'inégalité* of 1755.

---

[6] There are two different editions of this volume XXXII, both dated 1880. One of 515 pp. does not contain these marginal notes nor the *Sottisier*, and varies in some other respects from the edition of 627 pp., which is the one commonly used and which is referred to above in the present text.

[7] Pp. 272-84. Cf. my article in *Modern Language Notes*, XLVII (Jan., 1932), pp. 20-21, and *ibid.* (May, 1932), p. 325.

CHAPTER I

VOLTAIRE's COMMENTS ON ROUSSEAU's *Discours sur l'inégalité*

Rousseau's *Discours sur l'origine et les fondemens de l'inégalité parmi les hommes*, presented in 1754 in competition for the prize offered by the Académie de Dijon, was published by Rey at Amsterdam in 1755. Voltaire possessed the original octavo edition of lxii + 262 pages, probably the presentation copy sent him by Rousseau himself, though there is no dedication or other definite indication to this effect. All readers of Voltaire will recall his strikingly witty letter of August 30, 1755, in which politely, but with pointed irony, he acknowledged receipt of Rousseau's *Discours*. Voltaire wrote: "J'ai reçu, Monsieur, votre nouveau livre contre le genre humain, je vous en remercie. Vous plairez aux hommes à qui vous dites leurs vérités et vous ne les corrigerez pas. . . . On n'a jamais tant employé d'esprit à vouloir nous rendre bêtes. Il prend envie de marcher à quatre pattes,[1] quand on lit votre ouvrage. Cependant, comme il y a plus de soixante ans que j'en ai perdu l'habitude, je sens malheureusement qu'il m'est impossible de la reprendre, et je laisse cette allure naturelle à ceux qui en sont plus dignes que vous et moi."[2] After reading these pleasantries, one would not expect the tone of Voltaire's marginal comments upon this Discourse to be very favorable, and in fact, out of a total of forty-one such notes (two of which are omitted in Moland), all but one are distinctly hostile or critical. Voltaire did not here follow his own counsel as given in the *Préface du Poème sur le Désastre de Lisbonne* written in the following year, 1756. "Il serait bien plus raisonnable de ne faire attention qu'aux beautés utiles d'un ouvrage, et de n'y point chercher un sens odieux; mais c'est une des imperfections de notre nature d'interpréter malignement tout ce qui peut être interprété, et de vouloir décrier tout ce qui a eu

---

[1] Cf. Moland, I, 350. For similar phrases by Frederick the Great, cf. L. Ducros, *Jean-Jacques Rousseau*, II, 236, n. 1.
[2] The original text of this letter is reproduced in the *Correspondance générale de J.-J. Rousseau*, ed. by Dufour, Paris, 1924 ff., II, 203 ff., and differs substantially from the commonly cited text of Moland, XXXVIII, 446 ff.

du succès."³ Had Voltaire been introspective by nature, one might think this passage written with some of his own failings in mind, so applicable is it to many of his comments.

In addition to Voltaire's marginal notes, there are in many of his books a large number of bookmarks in the shape of long narrow slips of paper, or, as Wagnière calls them, "une quantité prodigieuse de *sinets*, sur lesquels il y a quelques mots écrits de sa main ou de la mienne."⁴ As has been indicated elsewhere,⁵ these appear for the most part to have been undisturbed since Voltaire's time. A few passages in Rousseau's Discourse have been merely marked without marginal notation. Let us now pass to a consideration of Voltaire's comments. The first of these occurs in connection with the fourth paragraph of the *Première Partie*, where Rousseau attributes the robust vigor of primitive man to his active and difficult outdoor life and sketches out a sort of principle of the survival of the fittest through the workings of natural selection. The passage has a bookmark on which, as often elsewhere, have been written the initials "N. M.," "Note marginale," probably placed there by Wagnière.

In reproducing Voltaire's notes, his somewhat capricious spelling, punctuation, and disregard of accents and capitalization have been followed. The text of Rousseau also differs frequently from modern usage.

ROUSSEAU (Rey, p. 14; Hachette, 1898, I, 85)	VOLTAIRE
La nature en use précisément avec eux comme la loi de Sparte avec les Enfans des Citoyens; elle rend forts, et robustes ceux qui sont bien constitués et fait périr tous les autres; différente en cela de nos sociétés, où l'état, en rendant les Enfans onéreux aux Pères, les tue indistinctement⁶ avant leur naissance.	obscur et mal placé

Voltaire's comment here is evidently stylistic and directed at a certain ambiguity of language from which Rousseau is not always

---

³ Moland, IX, 466-67.
⁴ See Havens and Torrey, PMLA., XLIII, 999.
⁵ *Ibid.*, 995.
⁶ Underlined by Voltaire.

free and which would be particularly calculated to annoy the clear and logical Voltaire.

The next passage, five paragraphs further on, is merely marked with a perpendicular line in the left margin, partially underlined, and indicated by a place-marker on which is written the word "Dépravé," referring obviously to the last word in the sentence.

ROUSSEAU (R., p. 22; H., 87)	VOLTAIRE
Si elle nous a <u>destinés à être sains</u>, j'ose presque assurer, que l'état de réflexion est un état contre Nature, et que l'homme qui médite est un animal dépravé.	(Written on a marker:) Depravé

In Voltaire's *Lettre au docteur Jean-Jacques Pansophe* of 1766, he harks back to this passage in these words: "Quoique, selon vous, *tout homme qui réfléchit soit un animal dépravé*,"[7] showing again clearly his disagreement with Rousseau over the question of education and culture.

Reading on, Voltaire makes no sign in Rousseau's text until he comes to Rousseau's discussion of the difference between man and animal.

ROUSSEAU (R., pp. 31-32; H., 90)	VOLTAIRE
La Nature commande à tout animal, et la Bête obéit. L'homme éprouve la même impression, mais il se reconnoît libre d'acquiescer, ou de résister; & c'est surtout dans la conscience de cette liberté que se montre la spiritualité de son âme.	voila une assez mauvaise métaphisique

Voltaire's inclination toward determinism during his later years is shown in *Le Philosophe ignorant*[8] of 1766 and elsewhere. As for the question of the soul, even as early as 1734 in the unpublished manuscript of *Le Traité de métaphysique*, he leaned toward the view that the soul was material and mortal.[9] Thus his comment here represents accurately his philosophical disagreement with Rousseau on these points. Voltaire's interest in the discussion is indicated by his selecting for comment two passages in the very next paragraph.

---

[7] Voltaire, *Œuvres* (Moland), XXVI, 21.
[8] *Ibid.*, XXVI, 55-57.
[9] *Ibid.*, XXII, 209-15.

Rousseau (R., pp. 32-33; H., 90)

Mais, quand les difficultés qui environnent toutes ces questions, laisseroient quelque lieu de disputer sur cette différence de l'homme & de l'animal, il y a une autre qualité très spécifique qui les distingue, & sur laquelle il ne peut y avoir de contestation, c'est la faculté de se perfectionner; faculté qui, à l'aide des circonstances, développe successivement toutes les autres, & réside parmi nous tant dans l'espéce, que dans l'individu, au lieu qu'un animal est, au bout de quelques mois, ce qu'il sera toute sa vie, & son espéce, au bout de mille ans, ce qu'elle étoit la première année de ces mille ans.

Voltaire

les animaux perfectionnent leur instinct par lusage

This passage and its marginal note are omitted in Moland. Rousseau here shows himself a believer in the fixed, unchanging characteristics of animal species as we see them now in the world. Without specifically discussing that question, on which it was still early in the development of biological and zoological science to venture an opinion, Voltaire does pronounce himself as holding that animals, as well as men, perfect themselves with practice. Hence, in his zeal against belief in spirituality of the soul, he attacks Rousseau's attempt to make an important distinction between animal and man along this line and perhaps approaches the conception of the basic unity of all life.

Rousseau (R. 34; H., 90)

Il seroit triste pour nous d'être forcés de convenir que cette faculté distinctive et presque illimitée est la source de tous les malheurs de l'homme; que c'est elle [la perfectibilité] qui le tire à force de temps de cette condition originaire dans laquelle il couleroit des jours tranquilles et innocens; que c'est elle qui, faisant éclore avec les siécles ses lumiéres & ses erreurs, ses vices & ses vertus, le rend à la longue le tiran de lui-même, & de la Nature.[x]

Voltaire

[x] les sauvages aplatissent le front de leurs enfans, afin qu'ils tirent aux oiseaux qui passent au dessus de leurs tetes

Voltaire writes a note on the lower margin of the page and identifies it with a cross-mark in the text and before the comment itself, in order to show that, since even savages deform nature, Rousseau's contention that man ever was, or would have remained, in "cette condition originaire dans laquelle il couleroit des jours tranquilles et innocens" is entirely without foundation in fact. While Voltaire's fundamental position here is sound enough, he is hardly happy in his choice of an example among the numerous cases of voluntary deformation among savages. It would be interesting to know from what source he drew his illustration.

Rousseau continues and traces briefly the development of civilization.

Rousseau (R. 38; H., 91)	Voltaire
Je montrerois en Egypte les arts naissant et s'étendant avec le débordement du Nil, je suivrois leur progrès chez les Grecs, où l'on les vit germer, croître, et s'élever jusqu'aux cieux & parmi les sables & les rochers de l'Attique, sans pouvoir prendre racine sur les bords fertiles de l'Eurotas; je remarquerois qu'en général les Peuples du Nord sont plus industrieux que ceux du Midi, parce qu'ils peuvent moins se passer de l'être.	cela nest pas vrai tous les arts viennent des pays chauds

While Rousseau in his idea of "perfectibility" and in his distinction between northern and southern peoples shows himself quite distinctly a forerunner of Mme de Staël, Voltaire contradicts him in favor of the south, though it is evident that Rousseau was not praising the north but only claiming that the very unfavorableness of the climate forced the people of northern countries to greater activity and industry, that progress came from the urge of necessity.

Characteristic is the next passage marked by Voltaire's pen. Rousseau sketches the development of the arts of agriculture.

Rousseau (R. 42; H., 92)	Voltaire
. . . toutes choses qu'il leur a falu [sic] <u>faire enseigner par les Dieux, faute de concevoir comment il les auroient apprises d'eux-mêmes.</u>	non, ils firent des dieux de leurs bienfaicteurs

After underlining the significant part of the passage, Voltaire clearly indicates by his comment, that he is opposed to the introduc-

DISCOURS SUR L'INÉGALITÉ

tion of a supernaturalistic explanation of the origin of agricultural arts among primitive people.

Passing now to the discussion of the development of language and arguing that it could not have arisen from the contacts of family life, because the family was not in primitive times a unit with a relatively permanent habitation, Rousseau states:

ROUSSEAU (R. 47; H., 93)	VOLTAIRE
Au lieu que, dans cet état primitif, n'ayant ni Maison, ni Cabanes, ni propriété d'aucune espéce, chacun se logeoit au hazard, & souvent pour une seule nuit.	ridicule supposition

Thus Voltaire manifests his characteristic disbelief in Rousseau's individualistic primitivism.

Continuing his discussion of language, Rousseau argues that the savage first perceived each object as distinct and gave it a different name. Voltaire, however, holds that generic resemblances would have been perceived from the beginning and would therefore have been reflected in speech.

ROUSSEAU (R. 54; H., 95)	VOLTAIRE
Si un Chêne s'appeloit *A*, un autre Chêne s'appeloit *B*.	il s'appelait au moins AB puisqu'il ressemblait a A

Stressing the difficulties and the long time required to develop complicated human speech, Rousseau at length gives up the attempt at a purely rationalistic explanation.

ROUSSEAU (R. 60; H., 96)	VOLTAIRE
Quant à moi, . . . convaincu de l'impossibilité presque démontrée que les Langues ayent pû naître & s'établir par des <u>moyens purement humains</u>.	pitoiable

Whether Rousseau was wholly sincere in this passage, whether he was affected by theological prudence or whether he simply and honestly felt reason bankrupt to offer an explanation of the origin of language, in any case Voltaire would have maintained his scornful comment. His underlining of "moyens purement humains" indicates clearly his recurring opposition to supernaturalistic explanations.

Rousseau now attacks the idea that men are by nature sociable and interdependent.

Rousseau (R. 60-61; H., 96)	Voltaire
En effet, il est impossible d'imaginer pourquoi dans cet état primitif, un homme auroit plutôt besoin d'un autre homme qu'un singe ˣ ou un Loup de son semblable.	ˣparce qu'il y a dans l'homme un instinct et une aptitude qui n'est pas dans le Singe

It is rather diverting to find that it is Voltaire this time who is defending a distinction between man and animal in contrast to the reverse situation apropos of perfectibility a little earlier in the Discourse.[10] Voltaire, the epitome of sociability, could hardly be expected to accept Rousseau's morose individualism, but he probably did not even suspect that he was on the borderline of self-contradiction.

Rousseau now turns to the discussion of primitivism, but pauses in passing to refute Hobbes. Voltaire adds his comment to the passage.

Rousseau (R. 66; H., 98)	Voltaire
Le méchant, dit-il [Hobbes] est un Enfant robuste.	le sauvage n'est méchant que comme un loup qui a faim

Here Voltaire's viewpoint seems practically identical with that of Rousseau, who at the beginning of the preceding paragraph had said: "Il paroît d'abord que les hommes dans cet état, n'ayant entre eux aucune sorte de relation morale ni de devoirs connus, ne pouvoient être ni bons ni méchans, et n'avoient ni vices ni vertus."[11] Likewise, a little below the passage commented upon by Voltaire, Rousseau had written: "On pourroit dire que les sauvages ne sont pas méchans précisément parce qu'ils ne savent pas ce que c'est qu'être bons."[12]

But, if Voltaire and Rousseau seem to meet for a moment in disagreement with Hobbes, they quickly diverge, for Rousseau continues his argument against society as a corrupting influence.

Rousseau (R. 72-73; H., 99-100)	Voltaire
C'est la raison qui engendre l'amour-propre.	Quelle idée! faut-il donc des raisonnements pour vouloir son bien-être?

Thus effectively Voltaire punctures Rousseau's primitivistic dream. On the same page the expression *s'argumenter*[13] has been

---

[10] Cf. above, p. 8.
[11] Hachette, I, 97.
[12] *Ibid.*, 98.
[13] R. 73; H., 100.

underlined by Voltaire, perhaps as a neologism,[14] perhaps as continuing the idea of rationalizing indicated by Rousseau above.

Rousseau now continues his well known and characteristic argument in favor of *pity* as the fundamental virtue of the savage in a primitive society.

ROUSSEAU (R. 74-75; H., 100)
C'est elle [la pitié] qui détournera tout Sauvage robuste d'enlever à un foible enfant, ou à un vieillard infirme, sa subsistance acquise avec peine, si lui-même espére pouvoir trouver la sienne ailleurs.

VOLTAIRE

ne dirait on pas que les iroquois sont plus compatissants que nous?

For some unknown reason, perhaps a copyist's negligence, this picturesque and characteristic comment has been entirely omitted in Moland.[15] In one of the numerous additions to the *Dictionnaire philosophique*, Voltaire wrote in 1771: "Plus de la moitié de la terre habitable est encore peuplée d'animaux à deux pieds qui vivent dans cet horrible état qui approche de la pure nature, ayant à peine le vivre et le vêtir, jouissant à peine du don de la parole, s'apercevant à peine qu'ils sont malheureux, vivant et mourant sans presque le savoir."[16] This passage is of special interest because, laying aside the wit and mockery so often used with telling effect elsewhere, Voltaire here treats the question seriously and exposes his humanitarian and matter-of-fact reasons for scorning primitivism., Numerous other examples could be given.[17]

These comments and those immediately following succeed each other closely. The subject is calculated to call forth Voltaire's keen interest.

ROUSSEAU (R. 76; H. 100)
Avec des passions si peu actives, & un frein si salutaire, les hommes plûtôt farouches que méchans, & plus attentifs à se garantir du mal qu'ils pourroient recevoir, que tentés d'en faire à autrui, n'étoient pas sujets à des démêlés fort dangereux.

VOLTAIRE

fou que tu es, ne sçais-tu pas que les americains septentrionaux se sont exterminés par la guerre?

[14] Littré gives only this one example of the use of *s'argumenter*, quoting Rousseau's *Discours*, a fact which may or may not have special significance.
[15] See Moland, XXXII, 469-70.
[16] *Ibid.*, XIX, 384.
[17] Cf. my article on "The Nature Doctrine of Voltaire," PMLA, XL (December, 1925), 857-61.

Here for the first time in his reading of Rousseau's Discourse Voltaire evidently loses patience completely and becomes violently personal, addressing himself directly and familiarly to the author. He is rude, but realistic. The passage recalls the one in his letter to Rousseau above referred to in which Voltaire explains why he cannot leave civilization for the joys of primitive life. "Je ne peux non plus m'embarquer pour aller trouver les Sauvages du Canada, premièrement parceque les maladies auxquelles je suis condamné me rendent un médecin d'Europe nécessaire; secondement parce que la guerre est portée dans ce pays-là, et que les exemples de nos nations ont rendu les sauvages presque aussi méchans que nous."[18] The tone in the letter is witty and ironical, while the marginal note is impatient and serious, but the fundamental attitude is the same in both cases. Voltaire's marginal comment here may well be his first protest against Rousseau on this particular point and the basis for the suave, but cutting, irony of his letter.

ROUSSEAU (R. 79; H., 101)	VOLTAIRE
Or il est facile de voir que le moral de l'amour est un sentiment factice, né de l'usage de la société, & célébré par les femmes avec beaucoup d'habileté & de soin pour établir leur empire, & rendre dominant le séxe qui devroit obéir.	pourquoy?

By his query accompanied by the underlining of the last three words, Voltaire has indicated clearly that he does not accept Rousseau's subordination of women to men, a theory which the latter was to develop and emphasize a few years later in his discussion of the relations of Emile and Sophie. As early as 1736, Voltaire had written in a letter to Berger, perhaps in part out of politeness with an eye to the chatelaine of Cirey, Mme du Châtelet, but probably not wholly so: "C'est une preuve de mon petit système que les femmes sont capables de tout ce que nous faisons, et que la seule différence qui est entre elles et nous, c'est qu'elles sont plus aimables."[19] In any case he wrote in 1771: "Il n'est pas étonnant qu' en tout pays l'homme se

---

[18] The text followed here is again that of the original version sent to Rousseau as reëstablished by Théophile Dufour in his *Correspondance générale de J.-J. Rousseau*, II, 203 (Paris, 1924). The Vulgate of Moland varies slightly in wording.
[19] Moland, XXXIV, 146.

DISCOURS SUR L'INÉGALITÉ

soit rendu le maître de la femme, tout étant fondé sur la force,"[20] though he goes on to say that women, sometimes very learned, are not original. In another passage of the *Dictionnaire philosophique* also written during this same year, he stated that owing to their physical constitution and to their domestic occupations, "elles sont partout moins barbares que les hommes."[21] Ten years earlier he had advocated for women a more complete and rational education.[22] Many of his references to the question are, however, inconsequential or facetious and permit of no conclusion as to Voltaire's real opinion. It is probable that he had never fully considered the influence of traditional restrictions and the lack of equal opportunities for experience and education in their effect upon women, nor envisaged the possible results of their being given complete freedom and equality. In any event, Voltaire's experience with witty and cultivated women of the salons contrasts sharply with Rousseau's liaison with Thérèse Levasseur and furnishes, without the need of additional considerations, sufficient explanation for their divergent viewpoints.

Continuing his emphasis upon biological, rather than psychological, aspects of love, Rousseau provokes from Voltaire a characteristically scornful comment.

Rousseau (R. 80; H., 101)	Voltaire
L'imagination qui fait tant de ravages parmi nous, ne parle point [de l'amour] à des cœurs Sauvages; chacun attend paisiblement l'impulsion de la Nature.	qu'en scais-tu as-tu vu des sauvages faire l'amour

Again Voltaire flings at Rousseau a challenge of his knowledge of fact and couches it in contemptuous, purely personal, form. His next comment is merely a revision of Rousseau's statement free from personalities.

Rousseau (R. 83; H., 102)	Voltaire
Or, aucun de ces deux cas n'est applicable à l'espéce humaine où le nombre des femelles surpasse généralement celui des mâles.	il nait plus de males mais au bout de vingt ans le nombre des femelles excede

---
[20] *Ibid.*, XIX, 98.
[21] *Ibid.*, XIX, 382.
[22] *Ibid.*, XXIV, 285-87.

Rousseau now starts to sum up his account of human development thus far.

ROUSSEAU (R. 84; H., 102)	VOLTAIRE
Concluons qu'errant dans les forêts, sans industrie, sans parole, sans domicile, etc.	c'est conclure un bien mauvais roman

Pouncing on the word "concluons," Voltaire thus gives his opinion of the Discourse in general up to this point. It is not an accurate history of the development of the human race; it is a romance merely, and a bad one.

Explaining in the next paragraph the reasons for insisting at length upon the characteristics of primitive life, Rousseau says:

ROUSSEAU (R. 86; H., 103)	VOLTAIRE
Si je me suis étendu si longtems sur la supposition de cette condition primitive, c'est qu'ayant d'anciennes erreurs & des préjugés invétérés à détruire, j'ai cru devoir creuser jusqu'à la racine, & montrer, dans le tableau du véritable état de Nature, combien l'inégalité, même naturelle, est loin d'avoir dans cet état autant de réalité & d'influence que le prétendent nos Ecrivains.	

Here Voltaire wrote no comment but merely underlined the words "de réalité," presumably by way of questioning the accuracy of Rousseau's whole exposition which suggested that inequality was of little moment in the state of nature.

Disappointed in love and not endowed with eighteenth-century wit, Rousseau characteristically attacks both.

ROUSSEAU (R. 88; H., 103)	VOLTAIRE
Là où il n'y a point d'amour, de quoi servira la beauté? Que sera l'esprit à des gens qui ne parlent point, & la ruse à ceux qui n'ont point d'affaires?	la beauté excitera l'amour et l'esprit produira les arts

Appreciative of love and beauty and the quick play of intelligence and wit, Voltaire equally characteristically answers Rousseau's rhetorical questions. Continuing now his attack upon society, Jean-Jacques argues that *perfectibility* could not operate of itself.

DISCOURS SUR L'INÉGALITÉ

> ROUSSEAU (R. 91; H., 104)
> Après avoir montré, que la perfectibilité, les vertus sociales, & les autres facultés que l'homme Naturel avoit reçues en puissance ne pouvoient jamais se développer d'elles-mêmes.

> VOLTAIRE
> quoi tu ne vois pas que les besoins mutuels ont tout fait

Although Rousseau had previously emphasized the significance of man's wants in urging him to progress,[23] he had not been content with a purely naturalistic explanation. Voltaire, however, insists constantly on pushing aside the supernatural in favor of the natural.

We come now to the Second Part of Rousseau's Discourse, which begins with his eloquent, though rhetorical, attack upon the institution of private property. This attack was the occasion for Voltaire's most important, and in many ways most characteristic, comment upon the *Discourse on Inequality*. Moreover, by some strange chance this particularly interesting note has been reproduced inaccurately in Moland so that the vigor and picturesqueness of the original have been much weakened.

> ROUSSEAU (R. 95; H., 105)
> Le premier qui ayant enclos un terrain, s'avisa de dire, *ceci est à moi*, & trouva des gens assés simples pour le croire, fut le vrai fondateur de la société civile. Que de crimes, de guerres, de meurtres, que de miséres & d'horreurs n'eût point épargnés au Genre-humain celui qui arrachant les pieux ou comblant le fossé, eût crié à ses semblables. Gardez-vous d'écouter cet imposteur; Vous êtes perdus, si vous oubliez que les fruits sont à tous, et que la Terre n'est à personne.[24]

> VOLTAIRE
> quoy celui qui a planté, semé, et enclos na pas droit au fruit de ses peines.
>
> quoy cet homme injuste ce voleur aurait été le bienfaiteur du genre humain! voyla la philosophie d'un gueux qui voudrait que les riches fussent volez par les pauvres

Rousseau's excoriation of private property is too much for Voltaire, the rich man, not yet of Ferney, but with large annuities, many investments at home and abroad, and a luxurious home just bought at Les Délices on the pleasant outskirts of Geneva overlooking the Rhone. Even at this distance in time one can feel his vibrating indig-

---
[23] Cf. above, pp. 6-7.
[24] A perpendicular line opposite "Gardez-vous" indicates Voltaire's particular reference to the last sentence of this passage. As given in Moland (XXXII, 471), "cet homme injuste, ce voleur," are weakened to: "un homme injuste et voleur," while the typical clause following "gueux" is omitted altogether. See the Frontispiece.

nation as he burst forth against "la philosophie d'un gueux qui voudrait que les riches fussent volez par les pauvres," a phrase which he repeated almost verbatim in additions to the *Dictionnaire philosophique* in 1771.[25] In the same passage occur the characteristic words: *voleur* and *bienfaiteur*. In 1768 likewise Voltaire not only attacked this passage of Rousseau, but used the similar terms: *quelque voleur de grand chemin*, and *un gueux fort paresseux*,[26] expressions which indicate definitely that his marginal note of thirteen to sixteen years before must have been directly before his eyes or engraved ineffaceably in his mind. Thus this marginal comment represents Voltaire's thought as it was dashed off spontaneously at white heat in his reading before it became later crystallized and was employed repeatedly in his published work.

In whatever respects Voltaire may be radical, it is obvious that this is not one of them. For him the institution of private property is necessary and well-nigh sacred. No socialism nor communism for him. There is no more vital point of cleavage between him and Rousseau than that revealed by his comment upon this passage. It is characteristic in its attitude and characteristic in the vividness of its expression.

Voltaire's next comment does not occur until ten pages later.

ROUSSEAU (R. 104-05; H., 107)	VOLTAIRE
Je parcours comme un trait des multitudes de Siècles, forcé par le tems qui s'écoule, par l'abondance des choses que j'ai à dire, et par le progrès presque insensible des commencemens; car plus les événemens étoient lents à se succéder, plus ils sont prompts à décrire.	ridicule

Voltaire marked the passage perpendicularly in the right-hand margin and commented thus succinctly and scornfully on the concluding clauses.

ROUSSEAU (R. 111; H., 109)	VOLTAIRE
La jalousie s'éveille avec l'amour; la Discorde triomphe, et la plus douce des passions reçoit des sacrifices de sang humain.	une passion qui reçoit des sacrifices

[25] See Moland, XIX, 380-81. The phrases are identical beginning with "gueux" except for the addition of "tous" before "les riches."
[26] Moland, XXVII, 339-40. Cf. also XV, 434, and XIX, 605.

DISCOURS SUR L'INÉGALITÉ 17

Voltaire's objection appears to be directed at the implied personification of passion and, in contrast to most of those preceding, seems to be purely stylistic in character.

>ROUSSEAU (R. 112; H., 109)
>Chacun commença à regarder les autres et à vouloir être regardé soi-même, et l'estime publique eut un prix.

VOLTAIRE

Voltaire underlined without comment the words *publique* and *un prix*, perhaps questioning whether there had ever been a time in the history of humanity when public honor had not exerted influence.

>ROUSSEAU (R. 114; H., 109)
>Plusieurs se sont hâtés de conclure que l'homme est naturellement cruel, et qu'il a besoin de police pour l'adoucir; tandis que rien n'est si doux que lui dans son état primitif.

VOLTAIRE

et quand il fallait disputer la nature.

Voltaire evidently again questions Rousseau's idealization of primitivism.

>ROUSSEAU (R. 115-16; H., 110)
>Ainsi, quoique les hommes fussent devenus moins endurans, & que la pitié naturelle eût déjà souffert quelque altération, ce période du développement des facultés humaines, tenant un juste milieu entre l'indolence de l'état primitif & la pétulante activité de notre amour-propre, dut être l'époque la plus heureuse & la plus durable.

VOLTAIRE

quelle chimere que ce juste milieu!

Here Rousseau is speaking of one of his pet theories, that of the supposed intermediate period between the pure state of nature and that of fully formed society, the ideal stage, the happiest period in the history of the human race, in his opinion, but Voltaire does not believe such a "juste milieu" ever existed.

>ROUSSEAU (R. 118; H., 110)
>La Métallurgie & l'agriculture furent les deux arts dont l'invention produisit cette grande révolution [dans la société]. Pour le Poëte, c'est l'or & l'argent; mais pour le Philosophe, ce sont le fer & le bled qui ont

VOLTAIRE

| les mexicains et les peruviens subjuguez par les sauvages espagnols etaient tres

civilisé les hommes & perdu le Genre- humain; ainsi l'un & l'autre étoient-ils in- connus aux Sauvages de l'Amérique, qui pour cela sont toujours demeurés tels. |

civilizes. mexico etait aussi beau qu'amsterdam.

Voltaire's comment, with a line indicating the passage referred to, is written in the lower margin. Rousseau presumably was thinking only of the North American Indians, when he mentioned the "sauvages de l'Amérique," while Voltaire characteristically turns the question about to defend the inhabitants of Mexico and Peru against "les sauvages espagnols," an attitude not unexpected in the author of *Alzire* and the inveterate enemy of the Inquisition.

ROUSSEAU (R. 119; H., 111)
Et l'une des meilleures raisons peut-être pourquoi l'Europe a été, sinon plus-tôt, du moins plus constamment, et mieux policée que les autres parties du monde, c'est qu'elle est à la fois la plus abondante en fer & la plus fertile <u>en bled</u>.

VOLTAIRE

faux

Voltaire underlined "en bled" to indicate the bearing of his laconic comment. In the *Questions sur l'Encyclopédie* in 1770, Voltaire discussed the importance of wheat, remarking that "l'Egypte devint la meilleure terre à fromont de l'univers"[27] and that "les provinces méridionales de la Russie en regorgent."[28] Elsewhere in the same work, he pointed out the large areas of the world whose inhabitants get along entirely without wheat.[29] He also listed the different countries of the world in respect to wheat production.[30] There is no question in Voltaire's mind[31] of the importance of this grain from the standpoint of national prosperity, so that he appears here to be denying merely the primacy Rousseau attributes to Europe in producing it. Moreover, it is significant that in discussing the fact of Holland's being wealthy without a large grain supply Voltaire stated that the grain trader is the one who enriches himself rather than the producer. "Qui est réellement possesseur du blé? c'est le

---

[27] Moland, XVIII, 7.
[28] *Ibid.*, XVIII, 15.
[29] *Ibid.*, XVII, 349.
[30] *Ibid.*, XVIII, 15.
[31] *Ibid.*, XVIII, 7, 8, 15.

DISCOURS SUR L'INÉGALITÉ

marchand qui l'achète du laboureur."[32] Thus there are many questions involved besides that implied in Rousseau's simple statement, though in general such a concrete explanation of the rise of civilization should have appealed to Voltaire.

Rousseau (R. 119-20; H., 111)

Il est très difficile de conjecturer comment les hommes sont parvenus à connoître & employer le fer. . . . D'un autre côté on peut d'autant moins attribuer cette découverte à quelque incendie accidentel que les mines ne se forment que dans les lieux arides, & dénués d'arbres & de plantes, de sorte qu'on diroit que la Nature avoit pris des précautions pour nous dérober ce fatal secret. /

Voltaire

|le fer est produit en masse dans les pirenées

This comment is written in the lower margin and is marked with a line referring back to another mark opposite "ce fatal secret." It is a characteristic denial of Rousseau's statement of fact and the argument based on it.

A paper place-marker without writing is found between pages 138 and 139 of this 1755 edition published by Rey. These pages, beginning with the phrase "(faire) tête à des forces unies" and ending with "Les plus honnêtes gens appri (rent),"[33] sum up Rousseau's account of the progress of social organization and touch at the end upon the rise of wars between nations and of "tous ces préjugés horribles qui placent au rang des vertus l'honneur de répandre le sang humain." It is quite possible that the passage was marked because of these words on war with which Voltaire was much more in accord than with Rousseau's general account of the rise of society, but no definite indication is available.

Rousseau (R. 153-54; H., 119)

Puffendorff dit que tout de même qu'on transfère son bien à autrui par des conventions & des contrats, on peut aussi se dépouiller de sa liberté en faveur de quelqu'un. C'est là, ce me semble, un fort mauvais raisonnement; car, premièrement le bien

Voltaire

tres beau

---
[32] *Ibid.*, XVIII, 9.
[33] Rousseau, Hachette, I, 115-116.

que j'aliène me devient une chose tout à fait étrangère, et dont l'abus m'est indifférent; mais il m'importe qu'on n'abuse point de ma liberté, & je ne puis sans me rendre coupable du mal qu'on me forcera de faire, m'exposer à devenir l'instrument du crime.

This comment is especially interesting as one of the few made by Voltaire on the *Discourse on Inequality* which appears enthusiastically favorable. Moreover, Rousseau's mention of Puffendorf in this connection probably called forth Voltaire's statement in 1771: "Puffendorf dit que l'esclavage a été établi 'par un libre consentement des parties, et par un contrat de faire afin qu'on nous donne.' Je ne croirai Puffendorf que quand il m'aura montré le premier contrat."[34] Wherever Rousseau's rationalism is to the fore, Voltaire is likely to find himself in accord with him and it is noteworthy that in spite of his general hostility he does not fail to acknowledge his agreement. It is improbable that his comment here is to be taken ironically.

ROUSSEAU (R. 155-56; H., 120)   VOLTAIRE

Les jurisconsultes qui ont gravement prononcé que l'enfant d'une Esclave naîtroit Esclave, ont décidé en d'autres termes qu'un homme ne naîtroit pas homme.

Il me paroît donc certain que non-seulement les Governemens n'ont point commencé par le Pouvoir Arbitraire, qui n'en est que la corruption, le terme extrême, & qui les ramène enfin à la seule Loi du plus fort, dont ils furent d'abord le remède; mais encore que quand même ils auroient ainsi commencé, ce pouvoir, étant par sa Nature illégitime, n'a pu servir de fondement aux Droits de la société ni par conséquent à l'inégalité d'institution.

On this passage there is no comment by Voltaire, but it has been marked, not only by the ribbon bookmark belonging to the volume (a circumstance not in itself significant), but also by a perpendicular mark in the margin extending from "l'enfant d'une Esclave" to "d'abord le remède." Thus it is evident that Voltaire continues to

[34] Moland, XVIII, 603.

show his interest in Rousseau's attack upon slavery as an institution without foundation in justice.

ROUSSEAU (R. 162; H., 121)
En un mot, d'un côté furent les richesses & les Conquêtes, & de l'autre le bonheur & la vertu.

VOLTAIRE

tarare

Rousseau has been contrasting monarchical and aristocratic governments with democracies, and has put riches and conquests on the one side in opposition to happiness and virtue on the other. Voltaire rules out such easy and uncritical generalization with a single scornful epithet.

ROUSSEAU (R. 170-71; H., 123)
Je montrerois que c'est à cette ardeur de faire parler de soi, à cette fureur de se distinguer qui nous tient presque toûjours hors de nous-mêmes, que nous devons ce qu'il y a de meilleur & de pire parmi les hommes, nos vertus & nos vices, nos Sciences & nos erreurs, nos Conquérans & nos Philosophes, c'est-à-dire une multitude de mauvaises choses sur un petit nombre de bonnes. Je prouverois enfin que si l'on voit une poignée de puissans & de riches au faîte des grandeurs & de la fortune, tandis que la foule rampe dans l'obscurité & dans la misère, c'est que les premiers n'estiment les choses dont ils jouissent qu'autant que les autres en sont privés, et que, sans changer d'état, ils cesseroient d'être heureux, si le Peuple cessoit d'être misérable.

VOLTAIRE

Singe de Diogene comme tu te condamnes toi meme!

comme tu outres tout! comme tu mets tout dans un faux jour.

For the second time during his reading of the Discourse Voltaire shows himself violently personal. The epithet "singe de Diogène" applied to Rousseau became a favorite with Voltaire. For example in *Les Honnêtetés littéraires* of 1767 it occurs in the variant forms "singe manqué de l'Arétin" and "bâtard du chien de Diogène."[35] In the poem *Les Deux Siècles* probably of 1771 Rousseau is compared to the "chien de Diogène,"[36] while already in a letter to

[35] Moland, XXVI, 131.
[36] *Ibid.*, X, 160.

Damilaville of June 4, 1762, Voltaire, speaking of the author of *Emile*, had said that "le chien qui suivait Diogène était moins méprisable que lui."[37] No one was more given to speaking of himself than Rousseau. Voltaire is quick to seize upon this weakness and fling it back into the face of his adversary here just as he was to do later at the beginning of Rousseau's *Lettre à M. de Beaumont*. As is to be expected, in his marginal comment at the end of this passage Voltaire, amid the luxury of Les Délices, quite naturally condemns Rousseau's blanket attack upon riches.

ROUSSEAU (R. 174; H., 124)	VOLTAIRE
De l'extrême inégalité des Conditions & des fortunes, de la diversité des passions & des talens, des arts inutiles, des arts pernicieux, des Sciences frivoles, sortirent des foules de préjugés, également contraires à la raison, au bonheur, & à la vertu: on verroit fomenter par les Chefs tout ce qui peut affoiblir des hommes rassemblés en les désunissant; tout ce qui peut donner à la Société un air de concorde apparente et y semer un germe de division réelle; tout ce qui peut inspirer aux différens ordres une défiance & une haine mutuelle par l'opposition de leurs Droits & de leurs intérêts, & fortifier par conséquent <u>ˣle pouvoir qui les contient tous.</u>	ˣSi le pouvoir roial contient et réprime touttes les factions, tu fais le plus grand éloge de la roiauté contre laquelle tu declames.

Voltaire does not touch Rousseau's fundamental contention that the rulers have fomented divisions among their subjects in order better to strengthen their own authority, but shows his own characteristic preference for monarchy by twisting Rousseau's words into an unconscious praise of the superlative value of its police power over society. Voltaire's use of the word "déclames" applied to Rousseau's writing forecasts the similar, and very frequent, use of "déclamation" a few years later in commenting upon many passages in *Emile*.[38]

This completes the marginal comments of Voltaire upon the

[37] *Ibid.*, XLII, 126. Cf. also *ibid.*, X, 117; XVI, 378.
[38] See below, Chapter IV.

actual text of the *Discours sur l'inégalité*, but the voluminous Notes which follow the Discourse did not fail also to draw forth written expressions of opinion.

ROUSSEAU (R. 201-202; H., 132)   VOLTAIRE
"La durée de la vie des Chevaux, dit M. de Buffon, est comme dans toutes les autres espèces d'animaux, proportionnée à la durée du temps de leur accroissement. . . . Comme les gros chevaux prennent leur accroissement en moins de tems que les chevaux fins, ils vivent aussi moins de tems, et sont vieux dès l'age de quinze ans." (Histoire naturelle du cheval.)

faux j ay eu deux chevaux de carosse qui ont vecu 35 ans.

In his anxiety to find fault with Rousseau, Voltaire unscientifically alleges two exceptions as overthrowing the general principle enunciated on Buffon's authority and quoted verbatim from him, in spite of the fact that Rousseau had also quoted the preceding clause from the same author: "Les exemples qui pourroient être contraires à cette règle sont si rares, qu'on ne doit pas même les regarder comme une exception dont on puisse tirer des conséquences." If Voltaire presumed to put his two exceptions against all the studies of Buffon, the outstanding authority of his age on natural history, it is not only because Rousseau had quoted him, but it is also no doubt because already as early as 1746 Voltaire in his *Dissertations sur les changements arrivés dans notre globe*[39] had started a controversy with Buffon which was not terminated until their reconciliation in 1774.[40] Regardless of the actual merits of the question, Voltaire is evidently venting his personal spleen against both authors at the same time and on evidence entirely inconclusive.

ROUSSEAU (R. 208-209; H., 134)   VOLTAIRE
L'homme Sauvage, quand il a dîné, est en paix avec toute la Nature, & l'ami de tous ses semblables. . . Mais chez l'homme en Société ce sont bien d'autres affaires; . . . de sorte qu'après de longues prospérités,

---

[39] See Moland, XXIII, 219-30.
[40] *Ibid.*, XLIX, 117-19, and n. Cf. A. Morize, *Candide*, édition critique, Paris, 1913, 1931, p. 144, n., and Daniel Mornet, *Les Sciences de la nature au XVIIIe siècle*, Paris, 1911, pp. 108-32.

après avoir englouti bien des trésors & désolé
bien des hommes, mon Héros finira par tout
égorger jusqu'à ce qu'il soit l'unique maître
de l'Univers. Tel est en abrégé le tableau
moral, sinon de la vie humaine, au moins
des prétentions secrétes du cœur de tout   et encore plus de tout sau-
homme Civilisé.   vage, s'il peut.

Thus at one stroke Voltaire brushes aside Rousseau's idealization of primitive life and takes his stand again in favor of the civilizing influence of society.

ROUSSEAU (R. 211; H., 135)   VOLTAIRE
Combien de moyens honteux d'empêcher   on a trouvé cette turpi-
la naissance des hommes, & de tromper la   tude établie en amérique; et
Nature? Soit par ces goûts brutaux & dé-   dans les livres juifs qu'on
pravés qui insultent son plus charmant ou-   nous fait lire y a-t-il un
vrage, gouts que les Sauvages ni les animaux peuple plus barbare que les
ne connurent jamais, & qui ne sont nés dans sodomites!
les païs policés que d'une imagination cor-
rompue.

Again Voltaire attacks primitivism, making a characteristic thrust at the Old Testament in passing.

ROUSSEAU (R. 212; H., 136)   VOLTAIRE
Que seroit-ce si j'entreprenois de mon-   ˣmalheureux jean jaque
trer l'espéce humaine attaquée dans sa source dont les carnosités sont assez
même, ˣ& jusque dans le plus saint de tous   conues. pauvre échapé de la
les liens....!   verole, ignores tu quelle
                                             vient des sauvages!

This comment continues the tendency of the two preceding, but with the addition of bitter personal innuendo directed at Rousseau and his illness. In his *Sentiments des citoyens* at the end of 1764, Voltaire was to call Rousseau publicly "un homme qui porte encore les marques funestes de ses débauches,"[41] a charge which called forth Rousseau's denial: "Jamais aucune maladie de celles dont parle ici l'auteur, ni petite, ni grande, n'a souillé mon corps. Celle dont je suis affligé n'y a pas le moindre rapport; elle est née avec moi," and he gives the names of five people as having known him from infancy and able to testify to the truth of this statement.[42] Probably Vol-

[41] *Ibid.*, XXV, 312.
[42] *Ibid.*, XXV, 312-13, n. 3. Cf. the fac-simile published in the Dufour edition of Rousseau's *Correspondance générale*, XII (Paris, 1929), p. 381.

taire's "information" is the product of Geneva gossip among Rousseau's enemies or malicious friends. Like the knowledge later of Rousseau's abandonment of his children, it may even have been spread by unprofessional indiscretions attributed to Dr. Tronchin,[43] physician both to Voltaire and Rousseau, though this possibility is no guarantee of the accuracy of the charge. It may be that more knowledge of the time when such rumors were first spread would permit the dating of this marginal comment, and perhaps by inference the others. If so, this would give it an importance quite out of proportion to its content. The nature of the personal attack suggests that it may have been made later than the other comments and some years after the first appearance of the Discourse.

Rousseau (R. 218; H., 138)	Voltaire
Quant aux hommes semblables à moi, dont les passions ont détruit pour toujours l'originelle simplicité, qui ne peuvent plus se nourrir d'herbes & de gland, ni se passer de Loix & de Chefs; Ceux qui furent honorés dans leur premier Père de leçons surnaturelles; . . . ceux, en un mot, qui sont convaincus que la voix divine appela tout le Genre-humain aux lumiéres & au bonheur des célestes intelligences; tous ceux-là tâcheront, par l'exercice des vertus qu'ils s'obligent à pratiquer en apprenant à les connoître, à mériter le prix éternel qu'ils en doivent attendre; ils respecteront les sacrés liens des Sociétés dont ils sont les membres; ils aimeront leurs semblables & les serviront de tout leur pouvoir.	galimatias

Voltaire's succinct comment seems to apply to the whole page and to be directed equally at the picture of primitivism and the introduction of the supernatural and the divine.

Rousseau (R. 220; H., 138-39)	Voltaire
Il y a eu, & il y a peut-être encore, des Nations d'hommes d'une taille gigantesque; & laissant à part la fable des Pygmées, qui	

---

[43] Cf. Louis Ducros, *Jean-Jacques Rousseau de l'Ile de Saint-Pierre à Ermenonville*, Paris, 1918, pp. 134-35, who gives this explanation, in the case of Rousseau's children, as a plausible, though unproved, inference.

peut bien n'être qu'une exagération, on sait
que les Lapons, & surtout les Groënlandois,
sont fort au-dessous de la taille moyenne de   faux
l'homme; on prétend même qu'il y a des
Peuples entiers qui ont des queües comme   faux
des quadrupèdes.

In a letter of January 8, 1763, Rousseau implies that the stature of the Lapps is around four feet,[44] though modern authorities have put the average around five for males and somewhat lower for females.[45] In any case, the Lapps and the Eskimos are both short races, so that the truth regarding the first point lies rather with Rousseau than with Voltaire. As for the second point, Rousseau has advanced it guardedly under an "on prétend même," so that he is less vulnerable to attack than usual in questions of fact.

Between pages 244 and 245[46] is a marker with the familiar letters *N.M.*, "Note marginale." Since, however, these pages have no mark or note of any kind, it is evidently one of the rare cases in which the marker has been displaced.

The two following pages have also a marker and on it is the notation "abomination de J. Jaques," which served Voltaire for later reference, as we shall see.

ROUSSEAU (R. 247; H., 147)   VOLTAIRE

Enfin M. Locke prouve tout au plus qu'il
pourroit bien y avoir dans l' homme un
motif de demeurer attaché à la femme
lorsqu'elle a un Enfant; mais il ne prouve
nullement qu'il a dû s'y attacher avant
l'accouchement & pendant les neuf mois de
la grossesse. Si telle femme est indifférente
à l'homme pendant ces neuf mois, si même
elle lui devient inconnue, pourquoi la se-
courra-t-il après l'accouchement? pourquoi   tout cela est abominable et
lui aidera-t-il à élever un Enfant qu'il ne   c'est bien mal connaitre la
sait pas seulement lui appartenir, & dont il   nature.
n'a résolu ni prévu la naissance?

The passage commented upon by Voltaire is part of a long note of Rousseau directed against Locke's contention that the family had a

---

[44] J.-J. Rousseau, *Correspondance générale*, éd. Dufour, VIII (Paris, 1927), 345-46.
[45] *Encyclopædia Britannica*, 11th ed., 1911, XVI, 204. Obviously, in Rousseau's day, accurate anthropological data regarding remote peoples hardly existed.
[46] Hachette, I, 146-47, from "douter que l'espèce humaine" to "prolongée dans un plus grand âge chez les . . ."

certain natural basis for relative permanency. Rousseau maintains that primitive man lived in isolation and that the society of the family was not an inevitable consequence of the relations between parents and children. In the *Dictionnaire philosophique* in his article *Homme*, first published in 1771, Voltaire included a citation from a part of the above passage and then commented: "Tout cela est exécrable; mais heureusement rien n'est plus faux.... Notre nature est bien différente de l'affreux roman que cet énergumène a fait d'elle."[47] Thus he remembered and utilized this "abomination de J. Jaques," which seems to accord so well with Rousseau's own abandonment of his children. There is some foundation, however, for the belief that Voltaire himself, with less justification, may have been open to the same charge.[48]

We have come now to the end of Voltaire's marginal notes on Rousseau's Discourse. There are forty-one such comments in all, besides two passages that are merely marked. As might be expected, since Rousseau's essay deals largely with a glorification of primitive, at the expense of civilized, man, nearly half of Voltaire's comments show his complete opposition to Rousseau upon that issue. Voltaire holds the more modern view that civilization has been a natural process of development urged on by man's constant attempts to satisfy his expanding wants and needs. Hence there is no inherent difference between primitive and civilized man, but only a difference in degree of refinement. Civilization is therefore obviously to be preferred. Rousseau's picture of human history is "un bien mauvais roman." Several comments show also that Voltaire favors throughout a naturalistic, instead of a supernaturalistic, explanation of human affairs. Consequently in a single metaphysical comment he shows himself by implication opposed to Free Will and the spirituality of the soul. Voltaire is especially vigorous in condemning Rousseau's attack upon private property. He opposes also Jean-Jacques' concept of the inferiority of women and the superiority attributed to democracy over monarchy. He agrees with Rousseau in his condemnation of slavery.

Several comments take issue with the author of the Discourse on questions of fact of varying importance; others deal with topics of

[47] Moland, XIX, 379.
[48] *Ibid.*, I, 319-20.

secondary interest; only two are purely personal in their invective, though a few others do give the effect of flinging the contradictions rudely back into the face of Voltaire's adversary. With not more than two or three exceptions, however, his comments here betray a sincere difference of opinion on which the impartial reader will be forced to agree with Voltaire as nearer right in most cases than Rousseau. The latter was too often inaccurate in his facts—and who better qualified to indicate this than the keen and sceptical Voltaire, even though he himself was not always free from this human weakness? It was upon his idealization of the past that Rousseau was too much inclined to base his attacks against the shortcomings of the present, and Voltaire, historian of humanity in the *Essai sur les mœurs* and admirer of "ce siècle de fer" in *Le Mondain,* was not likely to be slow in pointing this out.

On the question of private property, modern opinion is still far from agreed. We may hold that Rousseau was entirely justified in showing the dangers and abuses of wealth and the too great concentration of humanity's effort upon the owning of property and yet hold also that he was too rhetorical and sweeping and uncritical in his attack, that the problem in short offers no such easy and clear-cut solution as he suggests. On the other hand, Voltaire's view of this question is no less one-sided. He appears to accept without demur the organization of society which has allowed him to become rich. Perhaps because of Rousseau's very exaggeration Voltaire fails even to perceive the fundamental significance and legitimacy of the problem which the *Discourse on Inequality* raised.

This blindness would appear to be characteristic of Voltaire's general attitude toward Rousseau's essay as a whole. The former is keen enough—and generally right—in the details which he criticizes; he misses the legitimacy of the larger questions of social inequality and injustice which it is the merit of the Discourse to have flung as a challenge into the face of the public. What a *Discourse on Inequality* might have been written—if we may be allowed to imagine so impossible a situation—by a collaboration in which Rousseau would have revised his essay and published it only after successfully meeting all of Voltaire's objections and his challenge of the facts used in support of the argument!

CHAPTER II

VOLTAIRE'S COMMENTS ON ROUSSEAU'S *Extrait du Projet de Paix perpétuelle de M. l'Abbé de Saint-Pierre*

It was in 1756, according to the *Confessions*,[1] that Rousseau started upon a project suggested to him indirectly by the Abbé de Mably through the intermediary of Mme Dupin. Her *salon* the visionary, radical, but beneficent Abbé de Saint-Pierre had frequented during the last years before his death in 1743, thus barely coming within the view of the young and then entirely unknown Rousseau who had been introduced there the preceding year.[2] The proposal was that Rousseau publish with his own criticisms and commentary extracts of the Abbé de Saint-Pierre's suggestive, but diffuse, plans for humanitarian reform. As a result, Rousseau shortened and revised two of the Abbé's well-intentioned, though tiresome, works: his *Projet de paix perpétuelle*, first published in 1712,[3] and his *Discours sur la polysynodie* of 1718. There, however, the matter rested, and Rousseau, increasingly absorbed in the composition of his own masterpieces, the *Nouvelle Héloïse, Emile*, and the *Contrat social*, abandoned the rest of the Abbé de Saint-Pierre's sixteen volumes of *Ouvrages politiques* (1732-41) for more original work. The *Extrait du Projet de paix perpétuelle* was published in a separate edition at Paris without place indication in March, 1761. Voltaire's marginal notes thus focus upon this single brief volume[4] three diverse, but interesting, eighteenth-century minds. For this reason and because of its subject, the book is of unusual interest today.

Passing over the eloquent introductory paragraphs, Voltaire pauses for the first time to question the following interpretation of the Greek attitude toward the barbarian world.

---

[1] Hachette, VIII, 291-92.
[2] *Ibid.*, VIII, 203-206.
[3] In 1712 this work was entitled a *Mémoire pour rendre la paix perpétuelle en Europe*. The following year the word *Mémoire* was changed to *Projet*, as in subsequent editions.
[4] 114 pages in the original edition, 19 in Hachette.

30   VOLTAIRE ON ROUSSEAU

ROUSSEAU (p. 24; H. V, 311)   VOLTAIRE
Aussi les Grecs, raisonneurs & vains, dis-
tinguoient-ils, pour ainsi dire, deux espéces   quelle sottise. les grecs
dans l'humanité, dont l'une, sçavoir la leur,   avaient bien de la peine a
étoit faite pour commander; & l'autre, qui   ne pas porter les fers des
comprenoit tout le reste du monde, unique-   perses.
ment pour servir.

Voltaire's comment avoids entirely the fundamental issue of the Greek contempt for barbarians and the lack of unity of the European world in ancient times. A few lines below the word "Américain" is underlined without indication of the reason.[5]

Voltaire's comments now follow thick and fast.

ROUSSEAU (p. 25; H. V, 312)   VOLTAIRE
Mais quand ce Peuple, souverain par
nature, eût été soumis aux Romains ses   quelle pitié
esclaves.

By underlining, Voltaire indicated his contempt for the claim that the Greeks were inherently sovereign and the Romans with the other "barbarians" inherently their slaves.

ROUSSEAU (p. 25; H. V, 312)   VOLTAIRE
. . . le fameux décret de Claude, qui   non tous les sujets mais tous
incorporoit tous les Sujets de Rome au   ceux qui dans leurs villes
nombre de ses Citoyens.   avaient le droit de suffrage

ROUSSEAU (p. 26; H. V, 312)   VOLTAIRE
Le Code de Théodose, & ensuite les
livres de Justinien, furent une nouvelle
chaîne de justice & de raison, substituée à
propos à celle du pouvoir souverain.   sottise

The last four words were underlined by Voltaire.

ROUSSEAU (p. 27; H. V, 312)   VOLTAIRE
Ce supplément retarda beaucoup la dis-
solution de l'empire, & lui conserva long-
tems une sorte de juridiction sur les Bar-   louche
bares mêmes qui le désoloient. ─────

A horizontal mark at the end of the paragraph after "désoloient" indicates the bearing of Voltaire's comment on the ambiguity of Rousseau's sentence.

[5] Hachette, V, 312.

PROJET DE PAIX PERPÉTUELLE

ROUSSEAU (p. 27; H. V, 312)
L'on ne peut nier que ce ne soit surtout au Christianisme que l'Europe doit encore aujourd'hui l'espéce de société qui s'est perpétuée entre ses membres: tellement que celui des membres qui n'a point adopté sur ce point le sentiment des autres est toujours demeuré comme étranger parmi eux.

VOLTAIRE

que veut il dire?

The argument is that Christianity has produced a sort of solidarity of civilization in Europe to which non-Christian nations, as perhaps the Turks,[6] have remained strangers, but the sentence is somewhat vague and Voltaire affects not to understand it.

ROUSSEAU (p. 28; H. V, 312)
Après l'avoir si cruellement & si vainement persécuté, l'empire romain y trouva les ressources qu'il n'avoit plus dans ses forces; ses missions lui valoient mieux que des victoires; il envoyoit des Evêques réparer les fautes de ses Généraux.

VOLTAIRE

declamation!

Here appears a comment destined to become a favorite of Voltaire later in dealing with many passages in *Emile*, which likewise seem to him declamatory and merely rhetorical.

ROUSSEAU (p. 28; H. V, 312)
C'est ainsi que les Francs, les Goths, les Bourguignons, les Lombards, les Avares, & mille autres reconnurent enfin l'autorité de l'Empire après l'avoir subjugué, & reçurent, du moins en apparence, avec la Loi de l'Evangile celle du Prince, qui la leur faisoit annoncer.

VOLTAIRE

non ils se servirent des loix de l'empire comme d'un meuble des vaincus

ROUSSEAU (p. 29; H. V, 312)
Tel étoit le respect qu'on portoit encore à ce grand corps expirant, que jusqu'au dernier instant ses destructeurs s'honoroient de ses titres; on voyoit devenir Officiers de l'Empire les mêmes Conquérans qui l'avoient avili; les plus grands Rois accepter, briguer même, les honneurs Patriciaux, la Préfecture, le Consulat; & comme un lion

VOLTAIRE

[6] Cf. below, pp. 34-35.

qui flatte l'homme qu'il pourroit dévorer, non
on voyoit ces Vainqueurs terribles rendre clovis netait pas maitre de
hommage au Trône impérial, qu'ils étoient renverser lempire de con-
maîtres de renverser. stantinople

Voltaire, the historian, having thus given concrete expression to his many differences in viewpoint and interpretation as compared with Rousseau-Saint-Pierre, passes by the next nine pages without comment.

ROUSSEAU (p. 38; H. V, 314) VOLTAIRE
Une autre semence de guerre plus
cachée & non moins réelle, c'est que les
choses ne changent point de forme en
changeant de nature; que des Etats hérédi- ou sont ils
taires en effet, restent électifs en appa- mieux [?] du [?]
rence; qu'il y ait des Parlemens ou Etats parler des
nationaux dans des Monarchies, des Chefs fiefs d'italie
héréditaires dans des Républiques;

While part of Voltaire's note is not clearly legible, the meaning of the comment as a whole appears plain enough. He asks for concrete examples illustrating Rousseau's statement and suggests the fiefs of Italy as pertinent.

                VOLTAIRE
                sous les
ROUSSEAU (p. 39; H. V, 314) romains le[s]
. . . que tous les Peuples, soumis au tributaire[s]
même pouvoir, ne soient pas gouvernés par ne se
les mêmes loix, que l'ordre de succession gouvernai[ent]
soit différent dans les divers Etats d'un ils pas pa[r]
même Souverain; leurs loix
                municipa[les]

Rousseau's passage is a further development of the idea of the preceding citation immediately above. Voltaire's comment was evidently written in the book before binding as the margins have been cut and the final letters of the longer lines have been thus clipped off.

ROUSSEAU (p. 41, H. V, 315) VOLTAIRE
Le systême de l'Europe a précisément le quapelles t[u]
degré de solidité qui peut la maintenir dans renverser
une agitation perpétuelle, sans la renverser l'Europe
tout à fait;

PROJET DE PAIX PERPÉTUELLE

Voltaire again demands more precision of statement, though a less captious critic would doubtless understand Rousseau's implication of revolution or anarchy.

ROUSSEAU (p. 42; H. V, 315)   VOLTAIRE
En effet, ne pensons pas que cet équilibre si vanté ait été établi par personne, & que personne ait rien fait à dessein de le conserver: on trouve qu'il existe; & ceux qui ne sentent pas en eux-mêmes assez de poids pour le rompre, couvrent leurs vues particuliéres du prétexte de le soutenir.

les anglais et hollandais ont fait la guerre a louis XIV uniquement pr conserver l'equilibre.

Thus Voltaire takes issue with Rousseau and the Abbé de Saint-Pierre on the Balance of Power as a cause of war.

ROUSSEAU (pp. 44-45; H. V, 315)   VOLTAIRE
Où prendroit un prince européen des forces inattendues pour accabler tous les autres, tandis que le plus puissant d'entre eux est une si petite partie du tout, & qu'ils ont de concert une si grande vigilance? Aura-t-il plus de troupes qu'eux tous? . . .   bon
Aura-t-il plus d'argent? Les sources en sont communes, & jamais l'argent ne fit de   bon
grandes conquêtes.

This passage is of special interest because it shows Voltaire, in spite of his previous criticisms, ready to express unqualified approval of Rousseau's attack upon the possibility of universal conquest. Here at least the two rivals are completely in accord.

ROUSSEAU (p. 51; H. V, 316)   VOLTAIRE
Mais si le présent systême est inébranlable, c'est en cela même qu'il est plus orageux; car il y a entre les puissances européennes une action & une réaction qui, sans les déplacer tout à fait, les tient dans une agitation continuelle; & leurs efforts sont toujours vains & toujours renaissans, comme les flots de la mer, qui sans cesse agitent sa surface, sans jamais en changer le niveau; de sorte que les Peuples sont incessamment désolés, sans aucun profit sensible pour les Souverains.

pitoyable
louis 14 n'a
til pas donn[é]
lespagne a
son petit fi[ls]
que font
la tes flots

In spite of Voltaire's seeming matter-of-factness, it is Rousseau who appears nearer the fundamental truth; and the War of the Spanish Succession, though chosen by Voltaire as an example, is more apt to prove Rousseau's point that the people are constantly made to suffer without real gain, even to the rulers themselves.[7]

Rousseau (p. 52; H. V, 316-317)	Voltaire
Il me seroit aisé de déduire la même vérité des intérêts particuliers de toutes les cours de l'Europe; car je ferois voir aisément que ces intérêts se croisent de manière à tenir toutes leurs forces mutuellement en respect: mais les idées de commerce & d'argent ayant produit une espéce de <u>fanatisme</u> politique, font si promptement changer les intérêts apparens de tous les princes.	voyla un mot bien deplacé

While Voltaire in his more reflective moods might well have agreed with Rousseau and the Abbé de Saint-Pierre that the idea of gaining commercial advantage from war was illusory, his instinctive association of *fanaticism* with religious intolerance and persecution led him to underline the word and promptly criticize its use.

Rousseau (p. 53, n; H. V, 317, n.)	Voltaire
(a). Les choses ont changé depuis que j'écrivois ceci; mais mon principe sera toujours vrai. Il est, par exemple, très-aisé de prévoir que, dans vingt ans d'ici, l'Angleterre, avec toute sa gloire, sera ruinée, &, de plus, aura perdu le reste de sa liberté.	ah pauvre homme! encore profete?

Sharing the reaction against England which set in during the second half of the eighteenth century after the anglomania of its earlier years, Rousseau, like many other critics of that time and since, predicts England's proximate fall. Voltaire does not relish him in the rôle of prophet here any more than in the *Contrat social* the year following in connection with Russia.[8] The "encore" suggests a preceding reference which has not been located.

Rousseau (pp. 55-56; H. V, 317)	Voltaire
Il résulte de cet exposé trois vérités incontestables. L'une, qu'excepté le Turc,	

---

[7] Voltaire himself wrote elsewhere: "Depuis les anciens Romains, je ne connais aucune nation qui se soit enrichie par des victoires." (Moland, XIV, 525).

[8] See below, pp. 55-57.

PROJET DE PAIX PERPÉTUELLE 35

il règne entre tous les peuples de l'Europe une liaison sociale imparfaite, mais plus étroite que les nœuds généraux & lâches de l'humanité; la seconde, que l'imperfection de cette société rend la condition de ceux qui la composent pire que la privation de toute société entre eux; la troisième, que ces premiers liens, qui rendent cette société nuisible, la rendent en même tems facile à perfectionner; en sorte que tous ses membres pourroient tirer leur bonheur de ce qui fait actuellement leur misère, & changer en une paix éternelle l'état de guerre qui règne entre eux.

oublies tu que le turc a ete battu de la france

[illegible comment of one or two words]

chimerique

Voltaire's first comment hardly touches Rousseau's point that the Turk by religion, manners, and customs had always remained sharply separated from the rest of Europe. The second note has proved illegible, while the third shows Voltaire's characteristic scepticism, increasingly evident in following comments, regarding the possibility of establishing permanent peace.

ROUSSEAU (pp. 57-58; H. V, 318) VOLTAIRE
Mais il faut . . . que cette confédération [des nations] soit tellement générale, que nulle Puissance considérable ne s'y refuse; qu'elle ait un Tribunal judiciaire, qui puisse établir les loix & les règlemens qui doivent obliger tous les Membres; qu'elle ait une force coactive & coercitive pour contraindre chaque Etat de se soumettre aux délibérations communes.

chimere

Rousseau's analysis is excellent and forecasts the general form of the modern League of Nations as well as some of its present weaknesses, but Voltaire has no faith in the practicality of the proposal.

ROUSSEAU (p. 60; H. V, 318) VOLTAIRE
Il se peut faire que les Membres d'une de ces assemblées soient une fois douées du sens commun; il n'est pas même impossible qu'ils veuillent sincèrement le bien public.

trop cinique et révoltant

After opposing as chimerical the possibility of changing the current state of war into perpetual peace through a League of Nations and a World Court (Tribunal judiciaire), Voltaire rather inconsistently takes Rousseau to task as cynical for suggesting that some day an International Congress might chance to have enough common sense and public spirit to work for something else than national aggrandizement and try to build for world unity and peace. That Voltaire should be sceptical about the practicability of the proposed peace plan was entirely his right, but that he, who had so often flayed the weakness and corruption of mankind, and particularly the scourge of war, should object to Rousseau's implied criticism of governmental rulers as having adopted a foolish and selfish policy, is explicable only on an emotional, not on a rational, basis.

ROUSSEAU (pp. 62-63; H. V, 319)	VOLTAIRE
Par le troisième [article], la confédération garantira à chacun de ses Membres la possession & le gouvernement de tous les Etats qu'il possède actuellement, de même que la succession élective ou héréditaire, selon que le tout est établi par les loix fondamentales de chaque pays; &, pour supprimer tout d'un coup la source des démêlés qui renaissent incessamment, on conviendra de prendre la possession actuelle & les derniers Traités pour base de tous les droits mutuels des Puissances contractantes; . . . sans qu'il soit permis de s'en faire raison par voies de fait, ni de prendre jamais les armes l'un contre l'autre, sous quelque prétexte que ce puisse être . . .	chimère chimere
ROUSSEAU (p. 64; H. V, 319)	VOLTAIRE
Il sera encore convenu par le même Article qu'on armera & agira offensivement, conjointement, & à frais communs, contre tout Etat au ban de l'Europe, jusqu'à ce qu'il ait mis bas les armes.	tout le reste chimere

Sceptical of the proposal to renounce war forever in favor of judicial processes, sceptical of the nations' agreeing to take up arms together against any recalcitrant nation (the much discussed Article X of the modern League), the Patriarch of Ferney laid down his pen after commenting on the remaining half of the book: "tout le reste—chimère." It is evident that Voltaire at the age of sixty-seven, after all his reading of the wickedness and folly of mankind in preparation for his *Essai sur les mœurs* and after his own personal experiences with the shortcomings of human nature, was pessimistic and without faith in the Abbé de Saint-Pierre's humanitarian dreams. One wonders whether, with all his life-long attacks upon war, Voltaire had no hope of its elimination and no alternative plan to propose in remedy. "Quels que soient les dogmes des nations," he wrote in 1762, "elles feront toujours la guerre."[9]

Rousseau's own opinion after all, as expressed in his *Jugement sur la paix perpétuelle* unpublished until later, was hardly different from Voltaire's. He says: "Qu'on ne dise donc point que, si son système n'a pas été adopté, c'est qu'il n'étoit pas bon; qu'on dise au contraire qu'il étoit trop bon pour être adopté. . . . On ne voit point de ligues fédératives s'établir autrement que par des révolutions: et, sur ce principe, qui de nous oseroit dire si cette ligue européenne est à désirer ou à craindre? Elle feroit peut-être plus de mal tout d'un coup qu'elle n'en préviendroit pour des siècles."[10] It would be a mistake evidently to identify Rousseau's thought completely with that of the Abbé de Saint-Pierre upon which it was based, for the former tells us in his *Confessions:* "Je fis mon essai sur la *Paix perpétuelle*, le plus considérable et le plus travaillé de tous les ouvrages qui composoient ce recueil; et, avant de me livrer à mes réflexions, j'eus le courage de lire absolument tout ce que l'abbé avoit écrit sur ce beau sujet, sans jamais me rebuter par ses longueurs et par ses redites. Le public a vu cet extrait, ainsi je n'ai rien à en dire. Quant au jugement que j'en ai porté, il n'a point été imprimé, et j'ignore s'il le sera jamais; mais il fut fait en même temps que l'extrait."[11] Thus we must distinguish between the *Extrait*, which alone was commented upon by Voltaire,[12] and Rousseau's *Jugement* of it, at that

[9] Moland, XXIV, 423.
[10] Hachette, V, 335.
[11] *Ibid.*, VIII, 303.
[12] Voltaire published a satire of Rousseau's *Extrait* in the *Journal encyclopédique* for May 1, 1761. (Cf. Moland, XXIV, 231-33.) This satire had been composed in March, as is evident from a letter of the author to Cideville of March 26, 1761. (Cf. Moland, XLI, 242-43.) The pamphlet, *De la Paix perpétuelle par le docteur Goodheart* (1769) (Moland, XXVIII, 103-28), is little relevant, but is directed primarily at religious intolerance. It is interesting, however, to note in the opening lines a reference to the Abbé de Saint-Pierre's project as "une chimère," thus reproducing the favorite word of Voltaire's marginal comments.

time still unpublished, while still keeping in mind, however, the statement of Bastide, Rousseau's publisher: "Par la simplicité du titre il paroîtra d'abord à bien des gens que M. Rousseau n'a ici que le mérite d'avoir fait un bon *extrait*. Qu'on ne s'y trompe point, l'analyste est ici créateur à bien des égards."[13] Rousseau himself stated: "Il est vrai que j'ai vû l'objet sous un autre point de vûe que l'Abbé de Saint-Pierre, et que j'ai quelquefois donné d'autres raisons que les siennes."[14] Thus Voltaire was perhaps not entirely wrong in seeing Rousseau between the lines of the Abbé de Saint-Pierre's project.[15] Later, in the *Confessions*, Rousseau wrote of the good Abbé's projects that they were useful, but impractical, "par l'idée dont l'auteur n'a jamais pu sortir, que les hommes se conduisoient par leurs lumières plutôt que par leurs passions."[16] Voltaire himself could have said no more.

Agreed as to the desirability of abolishing war, Rousseau and Voltaire appear, therefore, to be agreed also that, human nature being what it is, the plan proposed by the Abbé was impracticable of execution, "une chimère," at least in the eighteenth century. Whether the Abbé de Saint-Pierre did not after all have a longer view on this question than either of his greater commentators, only the historian of the future can finally decide.

[13] *Correspondance générale de J.-J. Rousseau*, VI, 86.
[14] *Ibid.*
[15] "Voici un *Rescrit de l'empereur de la Chine sur la Paix perpétuelle* que ce Jean-Jacques va nous procurer." (Moland, XLI, 242-43.)
[16] Rousseau, *Œuvres* (Hachette), VIII, 302.

CHAPTER III

Voltaire's Comments on Rousseau's *Contrat social*

The *Contrat social* was released from the presses by Rey on April 13, 1762,[1] and announced by Rousseau as "imprimé" on the 25th of the same month.[2] Voltaire mentions it in a letter to Damilaville of June 25 of this year, in terms which sufficiently reveal his general attitude of hostility toward Rousseau at this time. "Ce *Contrat social* ou insocial n'est remarquable que par quelques injures dites grossièrement aux rois par le citoyen du bourg de Genève, et par quatre pages insipides contre la religion chrétienne. Ces quatre pages ne sont que des centons de Bayle. Ce n'était pas la peine d'être plagiaire. L'orgueilleux Jean-Jacques est à Amsterdam, où l'on fait plus de cas d'une cargaison de poivre que de ses paradoxes."[3] Since Voltaire had already as early as June 14[4] read *Emile*, published by May 22,[5] it is likely that he had received the *Contrat social* some weeks before the comment of June 25 mentioned above. In any case he was by no means slow in keeping up with all that Rousseau wrote at this time.

The edition of the *Contrat social* owned by Voltaire was one of those published by Rey at Amsterdam in 1762. His comments begin in the very first brief chapter. On the whole work Voltaire made fifty-eight marginal notes, fifty-six of which are reproduced, with a few inaccuracies, in Volume XXXII of the Moland edition of Voltaire.[6] All[7] are given here, including the two omitted by Moland. The tone of these notes is in general serious, indicating careful analysis of Rousseau's ideas.

After a few brief paragraphs introducing his subject, Rousseau begins his first chapter with the inflammatory words: "L'homme est

---

[1] Rousseau, *Correspondance* (Paris, Colin, 1927), VII, 187.
[2] *Ibid.*, 192.
[3] Voltaire, *Œuvres* (Moland), XLII, 142.
[4] *Ibid.*, 136. Cf. 125-26.
[5] Rousseau, *Correspondance* (Colin), VII, 232.
[6] Moland, XXXII, 474-82. Cf. above, p. 3, and n.
[7] I am very much indebted to my friend, Professor Norman L. Torrey, for aid in copying these notes on the *Contrat social*.

né libre, et partout il est dans les fers."[8] He then proceeds with his explanation.

ROUSSEAU (p. 3; H. III, 306)
Si je ne considérois que la force, & l'effet qui en dérive, je dirois: "Tant qu'un peuple est contraint d'obéïr, & qu'il obéït, il fait bien; sitôt qu'il peut secoüer le joug, & qu'il le secoüe, il fait encore mieux: car recouvrant sa liberté par le même droit qui la lui a ravie, ou il est fondé à la reprendre, ou l'on ne l'étoit point à la lui ôter."

VOLTAIRE
c'est tout le contraire. car sil est fondé a reprendre sa liberté, on ne letait pas a len priver.

Rousseau, however, had said at the beginning of his statement: "Si je ne considérois que la force, . . . je dirois." Thus he remarks simply that, if the law of force is to be admitted at all, it justifies revolting against any authority established by force. Rousseau offers two possibilities: either the same right, force, which has wrested man's liberty from him in the first place, justifies his recovering it at the earliest opportunity, or else man is justified in taking back his liberty because, if the right of force is disallowed altogether, man was unjustly enslaved in the first place. By implication therefore Rousseau suggests that the latter is really the case, thus agreeing with Voltaire. His double-barreled statement, with its tendency toward ambiguity, appears due to his desire to convince even those who, denying freedom based upon the abstract principle of justice, might appeal to the right of force. The next sentences commented upon by Voltaire follow immediately.

ROUSSEAU (p. 4; H. III, 306-07)
Mais l'ordre social est un droit sacré qui sert de base à tous les autres. Cependant ce droit ne vient point de la nature; il est donc fondé sur des conventions.

VOLTAIRE
cela est confus et obscur. ce droit vient de la nature, si la nature nous a fait des etres sociables.

Here, as has already been evident in connection with the *Discours sur l'inégalité*,[9] Voltaire and Rousseau diverge sharply on the question of whether man is by nature sociable or individualistic. Rousseau assumes society to be anti-natural, while Voltaire holds the opposite view.

[8] Hachette, III, 306.
[9] See above, p. 9.

CONTRAT SOCIAL 41

ROUSSEAU (p. 5; H. III, 307)
La plus ancienne de toutes les sociétés, & la seule naturelle, est celle de la famille.

VOLTAIRE
donc ce droit vient de la nature.

Rousseau appears here to contradict the extreme position taken in the *Discours sur l'inégalité* against the family as a natural social unit in primitive society.[10] Voltaire quite naturally observes the seeming contradiction between this statement and the one preceding.

ROUSSEAU (p. 5; H. III, 307)
La famille elle-même ne se maintient que par convention.

VOLTAIRE
mais il faut convenir que cette convention est indiquée par la nature.

Rousseau had just said that the ties of family ceased with the coming of children to age and independence, that, if the family continued to be united, it was not "naturellement" but "volontairement." Voltaire again disagrees.

ROUSSEAU (pp. 6-7; H. III, 307)
Grotius nie que tout pouvoir humain soit établi en faveur de ceux qui sont gouvernés: il cite l'esclavage en exemple.

VOLTAIRE
Grotius ne cite lesclavage que comme une exception, que comme le droit de la guerre.

ROUSSEAU (p. 8; H. III, 307-08)
Le raisonnement de ce Caligula revient à celui de Hobbes & de Grotius.

VOLTAIRE
lauteur se trompe. hobbés reconnait le droit du plus fort non comme une justice mais comme un malheur attaché a la misérable nature humaine.

ROUSSEAU (p. 17; H. III, 310)
Mais il est clair que ce prétendu droit de tuer les vaincus ne résulte en aucune maniére de l'état de guerre. Par cela seul que les hommes, vivant dans leur primitive indépendance, n'ont point entre eux de rapport assez constant pour constituer ni l'état de paix ni l'état de guerre, ils ne sont point naturellement ennemis.

VOLTAIRE

This passage is marked with a line in the right margin.

[10] See above, pp. 26-27.

ROUSSEAU (p. 18; H. III, 310)
La guerre n'est donc point une relation d'homme à homme, mais une relation d'Etat à Etat, dans laquelle les particuliers ne sont ennemis qu'accidentellement, non point comme hommes.

VOLTAIRE
tout cela me parait dun rheteur captieux. il est clair que la guerre d'état à état est la guerre dhomme a homme. *ordonnons a tous* nos sujets de leur courir sus.

From the beginning of the second passage above, "Mais il est clair," to the end of the paragraph of which the last passage cited comprises the first part,[11] there are marks in the margin, which seem to indicate that Voltaire's comment: "Tout cela me paraît d'un rhéteur captieux," may apply to the whole passage contained on pages 17, 18, and 19. While it is obviously true that individuals take part in wars, Rousseau appears right in contending that the men engaged in fighting are not inherently enemies. They have no private cause of quarrel but represent the states which have declared war. Evidence of the truth of this viewpoint is found in the tendency toward fraternization often remarked during lulls in the fighting.

ROUSSEAU (pp. 19-20; H. III, 311)
Même en pleine guerre, un prince juste s'empare bien, en pays ennemi, de tout ce qui appartient au public; mais il respecte la personne & les biens des particuliers; il respecte des droits sur lesquels sont fondés les siens.

VOLTAIRE

il fallait avant de parler du prince et des particuliers designer ce que cest que prince

ROUSSEAU (pp. 20-21; H. III, 311)
A l'égard du droit de conquête, il n'a d'autre fondement que la loi du plus fort. Si la guerre ne donne point au vainqueur le droit[x] de massacrer les peuples vaincus, ce droit qu'il n'a pas ne peut fonder celui de les asservir. On n'a le droit de tuer l'ennemi que quand on ne peut le faire esclave; le droit de le faire esclave ne vient donc pas du droit de le tuer: C'est donc un échange inique de lui faire acheter au prix de sa liberté sa vie, sur laquelle on n'a aucun

VOLTAIRE

[x] on na jamais droit de tuer un homme qu'a son corps deffendant.

supposition ridicule

---

[11] The paragraph ends: "Entre choses de diverses natures on ne peut fixer aucun vrai rapport."

CONTRAT SOCIAL

droit. En établissant le droit de vie & de mort sur le droit d'esclavage, & le droit d'esclavage sur le droit de vie & de mort, n'est-il pas clair qu'on tombe dans le cercle vicieux?

Rousseau and Voltaire here really hold the same view, but Voltaire, perhaps reading hastily, perhaps annoyed by the involved wording of Rousseau's argument, seems to go out of his way to criticize.

ROUSSEAU (pp. 21-22; H. III, 311)	VOLTAIRE
En supposant même ce terrible droit de tout tuer, je dis qu'un esclave fait à la guerre, ou un peuple conquis, n'est tenu à rien du tout envers son maître, qu'à lui obéir autant qu'il y est forcé. En prenant un équivalent à sa vie, le vainqueur ne lui en a point fait grâce: au lieu de le tuer sans fruit, il l'a tué utilement. Loin donc qu'il ait acquis sur lui <u>nulle</u> autorité jointe à la force, l'état de guerre subsiste entre eux comme auparavant, leur relation même en est l'effet; & l'usage du droit de la guerre ne suppose aucun traité de paix. Ils ont fait une convention; soit: mais cette convention, loin de détruire l'état de guerre, en suppose la continuité.	une non. il suppose continuité de faiblesse d'un côté et de force de l'autre.

In the text "nulle" is crossed out and "une" substituted for it. In his comment at the end of the passage, Voltaire again insists upon a merely verbal distinction. Rousseau had said simply that no real peace could be founded upon such unjust terms; that what really existed was a smoldering state of war ready at any favorable opportunity to break forth again. Rousseau is searching for an abstract principle justifying revolt against tyranny. Voltaire takes issue merely with his form of expression.

ROUSSEAU (p. 23; H. III, 312)	VOLTAIRE
Quand j'accorderois tout ce que j'ai réfuté jusqu'ici, les fauteurs du despotisme n'en seroient pas plus avancés.	bon

This is one of the three occasions where Voltaire expresses full agreement with a part of the *Contrat social*. He makes it definitely clear that, in spite of the verbal quibbles just noted, he does not, any more than his adversary, favor despotism.

ROUSSEAU (pp. 28-29; H. III, 313)

ˣ De plus, l'aliénation [de droits dans le contrat social] se faisant sans réserve, l'union est aussi parfaite qu'elle peut l'être, & nul associé n'a plus rien à réclamer.

VOLTAIRE

ˣ tout cela est faux. je ne me donne point a mes concitoiens sans reserve. je ne leur donne point le pouvoir de me tuer et de me voler a la pluralité des voix. je me soumets a les aider et a etre aidé; a faire justice et a la recevoir. point d'autre convention.

Here Moland has reproduced the wrong passage from Rousseau,[12] as is shown by Voltaire's cross-marks and by the repetition of the words "sans réserve" in both text and note.

Rousseau's point is that, by the social contract, the judgment in regard to all rights is removed from the individual to the state; that the individual in other words cannot take the law into his own hands. Voltaire's objection is that the contract must rest upon justice and is void in case of injustice. Nevertheless, Rousseau appears to be right in the sense that, even in the event of injustice to an individual, the latter has no recourse, assuming that all the courts have decided against him, except to submit or to make himself an outlaw. Such a revolt against society is in effect a return to primitive individualism and, if successful, constitutes a breaking down of the social contract in that particular instance.

ROUSSEAU (pp. 30-31, n; H. III, 313-14, n)

Le vrai sens de ce mot [la cité] s'est presque entièrement effacé chez les modernes: la plupart prennent une ville pour une cité, & un bourgeois pour un citoyen. Ils ne savent pas que les maisons font la ville, mais que les citoyens font la cité. . . Nul autre auteur françois [que D'Alembert], que je sache, n'a compris le vrai sens du mot *citoyen*.

VOLTAIRE

quelle pitié. ne voila til pas une chose difficile à comprendre! le gouvernement municipal existe en france. les citoiens de paris élisent le prevost des marchands les quartiniers elisent les echevins, le corps des marchands elit les consuls. cest pour cela qu'a londres la cité differe de la ville.

[12] Moland, XXXII, 476.

CONTRAT SOCIAL

Here again Moland has reproduced Voltaire's note inaccurately.[13] By omitting the first "élisent" after "les citoyens de Paris," the sense has been considerably changed. Rousseau is endeavoring, however clumsily, to bring out the rights of true citizenship, generally ignored in the eighteenth century in spite of Voltaire's slight correction.

ROUSSEAU (p. 34; H. III, 314) VOLTAIRE
Sitôt que cette multitude est ainsi réunie en un corps, on ne peut offenser un des membres[x] sans attaquer le corps, encore moins offenser le corps sans que les membres s'en ressentent.

[x] cela est pitoiable. si on donne le fouet a jean jaques Rousseau, donne t'on le fouet a la république

Rousseau holds that once the citizens of a republic have assembled in their deliberative body, their persons must be inviolate. It has in fact become the general practice in all free states to accord special immunities to members of legislative bodies on the floor of their place of assembly. Thus Rousseau is right in his idea. His expressions, however, are vague and confusing and provoke Voltaire to impatience over this theorizing about the social contract, so that he descends to personalities.

ROUSSEAU (p. 36; H. III, 315) VOLTAIRE
Afin donc que ce pacte social ne soit pas un vain formulaire, il renferme tacitement cet engagement, qui seul peut donner de la force aux autres, que quiconque refusera d'obéir à la volonté générale, y sera contraint par tout le corps: ce qui ne signifie autre chose sinon qu'on le forcera d'être libre; car telle est la condition qui donnant chaque citoyen à la Patrie, le garantit de toute dépendance personnelle; condition qui fait l'artifice & le jeu de la machine politique, & qui seule rend légitimes les engagemens civils, lesquels, sans cela, seroient absurdes, tyranniques, & sujets aux plus énormes abus.

tout cela nest pas exposé assez nettement.

Here Voltaire makes an objection to Rousseau's frequent lack of clear-cut precision, a defect which has evidently angered him all along. It is a criticism which is often just, and it is natural that Voltaire, the apostle of clarity and definiteness, should make it.

[13] *Ibid.*

ROUSSEAU (pp. 40-41; H. III, 316)

L'Etat, à l'égard de ses membres, est maître de tous leurs biens par le contrat social, qui dans l'Etat, sert de base à tous les droits; mais il ne l'est, à l'égard des autres Puissances, que par le droit de premier occupant, qu'il tient des particuliers.

VOLTAIRE

maitre de leur conserver tous leurs biens et tenu de les maintenir.

confus.

This interesting note shows Voltaire reiterating his belief that the social contract must secure the rights of individuals. Rousseau would doubtless have admitted this, but he would have held, what has always been true in practice, that individual rights must often bow to the right of the state, as for example in war time, or in peace in the right of the government to confiscate with suitable indemnity property needed for public purposes, even though the individual may be unwilling to sell. Voltaire's comment, however, is valuable in emphasizing the state's obligations on the other side, not brought out sufficiently by Rousseau. The note "confus" on the latter part of the passage has been omitted by Moland.[14] It is an entirely just comment. Again Voltaire might have said: "Tout cela n'est pas exposé assez nettement."

ROUSSEAU (p. 41; H. III, 316)

Voilà pourquoi le droit de premier occupant, si foible dans l'état de nature, est respectable en tout homme civil. On respecte moins dans ce droit ce qui est à autrui que ce qui n'est pas à soi.

VOLTAIRE

ouy quand ce premier occupant na pris que ce qui n'est a personne et quil nest pas un premier ravisseur.

Voltaire implies that first occupants of actually unused territory have been very rare in comparison with the cases where civilized nations have dispossessed savages of the land they already held.

ROUSSEAU (pp. 41-42; H. III, 316)

En général, pour autoriser sur un terrain quelconque le droit de premier occupant, il faut les conditions suivantes. Premièrement que ce terrain ne soit encore habité par personne; secondement, qu'on n'en occupe que la quantité* dont on a besoin pour subsister; / en troisième lieu qu'on en prenne possession, non par une vaine cérémonie, mais par le travail et la

VOLTAIRE

* bon
/ pourquoi? s'il napartient a personne je puis le prendre pour mes descendants.

[14] Moland, XXXII, 477.

culture, seul signe de propriété qui à défaut
de titres juridiques doive être respecté
d'autrui.

For the second time Voltaire expresses agreement with Rousseau's *Contrat social*. The "premier occupant" must actually be a "premier occupant," as implied by the preceding note already commented upon; the land appropriated must really be free and uninhabited. For the rest, Voltaire does not, however, feel that the quantity possessed must be limited to the immediate needs of the individual, as Rousseau does. The former would leave the way open to the acquisition of wealth, while the latter would not.

ROUSSEAU (p. 43; H. III, 317)
Quand Nuñez Balboa prenoit, sur le rivage, possession de la mer du sud et de toute l'Amérique méridionale au nom de la couronne de Castille, étoit-ce assez pour en déposséder tous les habitans & en exclure tous les Princes du monde?

VOLTAIRE
contradiction. ces terrains appartenaient dejà à d'autres.

Rousseau is merely amplifying his previous argument with a concrete illustration. There is therefore no contradiction, as Voltaire claimed, and no real disagreement between them, seeing that both have accepted the right of "premier occupant" as applied only to uninhabited territory.

ROUSSEAU (pp. 43-44; H. III, 317)
On conçoit comment les terres des particuliers réunies & contiguës deviennent le territoire public, & comment le droit de souveraineté, s'étendant des sujets au terrain qu'ils occupent, devient à la fois réel & personnel; ce qui met les possesseurs dans une plus grande dépendance, & fait de leurs forces mêmes les garans de leur fidélité. Avantage qui ne paroît pas avoir été bien senti des anciens monarques qui ne s'appelant que Rois des Perses, des Scithes, des Macédoniens, sembloient se regarder comme les chefs des hommes plutôt que comme les maîtres du pays. Ceux d'aujourd'hui s'appellent plus habilement rois de France, d'Espagne, d'Angleterre, etc. En tenant ainsi le terrain, ils sont bien sûrs d'en tenir les habitants.

VOLTAIRE

bien faux. les rois d'angleterre ne sont que Rois des anglais.

Probably the difference in attitude mentioned by Rousseau is the result merely of the greater fixity of territorial boundaries in modern, as compared with ancient, times and is not due to the conscious shrewdness which he suggests as the reason.

ROUSSEAU (p. 46, n; H. III, 318, n)　　　　VOLTAIRE
Sous les mauvais gouvernemens cette égalité n'est qu'apparente & illusoire; elle ne sert qu'à maintenir le pauvre dans sa misère & le riche dans son usurpation. Dans le fait les loix sont toujours utiles à ceux qui possédent & nuisibles à ceux qui n'ont rien: D'où il suit que l'état social n'est avantageux aux hommes qu'autant qu'ils ont tous quelque chose, & qu'aucun d'eux n'a rien de trop.

　　au contraire les loix protegent le pauvre contre le riche.

Very characteristic is the contrast in views made apparent by this passage and its comment. While Rousseau holds that laws protect owners of property and favor the rich as against the poor, Voltaire has exactly the opposite opinion. In reality, the laws undoubtedly do both, protect the rich and protect the poor also, leaning now one way and now the other in accordance with the trend of popular sentiment at a particular time, but with an almost inevitable tendency to leave an advantage in the hands of the man who has influence and the most money to spend on good lawyers. Voltaire, however, is right to this extent: if there were no laws, wealth supported by force would have free rein and the poor would be without the very considerable degree of protection which they do enjoy in consequence of legal safeguards.

ROUSSEAU (pp. 48-49; H. III, 318)　　　　VOLTAIRE
La souveraineté, n'étant que l'exercice de la volonté générale, ne peut jamais s'aliéner, & . . . le souverain, qui n'est qu'un être collectif, ne peut être représenté que par lui-même: le pouvoir peut bien se transmettre, mais non pas la volonté. . . . Si donc le peuple promet simplement d'obéir, il se dissout par cet acte, il perd sa qualité de peuple; à l'instant qu'il y a un maître, il n'y a plus de Souverain, & dès lors le corps politique est détruit.

　　louche

CONTRAT SOCIAL

Here is another note omitted by Moland.[15] Voltaire's objection is again directed against the ambiguity of Rousseau's thought, this time on popular sovereignty.

ROUSSEAU (p. 53; H. III, 319)
On a regardé l'acte de déclarer la guerre & celui de faire la paix comme des actes de souveraineté; ce qui n'est pas, puisque chacun de ces actes n'est point une loi mais seulement une application de la loi.

VOLTAIRE

ce qui est. car acte de souveraineté c'est acte de pouvoir.

Rousseau here appears in the realm of fine-spun theory, while Voltaire realistically puts his feet on the firm ground of actual fact.

ROUSSEAU (p. 55; H. III, 320)
Or, la vérité ne méne point à la fortune, & le peuple ne donne ni ambassades, ni chaires, ni pensions.

VOLTAIRE

tu aurais bien dû parler d'algernon Sidney.

Voltaire wrote in 1764: "Sidney écrivait d'après son cœur, et il scella ses sentiments de son sang."[16] Rousseau did mention Sidney in his *Lettres de la montagne* of the same year: "L'infortuné Sidney pensoit comme moi, mais il agissoit; c'est pour son fait et non pour son livre qu'il eut l'honneur de verser son sang."[17] As Sidney had an active public career in support of the Parliament against the King, held a position as plenipotentiary to Sweden, and was alleged to have received a pension from Louis XIV,[18] but was finally under Charles II condemned on a charge of treason and was beheaded after an unfair trial, it is not quite clear whether Voltaire here introduces his name for or against Rousseau's position. On the whole, it would seem that he might have mentioned the name in support of Rousseau's point.

ROUSSEAU (pp. 61-62; H. III, 321)
Tous les services qu'un citoyen peut rendre à l'Etat, il les lui doit sitôt que le Souverain les demande; mais le Souverain, de son côté, ne peut charger les sujets

VOLTAIRE

---

[15] *Ibid.*, XXXII, 477.
[16] Moland, XXV, 152, in a review of a translation of Sidney's *Discours sur le gouvernement*.
[17] Hachette, III, 206.
[18] Moland, XIV, 247-48, n. 2, here denied by the editors of Kehl.

d'aucune chaîne inutile à la communauté: il ne peut pas même le vouloir; car sous la loi <u>de raison</u> rien ne se fait sans cause, non plus que sous la loi <u>de nature</u>.

tu veux dire sous la loy de la physique et si lon fait des sottises sous la loy de raison! hem!

The contrasting phrases *de raison* and *de nature* have been underlined by Voltaire to indicate the bearing of his comment. Rousseau's position is that one cannot break the law of reason without thereby becoming *unreasonable* and hence left without sound justification. Voltaire, disregarding the theory of what ought to be, retorts with what may as a matter of fact occur, even though it be a "sottise." Rousseau would have expressed his meaning more accurately if he had written: "ne *doit* charger," "ne *doit* pas même le vouloir," "sous la loi de raison, rien ne *devrait* se faire sans cause," but this again is a case where his writing appears "louche."

ROUSSEAU (pp. 62-63; H. III, 322)
L'égalité de droit & la notion de justice qu'elle produit dérive[nt] de la préférence que chacun se donne, & par conséquent de la nature de l'homme; . . . la volonté générale pour être vraiment telle doit l'être dans son objet ainsi que dans son essence, . . . elle doit partir de tous pour s'appliquer à tous, & . . . elle perd sa rectitude naturelle lorsqu'elle tend à quelque objet individuel & déterminé; parce qu'alors, jugeant de ce qui nous est étranger nous n'avons aucun vrai principe d'équité qui nous guide.

VOLTAIRE

obscur et faux, cest sur un autre individu que s'exerce mon équité. quand je vote pour tous. cest pour moy cest par amour propre.

Again Rousseau's thought appears obscure and theoretical.

ROUSSEAU (pp. 63-64; H. III, 322)
En effet, sitôt qu'il s'agit d'un fait ou d'un droit particulier, sur un point qui n'a pas été réglé par une convention générale & antérieure, l'affaire devient contentieuse. C'est un procès où les particuliers intéressés sont une des parties, & le public l'autre, mais où je ne vois ni la loi qu'il faut suivre, ni le juge qui doit prononcer. Il seroit ridicule de vouloir alors s'en rapporter à une expresse décision de la volonté générale, qui ne peut être que la conclusion de l'une

VOLTAIRE

chacun est juge; et la loy naturelle est notre code.

des parties, & qui par conséquent n'est pour
l'autre qu'une volonté étrangère, particulière, portée en cette occasion à l'injustice
& sujette à l'erreur.

obscur et faux.

Rousseau's discussion still remains involved in abstractions whose interpretation in clear-cut terms is difficult.

ROUSSEAU (p. 71; H. III, 324)   VOLTAIRE
D'ailleurs tout malfaiteur attaquant le
droit social devient par ses forfaits rebelle
& traître à la patrie. . . . Les procédures, le
jugement, sont les preuves & la déclaration
qu'il a rompu le traité social, & par conséquent qu'il n'est plus membre de l'Etat.
Or, comme il s'est reconnu tel, tout au
moins par son séjour, il en doit être re-
tranché par l'exil comme infracteur du
pacte, ou par la mort comme ennemi public;
car un tel ennemi n'est pas une personne
morale, c'est un homme, & c'est alors que
le droit de la guerre est de tuer le vaincu.

tuo te gladio jugulas.

Coming, as this comment does, contemporary with, or shortly after, Rousseau's flight on June 9 due to the condemnation of *Emile*, it indicates how Rousseau's own words might be turned against him and made to justify his exile.

ROUSSEAU (p. 72; H. III, 324)   VOLTAIRE
Il n'y a point de méchant qu'on ne pût
rendre bon à quelque chose. On n'a droit
de faire mourir, même pour l'exemple, que   bon
celui qu'on ne peut conserver sans danger.

For the third time Voltaire agrees with Rousseau in definite and succinct terms. Here it is on the question of reducing capital punishment to the absolute minimum consistent with the welfare of society. In the midst of the antiquated judicial procedure of the time, the use of torture, and the excessive number of crimes expiated by capital punishment, there was especial need of such protests on the part of liberal minds. Rousseau's passage precedes by two years Beccaria's influential treatise, *Dei Delitti e delle Pene* (1764). For the French translation of this work in 1766 by the Abbé Morellet, Voltaire wrote an anonymous commentary, in which he said: "Les supplices inventés pour le bien de la société doivent être utiles à cette société."[19] Likewise in the *Dictionnaire philosophique* of 1764 Voltaire wrote: "Un homme pendu n'est bon à rien, et un homme condamné aux ouvrages publics sert encore la patrie et est une leçon vivante."[20] Thus these two outstanding writers of eighteenth-century France, Voltaire and Rousseau, agreed in this attitude which does honor to them both. It is interesting too that Voltaire does frankly give praise to Rousseau where he believes praise due.

Rousseau (p. 76; H. III, 325)   Voltaire
J'ai déjà dit qu'il n'y a point de volonté
générale sur un objet particulier. En effet
cet objet particulier est dans l'Etat ou hors
de l'Etat. S'il est hors de l'Etat, une volonté qui lui est étrangére n'est point gé-
nérale par rapport à lui; & si cet objet est   obscur
dans l'Etat, il en fait partie: Alors il se
forme entre le tout & sa partie une rélation
qui en fait deux êtres séparés, dont la partie est l'un, & le tout, moins cette même
partie est l'autre. Mais le tout moins une
partie n'est point le tout, & tant que ce
rapport subsiste il n'y a plus de tout mais
deux parties inégales: d'où il suit que la
volonté de l'une n'est point non plus
générale par rapport à l'autre.

Rousseau's language here is barbarous and resembles some of the fine-spun distinctions of scholastic theologians. Voltaire's comment therefore is not only accurate, but mild.

Rousseau (pp. 77-78; H. III, 325-26)   Voltaire
Quand je dis que l'objet des loix est
toujours général, j'entends que la loi con-
sidére les sujets en corps & les actions
comme abstraites, jamais un homme comme
individu ni une action particulière. . . . Elle
peut établir un Gouvernement royal & une
succession héréditaire, mais elle ne peut
élire un roi ni nommer une famille royale;   pourquoi non?

[19] Moland, XXV, 555.
[20] *Ibid.*, XIX, 626.

en un mot toute fonction qui se rapporte à un objet individuel n'appartient point à la puissance législative.

Rousseau continues his insistence that the legislative body should occupy itself exclusively with general principles and never with a particular application of them, but he does not specify here how a king might then be chosen. Presumably he means that a general election should be used in such cases in order to avoid any possibility of undue pressure upon the legislature. If so, such a procedure is undoubtedly the best safeguard that could be proposed.

ROUSSEAU (p. 86, n.; H. III, 328, n. 1)	VOLTAIRE
Ceux qui ne considérent Calvin que comme théologien connoissent mal l'étendue de son génie. La rédaction de nos sages Edits, à laquelle il eut beaucoup de part, lui fait autant d'honneur que son institution. Quelque révolution que le tems puisse amener dans notre culte, tant que l'amour de la patrie & de la liberté ne sera pas éteint parmi nous, jamais la mémoire de ce grand homme ne cessera d'y être en bénédiction.	fade louange d'un vil factieux, et d'un pretre absurde que tu detestes dans ton cœur.

Voltaire here shows himself unable to admit that Rousseau's admiration for Calvin as an administrator could possibly be sincere, though elsewhere, writing more moderately as a historian, Voltaire says of Calvin that his "dureté ... était jointe au plus grand désintéressement."[21] A modern authority quotes Renan, not likely to be too favorable, as calling Calvin "the most Christian man of his time,"[22] states that the execution of Servetus was generally approved by "all European Christendom" of the period, and testifies to the value of Calvin's contribution to civil administration in respect to trade, law, manufactures, police, the founding of the University of Geneva, and many other things upon which he was constantly called to give his judgment.[23] On this question the "citoyen de Genève" was undoubtedly in a much better position to judge accurately than

[21] *Ibid.*, XII, 309.
[22] *Encyclopædia Britannica*, 11th ed., Article *Calvin*.
[23] *Ibid.*

Voltaire, too exclusively influenced by his opposition to Calvin's theology and to the austerity of his government.

Rousseau (p. 91; H. III, 329)	Voltaire
La loi judaïque, toujours subsistante, celle de l'enfant d'Ismaël, qui depuis dix siècles régit la moitié du monde, annoncent encore aujourd'hui les grands hommes qui les ont dictées; & tandis que l'orgueilleuse philosophie ou l'aveugle esprit de parti ne voit en eux que d'heureux imposteurs, le vrai politique admire dans leurs institutions ce grand & puissant génie qui préside aux établissemens durables.	quoi! te contrediras tu toujours toi même!

Just before this passage Rousseau had said: "Les sages qui veulent parler au vulgaire leur langage au lieu du sien n'en sauroient être entendus. . . . Voilà ce qui força de tout tems les pères des nations de recourir à l'intervention du ciel & d'honorer les dieux de leur propre sagesse. . . . Cette raison sublime, qui s'élève au-dessus de la portée des hommes vulgaires, est celle dont le législateur met les décisions dans la bouche des immortels, pour entraîner par l'autorité divine ceux que ne pourroit ébranler la prudence humaine."[24] Voltaire's anger is caused, both by Rousseau's attack upon "l'orgueilleuse philosophie," and by his justification of an appeal to divine sanctions while at the same time admitting that these sanctions have no validity in themselves. Neither Voltaire nor Rousseau perceives that the idea of divine inspiration was so characteristic of primitive times as to affect the thought of the leaders as well as of the people, but Rousseau at any rate has progressed beyond the stage of describing these leaders as "d'heureux imposteurs." He at least recognizes the value of much of their work and the necessity of their speaking in the language of their age and not in terms of eighteenth-century rationalism. He is nearer here than Voltaire or many others of the philosophic party to an appreciation of the true meaning of historical relativity.

In Rousseau's discussion of Peter the Great, Voltaire has crossed out the "il" of the clause following the mention of Peter and written above it "le czar Pierre." From here down to the words "Précep-

[24] Hachette, III, 328-29.

teur françois,"[25] he has changed all the o's in the imperfect verb endings to a's, thus following the preference of his later years for a reformed spelling more in accord with the pronunciation.[26]

ROUSSEAU (p. 96; H. III, 330-31) VOLTAIRE
L'empire de Russie voudra subjuguer
l'Europe & sera subjugué lui-même. Les
Tartares ses sujets ou ses voisins deviendront
ses maîtres & les nôtres: Cette révolution   polisson. il te sied bien de
me paroît infaillible. Tous les Rois de   faire de telles prédictions!
l'Europe travaillent de concert à l'accélérer.

In addition to his personal animosity against Rousseau, which led to the sneering form of this criticism, and in addition to his disagreement with Rousseau's opinion regarding Russia, Voltaire was doubtless further angered by his presuming to set himself up as an authority in a field upon which Voltaire himself was at that very time doing pioneer work, the first volume of the *Histoire de l'empire de Russie sous Pierre le Grand* having been published in 1760 and the second, which appeared in 1763, being in preparation[27] at the time this marginal comment was probably written. Hence it is that Voltaire in several different works referred scornfully to Rousseau's prediction of the downfall of Peter's strenuous efforts before an invasion of Tartar barbarians, a prophecy bound to displease also Voltaire's Russian friends, including of course Catherine the Great.

Thus in his *Idées républicaines*, which Beuchot assigns to 1762 right on the heels of the *Contrat social*,[28] Voltaire quotes part of Rousseau's passage and adds: "Il lui paraît infaillible que de misérables hordes de Tartares, qui sont dans le dernier abaissement, subjugueront incessamment un empire défendu par deux cent mille soldats qui sont au rang des meilleures troupes de l'Europe. L'almanach du *Courier boiteux* a-t-il jamais fait de telles prédictions? La cour de Pétersbourg nous regardera comme de grands astrologues si elle

[25] Pp. 95-96 in the original edition.
[26] In an Avertissement to *Zaïre*, as early as 1736, Voltaire indicated his preference for, and use of, *ai* in *Français*, etc. (Moland, II, 555). In the *Supplément du Discours aux Welches* of 1764, Voltaire discussed also his antipathy to *oi* in imperfect verb endings. (*Ibid.*, XXV, 251.) Thus he evidently had the question particularly on his mind at the time when the *Contrat social* came into his hands.
[27] Moland, XVI, 373-74.
[28] *Ibid.*, XXIV, 413, n.

apprend qu'un de nos garçons horlogers a réglé l'heure à laquelle l'empire russe doit être détruit."[29]

Likewise in his Preface to his *Histoire de l'empire de Russie*, which in its present form dates from 1775,[30] Voltaire still has not forgotten Rousseau's prediction. "Mais un visionnaire plus avéré est l'écrivain qui prédit en 1762, dans je ne sais quel *Contrat social* ou insocial, que l'empire de Russie allait tomber. Il dit en propres mots: 'Les Tartares, ses sujets ou ses voisins, deviendront ses maîtres et les nôtres: cela me paraît infaillible.' C'est une étrange manie que celle d'un polisson qui parle en maître aux souverains, et qui prédit infailliblement la chute prochaine des empires, du fond du tonneau où il prêche, et qu'il croit avoir appartenu autrefois à Diogène. Les étonnants progrès de l'impératrice Catherine II et de la nation russe sont une preuve assez forte que Pierre le Grand a bâti sur un fondement ferme et durable."[31] Several familiar expressions recur here under Voltaire's pen. When he opened his copy of the *Contrat social* in order to be able to quote Rousseau "en propres mots," he doubtless saw once more after a lapse of years his marginal note and used again the word "polisson" in speaking of his rival. The phrase, "*Contrat social* ou insocial," it will be recalled, is a reminiscence of Voltaire's own first written comment on the work in his correspondence of June 25, 1762,[32] while the reference to Diogenes in connection with Rousseau is often repeated by Voltaire from the days of the *Discours sur l'inégalité*.[33] In 1765 also Voltaire incorporated into his *Dictionnaire philosophique* a similar comment upon this passage from "le *Contrat social* ou insocial du peu sociable Jean-Jacques Rousseau,"[34] thus again showing how much he enjoyed holding it up to ridicule in these terms.

Voltaire's concern for the susceptibilities of his Russian friends played some part in his zeal to refute Rousseau on this point as is shown by a letter to Catherine of October 1, 1772. "Comment se peut-il faire," he writes, "qu'il y ait encore chez nos Welches de prétendus raisonneurs et de prétendus politiques qui osent dire que

[29] *Ibid.*, 422-23.
[30] *Ibid.*, XVI, 377, n.
[31] *Ibid.*, 378-79.
[32] See above, p. 39.
[33] See above, p. 21.
[34] Voltaire, *Œuvres* (Moland), XX, 219-20.

'Pierre le Grand a tout épuisé pour former une armée, une flotte et un port, et que ses successeurs achèveront de tout ruiner pour soutenir l'ostentation de ces vains établissements?' Ce sont les propres paroles de la page 204 d'un nouveau livre intitulé *Histoire philosophique et politique des établissements et du commerce des Européens aux Indes*.[35] Il y a d'ailleurs de très-bonnes choses dans ce livre; mais cette sottise est pillée de ce fou de Jean-Jacques Rousseau, qui s'est avisé de juger souverainement tous les rois du haut de son grenier."[36]

In short, it appears that Rousseau's prediction has no bearing upon the recent revolution in Russia so long after the time of the *Contrat social*. It seems rather a guess somewhat rashly thrown out that Peter and his successors had gone too fast in their attempt to Europeanize their oriental empire. Rousseau may, however, have dimly perceived that the veneer of Russian civilization was very thin and was not grounded upon the sound basis of a general popular culture adequate to sustain it. In one of his characteristic generalizations he remarked: "Les Russes ne seront jamais vraiment policés, parce qu'ils l'ont été trop tôt."[37] Voltaire was inclined to be over-favorable toward Russia because of the inevitable influence of his aristocratic patrons in that country and their control of the documents furnished him for his history. Rousseau on the other hand, with perhaps some intuitive glimmerings of the fact that Russian progress had still but slightly touched a very small percentage of the total population, made a prediction too absolute and sweeping and not to be realized in any future at all proximate to the time either of Rousseau or of Voltaire.

Influenced no doubt by Montesquieu,[38] Rousseau in the next chapter develops the idea that there are limits to the size of an efficient government, "afin qu'il ne soit ni trop grand pour pouvoir être bien gouverné, ni trop petit pour pouvoir se maintenir par lui-même."[39] If the country is too large, its government falls under its own weight. This is the next passage commented on by Voltaire.

---

[35] By the Abbé Raynal.
[36] Moland, XLVIII, 182.
[37] Hachette, III, 330. (*Contrat social.*)
[38] Montesquieu, due partly to the slower methods of communication in his day, held that a republic should be small (*Esprit des lois*, Livre VIII, Chap. XVI), a monarchy of moderate size (*ibid.*, Livre VIII, Chap. XVII), and a despotism large (*ibid.*, Livre VIII, Chap. XIX.).
[39] Hachette, III, 331.

ROUSSEAU (p. 100; H. III, 332)
Et c'est ainsi qu'un corps [pays] trop grand pour sa constitution s'affaisse & périt écrasé sous son propre poids.

VOLTAIRE
miserable declamation. leurope est partagée en grands royaumes qui tous subsistent.

Voltaire's comment hardly touches the real issue raised by Rousseau.

ROUSSEAU (p. 102; H. III, 332)
Au reste, on a vu des Etats tellement constitués, que la nécessité des conquêtes entroit dans leur constitution même,ˣ & que, pour se maintenir, ils étoient forcés de s'agrandir sans cesse.

VOLTAIRE

ˣ il fallait les spécifier. cela en vaut bien la peine.

Voltaire's dry comment on Rousseau's generalization regarding the necessity of conquests in the case of some nations is most effective. Concrete examples are indeed much to be desired if the point is to be proved. Quite likely Rousseau, following Montesquieu's *Considérations sur les Romains* (1734), means Rome.

ROUSSEAU (pp. 105-106; H. III, 333)
Enfin il y a mille occasions où les accidens particuliers du lieu exigent ou permettent qu'on embrasse plus de terrain qu'il ne paroît nécessaire. Ainsi l'on s'étendra beaucoup dans un pays de montagnes, ... où un grand sol incliné ne donne qu'une petite base horizontale, la seule qu'il faut compter pour la végétation.

VOLTAIRE

tu nes pas geometre

Presumably Rousseau is referring to the scaling down of cultivable land through the terracing of hillsides. If this is so, then it is Voltaire who shows himself not "géomètre." Perhaps Rousseau's experience in the Swiss mountains gave him more accurate knowledge on this point than Voltaire's recent establishment at Ferney.

Thus far Voltaire's marginal comments have followed one another quite closely. Now he makes no comment for some ninety pages, going from Book II, Chapter X, to Book III, Chapter X. The immediately preceding Chapter IX has, however, a brief passage marked in the margin.

ROUSSEAU (p. 189; H. III, 354)
L'un est content quand l'argent circule, l'autre exige que le peuple ait du pain. Quand même on conviendroit sur ces points & d'autres semblables, en seroit-on plus avancé?

VOLTAIRE

Since there is no comment, it is probable that Voltaire approved of Rousseau's idea that individual preferences are too various to permit of absolute agreement on the ideal form of government. Voltaire now comments on a passage referring to Rome in connection with a long footnote on Venice.[40]

ROUSSEAU (p. 194, n; H. III, 356, n)
En effet, le peuple alors n'étoit pas seulement Souverain mais aussi magistrat et juge, le Sénat n'étoit qu'un tribunal en sous-ordre, pour tempérer & concentrer le Gouvernement.

VOLTAIRE

faux.

Rousseau is discussing the early struggles in Rome between the patricians and the plebs leading to the establishment of the tribunate. His statement that the Roman Senate thus became merely a subordinate tribunal seems, however, excessive and Voltaire's comment appears justified.

ROUSSEAU (p. 209; H. III, 360)
A l'instant que le Peuple est légitimement assemblé en corps Souverain, toute juridiction du gouvernement cesse, la puissance exécutive est suspendue, & la personne du dernier Citoyen est aussi sacrée & inviolable que celle du premier Magistrat, parce qu'où se trouve le Représenté, il n'y a plus de Représentant.

VOLTAIRE

faux, car si alors on commet un meurtre, un vol, le magistrat agit.

Voltaire in his *Idées républicaines,* also of 1762, comments upon this same passage in the following terms: "Cette proposition du *Contrat social* serait pernicieuse, si elle n'était d'une fausseté et d'une absurdité évidente. Lorsqu'en Angleterre le parlement est assemblé, nulle juridiction n'est suspendue; et dans le plus petit Etat, si pendant l'assemblée il se commet un meurtre, un vol, le criminel est et

[40] In this same footnote he has corrected the phrase *Serrar di consiglio* to read *del* instead of *di*. (p. 193, n.; H. III, 355, n.)

doit être livré aux officiers de la justice. Autrement une assemblée du peuple serait une invitation solennelle au crime."[41] Voltaire's repetition of the words "*meurtre* and *vol* and in the same order suggests the definite influence of his own marginal note in drawing up this slightly later passage. If Rousseau actually means the complete suspension of the executive power during the session of the popular assembly, then Voltaire is perfectly right in his criticism. Probably, however, Rousseau's real meaning, too ambiguously expressed, is that the executive has no jurisdiction over the members of the legislative, thus leaving them entirely free in their decisions from outside coercion. Thinking of Geneva and basing his opinion upon the very limited experience of the time in popular self-government, Rousseau, like Montesquieu,[42] conceives of democracy as applicable only in a very small territory and of the popular assemblies as composed of all, or nearly all, of the citizens.[43]

ROUSSEAU (p. 212; H. III, 360-61)   VOLTAIRE

Dans un Etat vraiment libre les citoyens font tout avec leurs bras & rien avec de l'argent: Loin de payer pour s'exempter de leurs devoirs ils payeroient pour les remplir eux-mêmes. Je suis bien loin des idées communes; je crois les corvées moins contraires à la liberté que les taxes.

The above passage is merely marked in ink by a vertical line in the left margin. Apparently this idea that citizens are interested in their government in proportion to the active part they take in it appealed to Voltaire as worthy of special consideration.

ROUSSEAU (p. 217; H. III, 362)   VOLTAIRE

Vos climats plus durs [les climats du nord] vous donnent plus de besoins: six mois de l'année la place publique n'est pas tenable, vos langues sourdes ne peuvent se

---

[41] Moland, XXIV, 420.

[42] *L'Esprit des lois,* Livre VIII, Chap. XVI. Note, however, that Montesquieu finds the federative republic adapted to a large territory. (*Ibid.,* Livre IX, Chap. 1.) This suggestion of Montesquieu appears to have been not without influence upon the American constitutional convention of 1787. See my article "James Madison et la pensée française," *Revue de littérature comparée,* III (1923), pp. 611-12.

[43] Cf. Rousseau's following chapter: "Sitôt que le service public cesse d'être la principale affaire des citoyens, & qu'ils aiment mieux servir de leur bourse que de leur personne, l'Etat est déjà près de sa ruine." Hachette, III, 360.

faire entendre en plein air, vous donnez
plus à votre gain qu'à votre liberté, & vous   tu ne songes pas que tous
craignez bien moins l'esclavage que la   les peuples du nord ont été
misère.   libres.

Rousseau's position here seems completely untenable. Voltaire points out the fallacy of his rival's too facile generalization by an equally sweeping generalization on the other side.

ROUSSEAU (pp. 242-43; H. III, 368)   VOLTAIRE
Le citoyen consent à toutes les lois, même
à celles qu'on passe malgré lui. . . . Quand
donc l'avis contraire au mien l'emporte,
cela ne prouve autre chose sinon que je
m'étois trompé, & que ce que j'estimois
être la volonté générale ne l'étoit pas. Si
mon avis particulier l'eût emporté, j'aurois
fait autre chose que ce que j'avois voulu,
c'est alors que je n'aurois pas été libre.   quel sophisme

Rousseau is insisting upon the necessity of the minority's accepting whole-heartedly the decision of the majority, if popular government is to succeed, but is unfortunate in his over-theoretical mode of expression.

ROUSSEAU (p. 248; H. III, 369-70)   VOLTAIRE
C'est une erreur de prendre le Gou-
vernement de Venise pour une véritable
Aristocratie. Si le peuple n'y a nulle part
au Gouvernement, la noblesse y est peuple   sophisme
elle-même. Une multitude de pauvres Bar-
nabotes n'approcha jamais d'aucune magis-
trature, & n'a de sa noblesse que le vain
titre d'Excellence & le droit d'assister au
grand Conseil. Ce grand Conseil étant   vanité ridicule
aussi nombreux que notre Conseil général
à Genève, ses illustres membres n'ont pas
plus de priviléges que nos simples Citoyens.

In his *Idées républicaines*, Voltaire cites and comments upon this passage as follows: "Tout cela est d'une fausseté révoltante. Voilà la première fois qu'on a dit que le gouvernement de Venise n'était pas entièrement aristocratique: C'est une extravagance à la vérité, mais elle serait sévèrement punie dans l'Etat vénitien. Il est faux que les sénateurs, que l'auteur ose appeler du terme méprisant de barnabotes, n'aient jamais été magistrats; je lui en citerais plus de cinquante qui ont eu les emplois les plus importants. Ce qu'il dit ensuite, que 'nos paysans représentent les sujets de terre ferme de la république de Venise,' n'est pas plus vrai. Parmi ces sujets de terre ferme, il se trouve à Vérone, à Vicence, à Brescia, et dans beaucoup d'autres villes, des seigneurs titrés, de la plus ancienne noblesse, dont plusieurs ont commandé les armées. Tant d'ignorance, jointe avec tant de présomption, indigne tout homme instruit. Lorsque cette ignorance présomptueuse traite avec tant d'outrages des nobles vénitiens, on demande quel est le potentat qui s'est oublié ainsi? Quand on sait enfin quel est l'auteur de ces inepties, on se contente de rire."[44]

The government of Venice during the eighteenth century is certainly to be classed as an oligarchy. If Rousseau had accepted this view and had classified Geneva in substantially the same way, his comparison would not have been out of place, since citizenship in Geneva at that time was distinctly a privilege enjoyed by not more than a thousand[45] of the then total of about 24,000 inhabitants.[46] His error is great, however, in turning the comparison in the opposite direction, though the *seigneur* of Ferney and of Tournay shows unnecessary aristocratic heat in taking the part of the Venetian nobles.

ROUSSEAU (p. 250; H. III, 370)	VOLTAIRE
Quand l'abbé de Saint-Pierre proposoit de multiplier les Conseils du Roi de France, & d'en élire les membres par Scrutin, il ne voyoit pas qu'il proposoit de changer la forme du Gouvernement.	il le voyait trés bien et il avait la folie de croire, comme toy que ses livres feraient des révolutions.

The reference is to the Abbé de Saint-Pierre's *Discours sur la polysynodie* (1718), of which Rousseau made an extract. Curiously enough Rousseau in his *Jugement sur la paix perpétuelle* of the Abbé (not published with the *Extrait* of the same work, which has been discussed in a previous chapter), referred to the means intended by Henri IV to accomplish the peace "que l'abbé de Saint-Pierre prétendoit faire avec un livre."[47] If Rousseau and Voltaire had lived until the French Revolution, they might have somewhat revised their opinions on the inadequacy of books to promote great changes.

[44] Moland, XXIV, 421-22.
[45] Louis Ducros, *Jean-Jacques Rousseau*, II (Paris, 1908), 321.
[46] D'Alembert, Article *Genève*, in Rousseau, Hachette, I, 348.
[47] Hachette, V, 335.

CONTRAT SOCIAL 63

ROUSSEAU (p. 251, n.; H. III, 370, n.)   VOLTAIRE
Le nom de *Rome*, qu'on prétend venir
de *Romulus*, est grec, & signifie force; le
nom de *Numa* est grec aussi, & signifie Loi.   proprement dureté. nomos
Quelle apparence que les deux premiers rois   a peu de raport a Numa et
de cette ville aient porté d'avance des noms   nul a Pompilius
si bien relatifs à ce qu'ils ont fait?

The words "force" and "Loi" have been underlined by Voltaire. Regardless of the controversy over the etymology of Numa Pompilius, second legendary king of Rome, it is interesting to note that Rousseau is convinced of the mythical character of early Roman history. Voltaire expresses the same attitude in his *Dictionnaire philosophique*.[48] Thus they are both in advance of Montesquieu, who is too inclined to accept these early legends as true history.[49]

On the next three chapters of the *Contrat social* Voltaire makes no marginal notes, but pauses again at Book IV, Chapter VIII.

ROUSSEAU (pp. 296-97; H. III, 382)   VOLTAIRE
De cela seul qu'on mettoit Dieu à la tête
de chaque société politique, il s'ensuivit
qu'il y eut autant de Dieux que de peuples.
Deux peuples étrangers l'un à l'autre, &
presque toujours ennemis, ne purent longtemps reconnoître un même maître: Deux
armées se livrant bataille ne sauroient obéir
au même chef. Ainsi des divisions nati-
onales résulta le polythéisme, & de là l'into-   très faux il n'y eut d'intolérance théologique & civile, qui naturelle-   lerance d'abord que chez les
ment est la même, comme il sera dit ci-   egyptiens et chez les juifs.
après.

Elsewhere Voltaire repeats this opinion: "Les Egyptiens semblent être les premiers qui ont donné l'idée de l'intolérance. ... Les Hébreux, voisins des Egyptiens, et qui prirent une grande partie de leurs rites, imitèrent leur intolérance, et la surpassèrent."[50] At the beginning of the same work in 1769, he says: "La seule paix perpétuelle qui puisse être établie chez les hommes est la tolérance."[51] The same passage of Rousseau is criticized in Voltaire's *Idées répu-*

---
[48] Moland, XIX, 348.
[49] Montesquieu, *Considérations sur les Romains*, Chap. I.
[50] Moland, XXVIII, 106.
[51] *Ibid.*, 103.

blicaines, already referred to: "Autant de mots, autant d'erreurs: les Grecs, les Romains, les peuples de la grande Grèce, reconnaissaient les mêmes dieux en se faisant la guerre: ils adoraient également les dieux *majorum gentium,* Jupiter, Junon, Mars, Minerve, etc. Les chrétiens, en se faisant la guerre, adorent le même Dieu. Le polythéisme des Grecs et des Romains ne résulta point de leurs guerres: ils étaient tous polythéistes avant qu'ils eussent rien à démêler ensemble; enfin il n'y eut jamais chez eux ni intolérance civile ni intolérance théologique."[52] Voltaire's glorification of antiquity[53] in this respect is certainly not unaffected by the desire to make an effective preachment for the benefit of contemporary and later generations.

ROUSSEAU (p. 297; H. III, 382)

La fantaisie qu'eurent les Grecs de retrouver leurs Dieux chez les peuples barbares, vint de celle qu'ils avoient aussi de se regarder comme les Souverains naturels de ces peuples. Mais c'est de nos jours une érudition bien ridicule que celle qui roule sur l'identité des Dieux de diverses nations: comme si Moloch, Saturne et Chronos pouvoient être le même Dieu! comme si le Baal des Phéniciens, le Zeus des Grecs et le Jupiter des Latins pouvoient être le même; comme s'il pouvoit rester quelque chose commune à des Etres chimériques portant des noms différens!

VOLTAIRE

cest toy qui es ridicule.
il est constant que le jupiter la junon le mars la venus des romains etaient les dieux des grecs.

Rousseau is doubtless weak in comparative religion, but it is to be noted that Voltaire, in criticizing him, carefully limits his comparison to the more obvious relationship of Roman to Greek gods.

ROUSSEAU (pp. 301-02; H. III, 383-84)

Enfin les Romains ayant étendu avec leur empire leur culte & leurs Dieux, & ayant souvent eux-mêmes adopté ceux des vaincus, en accordant aux uns & aux autres le droit de cité, les peuples de ce vaste empire se trouvèrent insensiblement avoir des multitudes de Dieux & de cultes, à peu près les mêmes partout: & voilà comment

VOLTAIRE

non sans doute les dieux de sirie et d'Egypte ceux du septentrion etaient fort différents ceux des perses et des indiens encor plus.

[52] *Ibid.*, XXIV, 423.
[53] Cf. *ibid.*, XXV, 40–41.

le paganisme ne fut enfin dans le monde
connu qu'une seule & même religion.   très faux.
    Ce fut dans ces circonstances que Jésus
vint établir sur la terre un royaume Spi-
rituel. . . . Or, cette idée nouvelle d'un
royaume de l'autre monde n'ayant pu jamais entrer dans la tête des payens, ils re-
gardèrent toujours les Chrétiens comme de
vrais rebelles qui, sous une hypocrite sou-
mission, ne cherchoient que le moment de
se rendre indépendans & maîtres, & d'u-
surper adroitement l'autorité qu'ils fei-   la vraie cause fut la désobé-
gnoient de respecter dans leur foiblesse.   issance de marcel de Lau-
Telle fut la cause des persécutions.   rent, et de tant d'autres.

    From Voltaire's criticism of the first part of this passage, it appears that Rousseau and he have changed places. Each seems to have reversed his position as compared with the passage and note immediately preceding. The last note is made clear by another passage of Voltaire dating from 1769. He says: "Un Marcel, en Afrique, jette son ceinturon par terre, brise son bâton de commandement, à la tête de sa troupe, et déclare qu'il ne veut plus servir que le Dieu des chrétiens; on fait un saint de ce séditieux! Un diacre, nommé Laurent, au lieu de contribuer comme un citoyen aux nécessités de l'empire, au lieu de payer au préfet de Rome l'argent qu'il a promis, lui amène des borgnes et des boiteux; et on fait un saint de ce téméraire!"[54] Actually the explanations given by Rousseau and by Voltaire of the reasons why the Christians were persecuted seem very similar. In both cases sedition seems the basic cause. Voltaire, however, rather captiously chooses to bring up a specific example as though it were fundamentally different. In any case, it seems clear that Voltaire in writing the later passage of 1769 utilized or at any rate remembered this marginal comment on Rousseau.

ROUSSEAU (pp. 303-05; H. III, 384)   VOLTAIRE
    Plusieurs peuples cependant, même dans
l'Europe ou à son voisinage, ont voulu conserver ou rétablir l'ancien système, mais
sans succès; l'esprit du christianisme a tout
gagné. Le culte sacré est toujours resté ou
redevenu indépendant du Souverain, & sans

[54] *Ibid.*, XXVIII, 110.

liaison nécessaire avec le corps de l'Etat. Mahomet eut des vues très saines; il lia bien son sistème politique; & tant que la forme de son Gouvernement subsista sous les Califes ses successeurs, ce Gouvernement fut exactement un, & bon en cela. Mais les Arabes, devenus florissans, lettrés, polis, mous & lâches, furent subjugués par des barbares: alors la division entre les deux puissances recommença; quoiqu'elle soit moins apparente chez les mahométans que chez les Chrétiens, elle y est pourtant, surtout dans la secte d'Ali; & il y a des Etats, tels que la Perse, ou elle ne cesse de se faire sentir. . . .   *très faux*

Partout ou le Clergé fait un corps, il est maître & législateur dans sa patrie. Il y a donc deux puissances, deux Souverains, en Angleterre & en Russie, tout comme ailleurs.   *point du tout*

Voltaire's admiration for the religion of Mahomet as a foil to Christianity, inherited perhaps from Bayle,[55] appears to exceed Rousseau's more qualified praise. In any case the former does not agree that Mahomedan lands later fell victims to churchly tyranny, nor does he find a similar dangerous division of secular power between Church and State in England or in Russia, as Rousseau holds to be the case. As long ago as 1734, Voltaire had written in the *Lettres philosophiques:* "Un Anglais, comme homme libre, va au Ciel par le chemin qui lui plaît."[56] Evidently he has not changed his opinion in the meantime.

ROUSSEAU (p. 308; H. III, 385)   VOLTAIRE

Il y a une troisième sorte de religion plus bizarre, qui, donnant aux hommes deux législations, deux chefs, deux patries, les soumet à des devoirs contradictoires, & les empêche de pouvoir être à la fois dévots & Citoyens. Telle est la Religion des Lamas, telles est celle des Japonois, tel est le christianisme Romain. On peut appeler celui-ci la religion du Prêtre.   les lamas et les japonais sont citez ici mal a propos. le gr. lama est souverain comme le pape. le Dairi nest quun mufti.

[55] Bayle, *Dictionnaire historique et critique*, art. *Mahomet.*
[56] Voltaire, *Lettres philosophiques*, Lanson ed., 2nd ed., Paris, 1915–17, I, 61.

In the *Essai sur les mœurs,* Voltaire wrote of the head of the Japanese church: "L'empereur ecclésiastique, nommé *dairi,* est une idole toujours révérée; et le général de la couronne, qui est le véritable empereur, tient avec respect le dairi dans une prison honorable."[57] Thus, according to Voltaire, in Japan the civil power is supreme. Of the Grand Lama he says: "Ce dalai-lama ... décide souverainement tous les points de foi sur lesquels les lamas sont divisés; enfin il s'est depuis quelque temps fait souverain du Thibet."[58] In this case therefore the religious head has made himself head also of the state. In both instances, according to Voltaire, there is unity of power, and not the division into two contradictory tendencies claimed by Rousseau.

Rousseau (pp. 310-11; H. III, 386)	Voltaire
Reste donc la Religion de l'homme ou le Christianisme, non pas celui d'aujourd'hui, mais celui de l'Evangile, qui en est tout à fait différent. Par cette Religion sainte, sublime, véritable, les hommes, enfans du même Dieu, se reconnoissent tous pour frères, & la société qui les unit ne se dissout pas même à la mort.	je suis venu aporter le glaive et non la paix diviser le pere et la mere le frere et la sœur.

In this comment Voltaire refers to the well-known passage in Matthew X, 34-35, which expresses the family divisions and heartbreaks caused by those who give up their former religion to become converts to Christianity. Voltaire interprets it unfairly against Rousseau without taking account of the context. In the *Dictionnaire philosophique,* he was to handle the passage for the benefit of the public in quite a different way. There he considers Jesus as having said exactly the opposite and having been misreported through a copyist's error: "Je leur dis que j'apportais la paix, et non le glaive."[59] This ingenious, but obvious, subterfuge cannot be reconciled with the second verse of the Biblical passage which speaks definitely of dividing members of the same family against each other. In neither case is it possible to believe that Voltaire was acting in good faith.

Rousseau (p. 312; H. III, 386)	Voltaire
Le christianisme est une religion toute	

[57] Moland, XII, 363.
[58] *Ibid.,* XI, 179.
[59] *Ibid,* XX, 347.

spirituelle, occupée uniquement des choses du Ciel; la patrie du Chrétien n'est pas de ce monde. les premiers chretiens etaient comme les esseniens les therapeutes les quakres.

In 1771 Voltaire returns to this comparison between the primitive Christians, the Essenians, the Therapeutics, and the Quakers. "La ressemblance s'y trouve en plusieurs points: confraternité, biens en commun, vie austère, travail des mains, détachement des richesses et des honneurs, et surtout horreur pour la guerre."[60] The four groups mentioned in his marginal note recur under his pen in this passage, probably through an association which had become definitely fixed in his mind.

Rousseau's work is now near its conclusion. We come here to his proposed "civic dogmas."

ROUSSEAU (p. 319; H. III, 388)

Il y a donc une profession de foi purement civile dont il appartient au Souverain de fixer les articles, non pas précisément comme dogmes de Religion, mais comme sentimens de sociabilité sans lesquels il est impossible d'être bon Citoyen ni sujet fidèle.

VOLTAIRE

tout dogme est ridicule funeste. toutte contrainte sur le dogme est abominable. ordonner de croire est absurde. bornez vous a ordoner de bien vivre.

In his comment upon this much-criticized passage of Rousseau, Voltaire stands upon firm ground. Whoever does not accept these dogmas of belief in a beneficent Providence, immortality, Heaven and Hell, the sacredness of the Social Contract and the laws, and—paradoxically—tolerance, must be banished, "non comme impie, mais comme insociable, comme incapable d'aimer sincèrement les lois, la justice, et d'immoler au besoin sa vie à son devoir."[61] This is the unexpected conclusion to which Rousseau in his *Contrat social* comes. Voltaire's comment, entirely free from personalities, goes directly to the heart of the question and shows the folly of any constraint upon religious belief. It is good conduct, not specific beliefs, that the laws should inculcate.

ROUSSEAU (p. 322; H. III, 389)

La raison sur laquelle on dit qu'Henri IV embrassa la Religion romaine la devroit faire quitter à tout honnête homme, & surtout à tout Prince qui sauroit raisonner.

VOLTAIRE

sa raison fut la couronne de france.

[60] *Ibid.*, XIX, 27. Cf. p. 25.
[61] Hachette, III, 388.

CONTRAT SOCIAL

In the *Essai sur les mœurs* likewise Voltaire wrote: "Sa conversion assurait sans doute son salut, je le veux croire; mais il paraît bien que l'amant de Gabrielle ne se convertit que pour régner."[62] Rousseau argues here from principle, Voltaire from expediency. There is no reconciling of the two viewpoints. Rousseau takes his religious convictions much more seriously than Voltaire ever would, or could. Provided tolerance was adhered to, the latter regarded the question of theological beliefs as of too slight importance to stand before the throne of France or before any other practical consideration. The question of personal integrity Voltaire does not raise, just as he, who will lie like a trooper to preserve a quasi-anonymity for his more dangerous works, regards Rousseau as an utter fool for insisting upon standing by his guns and publishing his writings under his own name.[63] This interesting passage, which with its comment emphasizes one of the most fundamental differences between the two men, was omitted by Moland.[64]

We have reproduced all of Voltaire's fifty-eight marginal notes on the *Contrat social*. The tone of the comments, as we have seen, is in general serious, indicating careful analysis of Rousseau's ideas. Such comments as: *confus et obscur, louche, obscur et faux, faux, quel sophisme, vanité ridicule, très faux, point du tout,* show Voltaire's sharp difference of opinion from Rousseau and his feeling that the latter is often lacking in definiteness, precision, or accuracy. At the same time, the subject treated does not in general call forth Voltaire's wrath and in consequence he is not often personal in his invective. An interesting exception to this general attitude appears when Rousseau predicts some type of governmental change or revolution in Russia. Voltaire's comment is distinctly *ad hominem:* "Polisson! il te sied bien de faire de telles prédictions."

One of the few cases where Voltaire records approval is when Rousseau condemns despotism. The former wrote in the margin the single word, *bon*. Likewise, when Rousseau says: "On n'a droit de faire mourir, même pour l'exemple, que celui qu'on ne peut conserver sans danger," Voltaire again commented: "Bon," thus showing that he also believed capital punishment should be restricted to

---
[62] Moland, XII, 546. Cf. *ibid.*, XXIV, 509–10; XXV, 484; XXVII, 289.
[63] Cf. below, pp. 136, 139.
[64] Moland, XXXII, 482.

the absolute minimum. The only other case of full agreement between them is when Rousseau limits lawful occupation of territory to that which is absolutely uninhabited, thus implicitly condemning the manner in which European nations dealt with the native occupants of America. All of Voltaire's other comments express disagreement or some degree of criticism. It should not be forgotten, however, that he probably took no exception to many passages upon which he did not comment. It is a natural human tendency to note points of disagreement more frequently than the opposite, and emphasis upon Voltaire's critical notations might easily give a false impression.

Among these hostile comments, very characteristic of the master of Ferney is the one which shows that, while Rousseau believes the tendency of the laws is to favor the rich against the poor, Voltaire has exactly the opposite opinion: "Au contraire, les loix protègent le pauvre contre le riche." An interesting comment occurs when Rousseau says that there have been nations so constituted that conquest was absolutely necessary for their continued existence: they must expand or perish. Voltaire writes drily: "Il fallait les spécifier. Cela en vaut bien la peine."

Book III has but three comments; Book IV has a few at the beginning and then none until the next to the last chapter which deals with "la Religion civile." Two marginal notes here are of special importance. Rousseau has spoken eloquently of Christianity, the Christianity of the Gospel with its emphasis upon unity and brotherly love. Voltaire's retort is to quote Christ's statement: "Think not that I am come to send peace on earth: I came not to send peace, but a sword." Obviously this is an unfair use of a passage without reference to its context. More important is Voltaire's clear-cut criticism of Rousseau's civic dogmas as basically intolerant and pernicious. This vigorous rejection of such an untenable position does honor to Voltaire's insight and common sense.

In his comments on the *Contrat social* Voltaire is by no means always right or always fair. He does not always have the better of the argument. In many instances where he is justified in his criticism of detail, we cannot conclude from what we know of his general opinions that he rejects the whole passage. In other cases, as has been pointed out above, he does convict Rousseau of inaccuracy or obscurity or of unsound opinion. Often the chief interest of his comments is to show upon what points they most sharply diverge. Obviously, no reader familiar with Rousseau will take these scattered comments as affording a complete or balanced estimate of the value of the *Contrat social*. That must be determined on other grounds. These notes of Voltaire should be taken frankly for what they are, criticisms of detail and criticisms primarily of faults. The reader might accept nearly all of Voltaire's strictures and yet conclude that Rousseau's work contains much of value in spite of such shortcomings. As for Voltaire, however, writing after Rousseau's violent break with him just two years before, it is clear enough that he held in no high regard what he called "ce Contrat social ou insocial"[65] and exempted from his unfavorable comments only three of the passages which he annotated.

[65] See above, p. 39.

CHAPTER IV

Voltaire's Comments on Rousseau's *Emile*

I. The Part of *Emile* before *Le Vicaire savoyard*

Emile was first printed at Paris by Duchesne under the name of Jean Néaulme, Amsterdam.[1] A copy was sent promptly to M. and Mme de Luxembourg on May 22, 1762.[2] On June 4, Voltaire wrote to Damilaville: "Je n'ai point encore cette *Education* de l'homme le plus mal élevé qui soit au monde. Je l'aurai incessamment."[3] On the 9th of June, Rousseau's work was condemned at Paris to be burned and a warrant was issued for the author's arrest.[4] Warned in advance and urged to flee from Montmorency, Jean-Jacques finally consented and left for Berne before the writ was served.[5] On the 11th, the *Contrat social* and *Emile* were both ordered seized at Geneva and there likewise were condemned on the 19th to be burned.[6] According to Rey, however, this action was taken only at the instance of France.[7] Meanwhile by the 14th Voltaire had received and read the book himself, for on this date he wrote again to Damilaville: "On a défendu à Genève les livres de Jean-Jacques. Je ne sais ce qu'on en fait à Paris. J'ai eu son *Education*. C'est un fatras d'une sotte nourrice en quatre tomes, avec une quarantaine de pages contre le christianisme, des plus hardies qu'on ait jamais écrites."[8] Thus promptly after its first publication did Voltaire form the general opinion of *Emile*—ridicule of Rousseau's educational theories with praise only for the *Vicaire savoyard*—which with little change was to remain his to the end.

That Voltaire made certain marginal notes on the *Vicaire sa-*

[1] Théophile Dufour, *Recherches bibliographiques sur Jean-Jacques Rousseau* (Paris, 1925), I, 149.
[2] Rousseau, *Correspondance* (Paris, Colin, 1927), VII, 232.
[3] Voltaire, *Œuvres* (Moland), XLII, 125.
[4] Rousseau, *Correspondance*, VII, 367-70.
[5] Rousseau, *Confessions* (Hachette), IX, 27-30.
[6] Rousseau, *Correspondance*, VII, 370-76.
[7] *Ibid.*, IX, 220-21.
[8] Voltaire, *Œuvres*, XLII, 136.

voyard has been known to modern scholars at least since 1858 when J. Gaberel reproduced some of them in his book, *Rousseau et les Genevois*,[9] but only since the publication of these notes by M. Bernard Bouvier in the *Annales Jean-Jacques Rousseau* for 1905[10] have they been available in complete form. Pierre-Maurice Masson made frequent reference to these notes in his masterly critical edition of the *Vicaire savoyard* published in 1914,[11] and since that time they have been commonly cited to show how even Voltaire could approve with a succinct "bon" certain parts of Rousseau's most important work on religion.

The volume in which these notes are found is now in the Archives Jean-Jacques Rousseau in the Bibliothèque publique at Geneva. It was given to that institution by a descendant of the Constant family several of whom in the eighteenth century had been neighbors and friends of Voltaire. In fact, the property adjoining Les Délices on one side was owned by Pictet de Saint-Jean[12] whose daughter Charlotte, the "Lolotte" of Voltaire's correspondence,[13] married in 1758 Samuel Constant de Rebecque. This Mme Samuel de Constant took part in the plays frequently produced by Voltaire after his removal to Ferney out of Genevan jurisdiction. In fact she was so often a visitor there that her letters furnished Perey and Maugras with some of the best of their material on *La Vie intime de Voltaire aux Délices et à Ferney*.[14] It is therefore not strange that a volume utilized by Voltaire should have found its way into the library of the Constant family, but whether they lent the book to Voltaire or whether he gave it to them, one can only speculate as does M. Bouvier,[15] though it seems unlikely that Voltaire would have annotated a borrowed copy. It is interesting to note in this connection an incident related by the Prince de Ligne as having occurred during his visit at Ferney in 1763. He says: "M. de Constant lui demanda [à Voltaire], en ma présence, son *Histoire de Russie*."[16] This shows that Voltaire

[9] Cf. *Annales Jean-Jacques Rousseau*, I (1905), 272, n.
[10] *Ibid.*, pp. 272-84.
[11] Paris, Hachette.
[12] Cf. Perey and Maugras, *La Vie intime de Voltaire aux Délices et à Ferney*, Paris (1885), p. 192, n.
[13] Moland, XXXVIII, 540; XXXIX, 13, 373-74.
[14] Cf. in this work, pp. 83-84, 187-95, and *passim* to p. 390.
[15] *Annales Jean-Jacques Rousseau*, I, 272-73.
[16] Moland, I, 351.

might very well, upon some other occasion, have lent or given M. de Constant a duplicate copy of *Emile* in which there were already marginal annotations. Some duplication of important books in Voltaire's library was rendered inevitable by his possession for a time of several residences in and near Switzerland and is in fact suggested by passing references in his correspondence.[17]

That the Constant *Emile* was not the only copy possessed and annotated by Voltaire is made clear by an examination of the Leningrad library. In fact the *Emile* at Leningrad contains, besides many passages marked without comment, seventy-one marginal notes in contrast to forty-one or, according to my count, forty-three in the copy at Geneva. Moreover, the notes at Leningrad are not, like those studied by M. Bouvier, practically limited to the *Vicaire savoyard*. The copy of *Emile* which remained permanently in Voltaire's possession naturally engaged his major attention. It is therefore particularly worthy of close study.

The question of the date when these two sets of annotations were made is interesting, but at present impossible of positive solution. The Leningrad *Emile* is the duodecimo edition in four volumes bearing on its title page the name of Jean Néaulme, Amsterdam, but in reality printed, as we have seen,[18] by Duchesne at Paris in the spring of 1762. This is the original edition. The Geneva *Emile* is also duodecimo in format and M. Bouvier thought it too was printed by Duchesne, though its title page bears, not the name of Néaulme, Amsterdam, but that of "Les Héritiers de G. Weidmann & Reich," Leipzig.[19] According to Masson, however, this edition was printed, not at Leipzig, but in all probability by Bruyset at Lyons with the complicity of Duchesne. If this is the case, it appeared simultaneously with that at Paris[20] and may have reached Voltaire first, as Masson surmises. On the other hand, the fact that the annotations in the

---

[17] "Je ne peux vivre sans livres: une campagne sans eux serait pour moi une prison." (Moland, XXXVIII, 157). "J'aurai une chambre pour vous [à Monrion], . . . quelques livres qui n'en sortiront point." (*Ibid.*, 508). "J'avais fait venir, il y a six mois, les mêmes volumes de Londres. Les uns seront dans mon cabinet des Délices; les autres, dans celui de Ferney." (*Ibid.*, XXXIX, 527).

[18] Cf. above, p. 72.

[19] *Annales Jean-Jacques Rousseau*, I, 273, n. 2.

[20] Masson, *La Profession de foi du Vicaire savoyard*, Paris, 1914, pp. lxxxvii-lxxxviii. Cf. Th. Dufour, *Recherches bibliographiques sur les œuvres de Jean-Jacques Rousseau*, I, 175-76.

Leningrad *Emile* are scattered through the whole book would seem to suggest a reader going through the entire work from beginning to end for the first time. The edition preserved at Geneva from the Constant library might therefore have been picked up by Voltaire later when he was rereading the only part of *Emile* for which he had esteem, the *Vicaire savoyard*. Such an explanation would account for the fact that his marginal notes in this edition are limited to Book IV and, with a few exceptions, deal only with the words of the priest who is the mouthpiece for Rousseau's religious ideas. However, the argument might be reversed and the matter remains doubtful. In only a few instances do the annotations in these two different editions deal with the same passages.

We are now ready to pass to Voltaire's marginal comments as found in the *Emile* in the Leningrad library.

Near the beginning of Book I, after laying down his fundamental principle: "Tout est bien, sortant des mains de l'Auteur des choses, tout dégénère entre les mains de l'homme,"[21] Rousseau explains more fully what he means by Nature as applied to man, calls attention to the limitations of an exclusive patriotism, which looks with contempt upon the foreigner, but concludes that this is an inevitable human defect and preferable to a cosmopolitanism which exalts the foreign at the expense of compatriots near at hand.

ROUSSEAU (I, 10; H. II, 6)	VOLTAIRE
Défiez-vous de ces cosmopolites qui vont chercher au loin dans leurs livres des devoirs qu'ils dédaignent de remplir autour d'eux. Tel Philosophe aime les Tartares, pour être dispensé d'aimer ses voisins.	quel philosophe a donc jamais aimé les tartares

Voltaire partially underlined "Philosophe" and "Tartares." Perhaps he saw in this passage a reference to his *Orphelin de la Chine* of 1755. Admiration for the Chinese was in any case very common among the adherents of the philosophic party, furnishing them with a useful foil for comparisons unfavorable to contemporary France. Rousseau himself, in his enthusiasm for primitivism, was after all but going a step farther in a similar direction. In any event, the derogatory reference to the *philosophe* piqued Voltaire as indicating

[21] Rousseau, *Œuvres* (Hachette), II, 3.

that Rousseau had turned from a protégé to an enemy of the philosophic party.

Immediately following is this passage:

ROUSSEAU (I, 10; H. II, 6)   VOLTAIRE
L'Homme naturel est tout pour lui; il est l'unité numérique, l'entier absolu, qui n'a de rapport qu'à lui-même ou à son semblable. L'homme civil n'est qu'une <u>unité fractionnaire</u> qui tient au <u>dénominateur</u>.   quel stile

Voltaire has underlined the words "unité fractionnaire" and "dénominateur" to indicate the reason for his scorn.

Insisting upon his distinction, Rousseau maintains that a citizen of Rome for example sacrificed his independent human individuality to devote himself exclusively to his country.

ROUSSEAU (I, 11; H. II, 6)   VOLTAIRE
Un citoyen de Rome n'étoit ni Caïus ni Lucius; c'étoit un Romain: même il aimoit la patrie exclusivement à lui. <u>Régulus</u> se prétendoit <u>Carthaginois,</u> comme étant devenu le bien de ses maîtres. . . . Il s'indignoit qu'on voulût lui sauver la vie. Il vainquit, & s'en retourna triomphant mourir dans les supplices. Cela n'a pas grand rapport, ce me semble, aux hommes que nous connoissons.   quelle supposition ridicule!

     et laventure nest pas vraie

Again Voltaire's underlining of the two important words "Régulus" and "Carthaginois" shows the direction of his comment. He manifests impatience at Rousseau's supposition that Regulus claimed himself Carthaginian as a result of the fortunes of war. His scepticism regarding the legend of Regulus' death[22] is shared by modern authorities. Voltaire is a historian, Rousseau is not.

Immediately following at the beginning of the next paragraph is this passage.

---

[22] "The tale was probably invented by the annalists to excuse the cruel treatment of the Carthaginian prisoners by the Romans." *Encyclopædia Britannica*, 11th ed., XXIII, 48. Cf. Moland, XI, 153; XIX, 360.

EMILE

ROUSSEAU (I, 11; H. II, 6)   VOLTAIRE
Le Lacédémonien Pédarète se présente pour être admis au conseil des trois cens; il est rejetté. Il s'en retourne tout joyeux de ce qu'il s'est trouvé dans Sparte trois cens hommes valant mieux <u>que lui.</u>

tarare!

Voltaire's scornful epithet indicates his disbelief in this story as one of Plutarch's idealizations.

After expressing admiration for Plato's *Republic* as really the finest treatise on education ever written, Rousseau holds that institutions of public education in the true sense of the term cannot exist under modern forms of society as at present organized.

ROUSSEAU (I, 14; H. II, 7)   VOLTAIRE
Je n'envisage pas comme une institution publique ces risibles établissemens qu'on <u>appelle collèges.</u>

those reverend bedlams colleges and scools.

It is interesting to note that Voltaire here makes his comment in English, recalling apparently an apropos phrase from his reading.

ROUSSEAU (I, 16; H. II, 8)   VOLTAIRE
En Egypte, où le fils étoit obligé d'embrasser l'état de son père, l'éducation du moins avoit un but assuré; mais parmi nous où les rangs seuls demeurent & où les hommes en changent sans cesse, nul ne sait si en élevant son fils pour le sien il ne travaille pas contre lui.

quelle phrase!

Ignoring the content here, Voltaire apparently objects to Rousseau's sentence as involved and awkward.

Calling for a more general and active education, Rousseau says this education should prepare for an abundant, vigorous life.

ROUSSEAU (I, 20; H. II, 9)   VOLTAIRE
L'homme qui a le plus vécu n'est pas celui qui a compté le plus d'années, mais celui qui a le plus senti la vie. Tel s'est fait enterrer à cent ans, qui mourut dès sa naissance. Il eût gagné de mourir jeune; au moins eût-il vécu jusqu'à ce tems-là.

quel contresens!

Again Voltaire's objection is stylistic.

ROUSSEAU (I, 23; H. II, 10)

VOLTAIRE

Les pays où l'on emmaillotte les enfans sont ceux qui fourmillent de bossus, de boiteux, de cagneux, de noués, de rachitiques, de gens contrefaits de toute espèce. De peur que les corps ne se déforment par des mouvemens libres, on se hâte de les déformer en les mettant en presse.

cela arrive aux enfans des ouvriers dont le métier déforme le corps.

Between these pages 22 and 23 is a marker with the words: "Note margi assassiner." It seems not to be relevant to these pages and has probably been misplaced from pages 296-97 of the second volume of Rousseau's work mentioned later in this chapter. Voltaire's comment is directed at pointing out that the use of tight swaddling clothes is not the only cause of such bodily deformities as Rousseau mentions.

Insisting now upon the necessity of children in order to give permanence to family life, Rousseau continues:

ROUSSEAU (I, 31; H. II, 13)

VOLTAIRE

[Sans enfants] il n'y a point de <u>résidence</u> dans les familles.

Voltaire merely underlined *résidence* without comment, struck perhaps by Rousseau's use of the word.

ROUSSEAU (I, 47; H. II, 17)

VOLTAIRE

Quelqu'un dont je ne connois que le rang m'a fait proposer d'élever son fils. Il m'a fait beaucoup d'honneur sans doute; mais loin de se plaindre de mon refus, il doit se louer de ma discrétion. Si j'avois accepté son offre, & que j'eusse erré dans ma méthode, c'étoit une éducation manquée: si j'avois réussi, c'eût été bien pis. Son fils auroit renié son titre; il n'eût plus voulu être Prince.

quel sot amour propre qu'importe au public qu'on t'ait proposé d'etre précepteur!

Voltaire here descends to uncalled for personalities in comment upon Rousseau's perfectly legitimate statement. In his *Dialogues d'Evhémère* of 1777, Voltaire clearly has this passage still in mind, or probably has turned again to it. He writes: "D'abord l'auteur, demi-Gaulois, demi-Allemand, déclare qu'un grand prince l'a supplié de vouloir bien lui faire l'honneur d'être précepteur de son fils; qu'il

EMILE

l'a refusé, et qu'il ne sera jamais précepteur. Aussitôt il nous apprend qu'il l'est d'un jeune homme de qualité."[23]

Now Voltaire appears to be reading rapidly, for he passes by more than fifty pages without comment.

ROUSSEAU (I, 99-100; H. II, 33)   VOLTAIRE
On a longtems cherché s'il y avoit une Langue naturelle & commune à tous les hommes: sans doute, il y en a une; & c'est celle que les enfans parlent avant de savoir parler. Cette Langue n'est pas articulée, mais elle est accentuée, sonore, inintelligible. L'usage des nôtres nous l'a fait négliger au point de l'oublier tout-à-fait. Etudions les enfans, & bientôt nous la rapprendrons auprès d'eux.   que de futilitez ecrites avec arrogance!

Voltaire's impatience is increasing. He is easily exasperated by Rousseau's suggestion that adults might profitably spend time relearning child language. Rousseau, on his side, over-serious and lacking in sense of humor, has expressed himself in such a way as to rouse opposition in any one at all inclined in that direction.

Voltaire continues to hurry on, but pauses a moment fourteen pages later.

ROUSSEAU (I, 114; H. II, 38)   VOLTAIRE
Les longues pleurs d'un enfant qui n'est ni lié ni malade & qu'on ne laisse manquer de rien, ne sont que des pleurs d'habitude & d'obstination.   pleurs est masculin

Rousseau in his manuscript[24] had used *pleurs* in the feminine, as did Régnier,[25] and so it was reproduced in the duodecimo edition of Duchesne which Voltaire read. In the octavo edition of the same publisher, this passage and another ten pages earlier were both corrected to the masculine,[26] which is followed in modern editions.

This is the last comment in Book I of *Emile*. Voltaire passes to Book II. Between pp. 148-49[27] is a paper bookmark, but it is unac-

[23] Moland, XXX, 529.
[24] Th. Dufour, *op. cit.*, I, 172.
[25] Littré, *Dictionnaire de la langue française*, III (1881), p. 1163. "Régnier a fait pleur du féminin; c'est une faute que rien n'excuse."
[26] Th. Dufour, *loc. cit.*
[27] Extending from the last paragraph on p. 47 in the Hachette edition to the word *nécessaire* in l. 21 on p. 48.

companied by commentary. The passage deals with Rousseau's advice that man should gain happiness by reducing his wants within his physical limitations. Similarly marked without comment is the interesting passage on pp. 158-59[28] where Rousseau continues the development of the same idea and shows how a ruler, like the common man, is limited by his faculties and is in reality enslaved to those who serve him. The implied satire of court life might indeed have interested the author of the first of the seven *Discours sur l'Homme*, "De l'égalité des conditions" (1738), who since its publication had had bitter experience also of the potent hostility of the King's mistress, Mme de Pompadour. A marker is found likewise between pp. 174-75[29] which protest against allowing children, royal or otherwise, to enforce their will upon adults. There is no doubt but that the markers used by Voltaire in his books have in a large number of cases been left undisturbed in their original position,[30] but in the instances just cited there is no definite evidence, except the probability that the passages in question might interest, rather than aggravate, Voltaire, to permit us to say positively that he marked them for future reference.

A marker also stands between pp. 178-79,[31] which give an imagined conversation between teacher and child in order to show that it is impossible to make children understand moral ideas and the reasons why certain things are forbidden. This time, however, there is an accompanying comment. The child asks:

Rousseau (I, 179; H. II, 57)	Voltaire
Quel mal y a-t-il à faire ce qu'on me défend?	Vous etes un sot monsieur le maitre il faut dire parce que vous offensez votre mere qui vous a donné la vie et lenfant ne vous fera plus de questions.

Rousseau's imaginary conversation is over-theoretical and rather far-fetched. Voltaire on his side shows himself eminently practical,

---

[28] Beginning with *comme* in l. 4, p. 51, Hachette, and ending with *parce* in l. 30.

[29] Beginning with the last paragraph on p. 55 of Hachette and ending with *imposé* in l. 18 on p. 56.

[30] See G. R. Havens and N. L. Torrey, "The Private Library of Voltaire at Leningrad," PMLA, XLIII, 995.

[31] Hachette, II, 57.

EMILE

though parents well know that his suggested answer will not always suffice.

There now follow seven passages, two in Volume I and five in Volume II, which are without marginalia but are marked in other ways. The first two of these have bookmarks only and are therefore subject to the same uncertainties as those just mentioned above. The last five have no bookmarks, but are checked in ink with a crossmark in the margin. The first passage is in Volume I, pp. 180-81[32] and continues the conversation of teacher and child. The second is on pp. 244-45[33] of the same volume and discusses the ability of children to reason. Possibly, from what we know of a later comment of Voltaire on the *Vicaire savoyard*, he may have been interested in the contrast between the sensations as "passives" and the judgment as "actif,"[34] perhaps it was rather Rousseau's statement of the tendency of children to deal with geometry by rote rather than by reasoning which caught Voltaire's eye. Again we can only speculate without being sure.

From this point, through all the latter half of Book II and the first half of Book III, Voltaire leaves behind him no concrete sign of being interested. At about the middle of Book III, Volume II, p. 77,[35] a check mark in ink is found at the beginning of the paragraph which reads: "Que deviendront vos élèves, si vous leur laissez adopter ce sot préjugé, si vous le favorisez vous-même, s'ils vous voient, par exemple, entrer avec plus d'égards dans la boutique d'un orfèvre que dans celle d'un serrurier?" Four pages later, Volume II, p. 81,[36] a similar check mark in ink is found opposite the sentence which says that Emile "n'est presque encore qu'un être physique." Voltaire's violent hostility[37] to the non-intellectual character of Rousseau's program of early education may well have led him to mark this passage in a sort of sardonic agreement. Likewise, on the follow-

---

[32] *Ibid.*, 57, "On vous punit pour avoir désobéi," to p. 58, ll. 4-5, "ou, qui pis est, la" . . .

[33] *Ibid.*, 76, l. 9, "être seule dans l'esprit," to the 2nd line in the last paragraph, "raisonnement."

[34] Cf. below, p. 99.

[35] Hachette, II, 157.

[36] *Ibid.*, 158.

[37] Cf. Moland, X, 160: "Je fais d'un gentilhomme un garçon menuisier." (*Les Deux Siècles*, 1771?); XXX, 573: "Dans un roman nommé *Emile*, dont le héros est un gentilhomme menuisier."

ing pages,[38] after Rousseau's statement that his pupil values things according to their utility, a check has been placed opposite the sentence: "Il honore beaucoup plus un cordonnier, un maçon, qu'un L'Empereur, un Le Blanc, & tous les joailliers de l'Europe." It is unlikely that Voltaire, the partisan of luxury, would have shared this point of view in such sharp contrast to his own admiration for "Le superflu, chose très-nécessaire."[39] On p. 85[40] Rousseau classifies the mechanical arts in the order of their importance as they appear to him and attacks the refinement of specialization to which they have been brought. These words have been checked in the same fashion: "Que pensera-t-il en voyant que les arts ne se perfectionnent qu'en se subdivisant, en multipliant à l'infini les instruments des uns & des autres? Il se dira: 'Tous ces gens-là sont sottement ingénieux.'" Similar reasons have led to the checking of a passage on p. 93[41] attacking luxury: "Que pensera-t-il du luxe, quand il trouvera que toutes les régions du monde ont été mises à contribution, que vingt millions de mains peut-être ont longtems travaillé, qu'il en a coûté la vie peut-être à des milliers d'hommes?" On p. 95[42] a check mark is found also opposite the sentence: "Ce pain bis, que vous trouvez si bon, vient du bled recueilli par ce paysan." The similarity in tone of all these passages and the fact that it is easy to see why they would all be objectionable to Voltaire makes it reasonably certain that the check marks are from his pen. This probability is increased by the fact that marginal notes on the pages closely following indicate that he was reading attentively this part of *Emile*.

Making concrete his preference for simplicity over luxury, Rousseau offers Emile a choice between a dinner amid all the trappings of wealth and social splendor and a plain repast with friends in a neighboring village.

ROUSSEAU (II, 97; H. II, 163)   VOLTAIRE
Le choix d'Emile n'est pas douteux: car
il n'est ni babillard ni vain.   c'est un

The rest of the note was cut off by the bookbinder, which is a

---

[38] II, 82; Hachette, II, 158.
[39] Moland, X, 84.
[40] Hachette, II, 159.
[41] *Ibid.*, 162.
[42] *Ibid.*

further indication that these comments were probably made early after Voltaire's first receipt of the book. The missing word is in all likelihood "babillard," the use of which would accord with Voltaire's frequent practice of directly contradicting Rousseau by throwing back at him his own words.[43]

Between the following two pages, pp. 98-99,[44] is a marker with the initials, "N.M.," *Note marginale*. There is no written comment in the margin, however, but only another check mark, which would seem to indicate that the marker was put there by Wagnière to designate a passage marked by Voltaire himself. If so, this is further evidence in support of the probability that these check marks are all by Voltaire as well as the marginal notes themselves. The passage checked here is the following: "On n'imaginera pas que, dans l'espace de trois ou quatre ans que nous avons à remplir ici, nous puissions donner à l'enfant le plus heureusement né, une idée de tous les arts & de toutes les sciences naturelles, suffisante pour les apprendre un jour de lui-même." Judging from Voltaire's marginal note on the very next page, he probably marked this passage in renewed scorn of Rousseau's whole program.

ROUSSEAU (II, 99; H. 164)	VOLTAIRE
Ce que nous nous proposons d'acquérir est moins la science que le jugement.	ni lun ny lautr

It is again the binder who is responsible for cutting off the final *e* and part of the *r* of *autre*.

In the course of the next thirty-four pages there are sixteen passages with marginal check marks in ink, but without written comments. The first of these is opposite footnote 8 on p. 106,[45] the footnote to Rousseau's famous forecast of approaching revolutions:[46] "Je tiens pour impossible que les grandes monarchies de l'Europe aient encore longtemps à durer: toutes ont brillé, & tout Etat qui brille est sur son déclin. J'ai de mon opinion des raisons plus particulières que cette maxime, mais il n'est pas à propos de les dire, & chacun ne les voit que trop." In the *Contrat social* Rousseau had predicted a revo-

---
[43] Cf. below, pp. 88, 89, 150, 151, 152, 177.
[44] Hachette, II, 163.
[45] *Ibid.*, 166, n. 1.
[46] "Nous approchons de l'état de crise et du siècle des révolutions." Hachette, II, 166.

lution in Russia and Voltaire had commented: "Polisson, il te sied bien de faire de telles prédictions!"[47] likewise a passage in the same work on the territorial limitations of effective government was annotated by Voltaire: "Misérable déclamation! L'Europe est partagée en grands royaumes qui tous subsistent."[48] Remembering these passages, we can easily see that Rousseau's prophecy of the fall of monarchies would not appeal to the politically conservative Voltaire.

On the next page[49] Rousseau praises that rare king able to rise even above the loss of his crown and philosophically maintain his dignity as a man. This passage is checked. "Du rang de roi, qu'un lâche, un méchant, un fou peut remplir comme un autre, il [un roi détrôné] monte à l'état d'homme, que si peu d'hommes savent remplir." Rousseau's democratic scorn of kings, based upon the low average character of most of those known to history, does honor both to his frankness and his courage. Whether Voltaire, the admirer of Henri IV, accepted this viewpoint is doubtful. His experiences with Louis XV and with Frederick might, however, have prepared him by this time to look upon it with more favor than otherwise.

The next passage checked is on p. 109:[50] "Celui qui mange dans l'oisiveté ce qu'il n'a pas gagné lui-même le vole." This is vigorous language, and perhaps much too socialistic for Voltaire, although, remembering the trenchant conclusion of the tenth of the *Lettres philosophiques*,[51] we can hardly be sure. Many years had elapsed, however, since 1734. Then Voltaire had only recently returned from his English exile. In 1762 he was established in riches and independence at Ferney. There was time and cause for a change in viewpoint. Moreover, there is a great difference, after all, between Voltaire's praise of big merchant princes and Rousseau's esteem for the manual laborer.

[47] Cf. above, p. 55.
[48] Cf. above, p. 58.
[49] Hachette, II, 166.
[50] *Ibid.*
[51] "Je ne sçais pourtant lequel est le plus utile à un Etat, ou un Seigneur bien poudré qui sçait précisément à quelle heure le Roi se léve, à quelle heure il se couche, & qui se donne des airs de Grandeur en jouant le rôle d'esclave dans l'antichambre d'un Ministre, ou un Négociant qui enrichit son Païs, donne de son Cabinet des ordres à Suratte & au Caire, & contribue au bonheur du monde." *Lettres philosophiques* (1734), Lanson ed., 1915-17, I, 122.

EMILE

On the following page[52] in fact Rousseau shows even more clearly that he holds manual labor in honor as nearest the state of nature, while the artisan he believes to be freer than the farm laborer. "L'artisan ne dépend que de son travail; il est libre, aussi libre que le laboureur est esclave: car celui-ci tient à son champ dont la récolte est à la discrétion d'autrui." Perhaps the checking of this passage was due to the feeling which later inspired the defender of the serfs of Mont-Jura in 1772.[53]

In consequence of his conviction that the artisan is most truly free, Rousseau on the next page urges that Emile learn a trade. "Un métier à mon fils! mon fils artisan! Monsieur, y pensez-vous? —J'y pense mieux que vous, Madame, qui voulez le réduire à ne pouvoir jamais être qu'un Lord, un Marquis, un Prince, & peut-être un jour moins que rien."[54] Louis XVI, who was so much better as a locksmith than as a king, held doubtless something of Rousseau's point of view. It is unlikely, however, that the "Gentilhomme ordinaire de la Chambre du Roi," the "comte de Tournay," and the master of Ferney would relish this putting of an artisan's trade above titles like those which he had been at so much pains to win for himself. The checking of this passage is probably due to the same feeling which caused Voltaire to call Emile scornfully "un gentilhomme menuisier."[55]

On the same page there is a check mark opposite the phrases: "Eh! tant pis, tant pis pour vous!"[56] Probably Voltaire, if he checked this passage, as seems likely, meant merely to manifest his hostility to Rousseau's theories by turning his own words back upon him.

Continuing on the next page[57] his discussion of this theme, Rousseau speaks of those fathers with foresight who had endeavored to provide their sons with such knowledge as would make it possible for them to gain a living later in case of unexpected necessity. The passage checked is the following: "Ces pères prévoyans croient beaucoup faire; ils ne font rien; parce que les ressources qu'ils pensent ménager à leurs enfans, dépendent de cette même fortune au-dessus

---
[52] II, 110; H. II, 167.
[53] Moland, XXVIII, 567-75.
[54] II, 111; H., II, 167.
[55] Moland, XXX, 573.
[56] II, 111; H., II, 167.
[57] II, 112; H., II, 167.

de laquelle ils les veulent mettre." In the same spirit is the passage checked on the following page:[58] "Vous avez étudié la politique & les intérêts des Princes: voilà qui va fort bien; mais que ferez-vous de ces connoissances, si vous ne savez parvenir aux ministres, aux femmes de la cour, aux chefs des bureaux; si vous n'avez le secret de leur plaire, si tous ne trouvent en vous le fripon qui leur convient?" Who should know this better than the Voltaire who had paid his court to nearly every one of influence in his day, but who at this very time was so out of favor with Mme de Pompadour and Louis XV that he dared not return to the Paris he had left so blithely in 1750 at the invitation of Frederick?

On p. 116, three pages further on,[59] Rousseau states his belief that the trained artisan, without the necessity of intrigues or dishonesty, has only to ask for work to get it. "Maître, j'ai besoin d'ouvrage; compagnon, mettez-vous là, travaillez." This passage is checked like those preceding. Could this perhaps have appealed to the lord of Ferney interested in the development of the industries of watch and clock making and of pottery? On p. 117,[60] Rousseau limits the trades worth learning to those "utiles au public," and a check mark has been placed opposite the passage: "Je ne veux point qu'il soit brodeur, ni doreur, ni vernisseur, comme le gentilhomme de Locke; je ne veux qu'il soit ni musicien, ni comédien, ni faiseur de livres." All these are occupations to which Voltaire as a partisan of luxury, literature, and the theater could hardly be hostile. Hence he would certainly oppose condemnation of them by Rousseau. The same comments hold good for the characteristic sentences: "J'aime mieux qu'il soit cordonnier que poëte"[61] and the reference to "les professions oiseuses, futiles, ou sujettes à la mode,"[62] both of which are likewise checked.

Rousseau condemns sedentary occupations for men and a check mark is found opposite this sentence on p. 125:[63] "Tout homme foible, délicat, craintif, est condamné par elle [la nature] à la vie sédentaire; il est fait pour vivre avec les femmes, ou à leur manière."

[58] II, 113; H., II, 168.
[59] H., II, 169.
[60] Ibid.
[61] II, 119; H., II, 169.
[62] Ibid.
[63] Ibid., 171.

We can only speculate as to whether Voltaire saw in this a condemnation of his well-loved *salon* life or whether rather, in his own multifarious activities tending to develop his lands at Ferney, he was perhaps ready to agree in part with Rousseau. There can be no doubt that he agreed with the next passage checked: "J'en dis trop pour mes agréables contemporains,"[64] though the agreement is not of the kind Rousseau would have sought. It is easy also to see why, in view of the frequent scorn Voltaire heaped upon Emile's trade of carpentry,[65] the following passage should have been checked: "Tout bien considéré, le métier que j'aimerois le mieux qui fût du goût de mon élève est celui de menuisier. Il est propre, il est utile, il peut s'exercer dans la maison."[66] It is probably for similar reasons that this next passage on p. 131[67] was checked. "Je suis donc d'avis que nous allions toutes les semaines une ou deux fois, au moins, passer la journée entiére chez le maître, que nous nous levions à son heure." Finally, Voltaire would certainly not have accepted seriously Rousseau's condemnation of wide knowledge, life in Paris, and riches: "Si ton fils sait beaucoup de choses, défie-toi de tout ce qu'il sait; s'il a le malheur d'être élevé à Paris, & d'être riche, il est perdu."[68]

In sum, while one cannot state positively that these numerous passages just cited were checked by Voltaire himself, the presumption is entirely in favor of such a conclusion. From what we know of Voltaire's thought as expressed elsewhere, it is almost always possible to see why he would have been likely to mark those particular passages. Moreover, in the pages immediately following, similarly checked passages are closely mingled with others which are annotated in Voltaire's own hand.

We now come again to frequent written comments on his part. Characteristically, Rousseau attacks knowledge as fostered by the numerous scientific academies of the eighteenth century.

Rousseau (II, 142; H. 176)	Voltaire
Il y a plus d'erreurs dans l'Académie des Sciences que dans tout un peuple de Hurons.	quelle impertinence absurde

[64] II, 127; H., II, 172.
[65] Moland, XVII, 44; XXIV, 420-21; XXX, 529, 573.
[66] II, 129; H., II, 172.
[67] H., II, 173.
[68] II, 133; H., II, 174.

In addition to Voltaire's comment, there is opposite this passage a check mark, which is another interesting confirmation of the conclusion that the passages which we have been studying just previously were likewise checked by Voltaire as he read rapidly along. Rousseau's enthusiasm for primitivism, or at least his desire to attack the science of the philosophic party, has led him to an absurd overstatement, which is not inaccurately characterized by Voltaire's scornful comment. The future author of *L'Ingénu* will have his turn later at a glorification of the Hurons at the expense of civilized society, but not in too serious a tone.

The sentence immediately following: "Puisque plus les hommes savent, plus ils se trompent, le seul moyen d'éviter l' erreur est l'ignorance,"[69] is checked without comment, but obviously for similar reasons.

Eight pages later Rousseau defends himself against those who might think he was overloading his pupil with knowledge. As might be expected, this but lays him the more open to Voltaire's irony.

Rousseau (II, 151; H. II, 179)	Voltaire
Vous craignez que je n'accable son esprit sous ces multitudes de connoissances. C'est tout le contraire; je lui apprends bien plus à les ignorer qu'à les savoir. Je lui montre la route de la science aisée, à la vérité; mais longue, immense, lente à parcourir. Je lui fais faire les premiers pas pour qu'il reconnoisse l'entrée; mais je ne lui permets jamais d'aller loin.	sans d[oute] je le croi[s]

The cutting down of the pages at the bindery has eliminated the final letters, but there appears no doubt of the correct reading and the comments are self-explanatory. Voltaire is but too ready to acknowledge that Rousseau will not take his pupil far intellectually. Rousseau now continues the same thought.

Rousseau (II, 152; H. II, 179)	Voltaire
Dans le petit nombre des choses qu'il sait & qu'il sait bien, la plus importante est, qu'il y en a beaucoup qu'il ignore & qu'il peut savoir un jour.	[il]ny entens[sic] [r]ien

[69] II, 143; H., II, 176.

EMILE

It seems more logical to read *il* here rather than *je* because *il* harmonizes with Voltaire's frequent practice of directly contradicting Rousseau in wording the same, or similar to, the latter's own. The use of a first-person verb form is not conclusive for reading *je*, since four pages below Voltaire writes: "C'est une brute qui ne *connais* pas." With either reading, however, Voltaire's scorn for Rousseau's emphasis upon non-intellectual education is clear.

Rousseau (II, 155; H. II, 180)	Voltaire
En un mot Emile a de la vertu tout ce qui se rapporte à lui-même. Pour avoir aussi les vertus sociales, il lui manque uniquement de connoître les relations qui les exigent.	il lui m[anque] tout

Although all but the first letter of the verb is cut off at the margin, the reading is clear, in view of Rousseau's text, and the comment carries out the idea of those just preceding.

Rousseau (II, 156; H. II, 180)	Voltaire
Trouvez-vous qu'un enfant ainsi parvenu à sa quinzième année ait perdu les précédentes?	Oui car c'est une brute qui ne connais [sic] pas une seulle vertu socialle.

With this rhetorical question Rousseau brought the third book of *Emile* to a close. Voltaire's reply is entirely in harmony with the five marginal comments immediately preceding. He catches up Rousseau's reference to "social virtues" in the passage commented upon just before and flings back a sharp denial that Emile possesses any of them. No doubt Voltaire is right, if with him we think mainly of the social graces of those who frequented the *salon* life of the time. Voltaire does not perceive, however, that Rousseau is aiming at a deeper and more democratic comprehension of social relations. Certainly he, as a teacher, could not have been successful in inculcating this comprehension himself. Certainly the ideal, as Rousseau admits elsewhere, is too high for perfect attainment by any one. It remains nevertheless, in spite of defects and excesses due to overemphasis in one direction, a valuable and potentially fruitful ideal if understood rightly and practiced with judgment.

There now follow early in Book IV three passages which are merely checked with a cross mark.

The first of these passages deals with the conformity in appearance of children regardless of sex. "Les mâles en qui l'on empêche le développement ultérieur du sexe, gardent cette conformité toute leur vie; ils sont toujours de grands enfans: & les femmes, ne perdant point cette même conformité, semblent, à bien des égards, ne jamais être autre chose."[70] We have seen previously in studying Voltaire's comments on the *Discours sur l'inégalité*[71] that he did not accept Rousseau's idea of the inferiority of women. This passage may have been marked for that reason or perhaps only as a curious detail.

On p. 165[72] the following passage has been checked: "Ce qui nous sert, on le cherche; mais ce qui nous veut servir, on l'aime: ce qui nous nuit, on le fuit; mais ce qui nous veut nuire, on le hait." Rousseau says that we seek out what is advantageous and avoid what is harmful. Only when these things show themselves as animals or persons capable of purposive good or bad toward us, do they call forth in us sentiments of love or hate. This passage may have been checked as an interesting explanation of the origin of the sentiments and passions. No reason either for approval or disapproval is apparent. Likewise, when Rousseau speaks of a sincere, deep love as being in accord with reason, not against it: "Ce choix qu'on met en opposition avec la raison nous vient d'elle,"[73] the check mark indicates probably interest in the observation as such. Perhaps Voltaire was thinking still of his long attachment to Mme du Châtelet.

We must now turn more than a hundred pages before coming upon any other concrete sign of interest on the part of Voltaire. The passage next commented upon was well calculated to arouse Voltaire from his seeming indifference, for it raises the question of how literary excellence is attained and suggests that it is merely a matter of genius to which there is attached no individual merit.

ROUSSEAU (II, 278; H. II, 216)	VOLTAIRE
Qu'a fait Racine, pour n'être pas Pradon? qu'a fait Boileau, pour n'être pas Cotin?	ils ont travaillé, consulté, corrigé

Though Voltaire, if pressed, would certainly not have failed to admit the necessity of original genius for the highest literary attain-

[70] II, 159; H., II, 181.
[71] See above, pp. 12-13.
[72] H., II, 183.
[73] II, 169; H., II, 184.

EMILE

ment, his comment here is to be understood as supplementing and correcting Rousseau's extreme statement in the opposite direction. Speaking from his own long experience in reworking his plays and his verse and in constantly taking counsel of his friends, Voltaire insists that a very important part of literary excellence is due to the entirely controllable element of hard, unremitting labor toward perfection.

Passing over the next nine pages, Voltaire stops at a long footnote of Rousseau dealing with the question of what Emile, who is in no way quarrelsome, will do if wantonly provoked.

ROUSSEAU (II, 297, n. 20;   VOLTAIRE
H. II, 221, n. 1)
Un soufflet & un démenti reçu & enduré ont des effets civils, que nulle sagesse ne peut prévenir & dont nul Tribunal ne peut venger l'offensé. L'insuffisance des loix lui rend donc en cela son indépendance; il est alors seul Magistrat, seul Juge entre l'offen-   erreur punissable
seur & lui.

This passage is further marked with a slip of paper between the leaves. On it is written "Note margi" and the single word "assassiner." It is identical with a marker between pages 22-23 of the first volume of Rousseau's work. Obviously this bookmark with so definite an indication was put here so that this passage could be quickly found again. As a matter of fact, at least twice many years later Voltaire did make use of it. In 1770 he wrote in the *Questions sur l'Encyclopédie*: "Il [Rousseau] veut que ce gentilhomme menuisier, quand il a reçu un démenti ou un soufflet, au lieu de les rendre et de se battre, *assassine prudemment son homme.*"[74] As late as 1777, one year before his death, this passage still annoyed him and he commented: "Enfin il lui dit qu'il est bien plus sage d'assassiner son ennemi que de le combattre noblement."[75] In this case the Kehl editors give the exact volume and page reference to this edition of *Emile* which Voltaire used. Here then we have one more instance of the way in which Voltaire sometimes utilized long afterward passages which he had commented on and marked for reference. Here is concrete evidence that some of these markers remain still in

---

[74] Moland, XVII, 444. Rousseau clarified his meaning by further discussion of the subject in a letter of March 14, 1770. Cf. Hachette, XII, 206-07.
[75] *Ibid.*, XXX, 529.

the position in which they were placed originally. In this instance, Voltaire appears as still under the influence of the code of honor in favor of duelling,[76] the fallacy of which Rousseau clearly perceives. The inference of "assassination" is an extreme one drawn from Rousseau's intentional vagueness about the measures to be taken by Emile in his own defense, a vagueness due to the uncertainty as to what would be necessary in particular varying cases and due also to the fact that Rousseau was introducing an idea shocking to current prejudices.[77] While his declaration is not wholly satisfactory and one may sympathize with Voltaire's criticism of the idea of allowing Emile to take the law into his own hands, Rousseau's statement is probably as good as the inadequacy of legal procedure and the current *mores* would permit. In any case, Rousseau is looking toward the future, and Voltaire, unlike Zadig, is standing pat on an "ancien abus."[78]

II. *Le Vicaire savoyard*

We come now to Rousseau's important work on religion which is known as *La Profession de foi du Vicaire savoyard*. It forms the middle third of Book IV of *Emile*, and on it, as might be expected, Voltaire has made many marginal comments and almost certainly himself marked other passages which are not annotated. In both the copies of *Emile* used by Voltaire, the *Vicaire savoyard* begins on p. 19 of Volume III. In the Geneva *Emile*, studied by M. Bouvier, Voltaire's marginal notes begin on p. 21, very near the commencement of the Vicar's Profession, and there are also numerous notes on the pages immediately following. In the Leningrad *Emile*, the first note is found on p. 59, thirty-eight pages later. With only a few exceptions, the two series of annotations deal throughout with different passages and but rarely overlap. It will be profitable to keep in mind for comparison or contrast both series of notes, since the attitude of Voltaire toward the religious ideas of Rousseau is of much

[76] Unless he merely assumes this position for the purpose of belaboring Rousseau and discrediting him with the nobility.

[77] Steele's notable attack upon duelling in his play, *The Conscious Lovers*, appeared in 1722. The play had been translated into French by Prévost in his *Pour et Contre* in 1736. Sedaine's attack on duelling in *Le Philosophe sans le savoir* is three years later than *Emile*.

[78] Voltaire, *Zadig*, Ascoli ed., Paris, 1929, I, 53.

LE VICAIRE SAVOYARD

more significance than his almost wholly scornful and contemptuous treatment of the latter's educational program, of which Voltaire easily perceives the defects without apparently at all sensing its originality and value as a stimulating new approach to an old problem. In his educational views Voltaire was distinctly conservative.

The first fourteen notes in the Geneva *Emile* are found on the nineteen pages included between pp. 21-39. Without repeating here what M. Bouvier has already given in detail, it is sufficient to remark that only one of these fourteen comments is wholly favorable, approving with a laconic "bon" Rousseau's statement that, since the Catholic church permits no element of doubt, the rejection of a single point of doctrine forces the rejection of all the rest.[1] Voltaire also approves of Rousseau's admiration for the Englishman Samuel Clarke, so far as the first volume of his *Being and Attributes of God* (1705) is concerned, but not as regards the second which he calls "ridicule."[2] The other twelve notes on these pages are entirely hostile.

In this edition at Geneva no more marginal notes are found until p. 134 and M. Bouvier in consequence made the inference that Voltaire must have passed hurriedly over the important section between. He writes: "On dirait qu'il a seulement feuilleté la longue démonstration que fait le vicaire du 'théisme ou de la religion naturelle.' Car, à la lire de près, l'auteur du poème sur *Le Désastre de Lisbonne* y aurait sans doute trouvé à redire. Rousseau y reprend plusieurs des arguments qu'il lui avait opposés dans sa *Lettre sur la Providence,* et l'hommage enthousiaste que le vicaire rend à la conscience, interprète de la loi morale et guide de notre conduite plus éclairé que la raison même, semblait fait pour exciter la mauvaise humeur, tout au moins les railleries de Voltaire. Mais il a passé sans mot dire sur tout cela, et ses remarques prochaines nous le montrent dans une heureuse humeur."[3] This very natural conclusion, true for the Geneva *Emile,* does not hold for the copy in the Voltaire library at Leningrad, which here fills an important gap, for on these pages in this latter edition there are many important notes. The first of these, as has been stated, is found on p. 59.

---

[1] *Annales Jean-Jacques Rousseau,* I, 275.
[2] *Ibid.,* 276.
[3] *Ibid.,* 277.

ROUSSEAU (III, 59; H. II, 248; M. 153)[4]
Ce qu'il y a de plus injurieux à la Divinité n'est pas de n'y point penser, mais d'en mal penser.

VOLTAIRE
et que luy importe que tu en penses bien ou mal?

Voltaire's attitude here seems to indicate quite definitely that his idea of God is a philosophical concept without the traits of personality which Rousseau's religion accords to divinity. To Voltaire's God what matters the attitude of men?

The next passages commented on follow in close succession, indicating that Voltaire is reading the text with care. In the paragraph immediately following, Rousseau gives his reasons for putting man at the top of creation.

ROUSSEAU (III, 59; H. II, 248; M. 153, 155)
Car, par ma volonté & par les instrumens qui sont en mon pouvoir pour l'exécuter, j'ai plus de force pour agir sur tous les corps qui m'environnent, ou pour me prêter ou me dérober comme il me plaît à leur action, qu'aucun d'eux n'en a pour agir sur moi malgré moi par la seule impulsion physique.

VOLTAIRE

et le Soleil? ne vaut il pas mieux que toy

Voltaire obviously is not in a favorable mood. In order to register an objection against Rousseau, he is even willing to use one which does not meet at all the argument based on freedom of voluntary action in contrast to the greater regularity of inanimate nature.

ROUSSEAU (III, 60; H. II, 248; M. 155, 157)
Qu'y a-t-il de si ridicule à penser que tout est fait pour moi, si je suis le seul qui sache tout rapporter à lui?

VOLTAIRE

quel sophisme!

Rousseau's argument is an old one and is still in use. Its acceptance or rejection depends largely upon whether purpose is assumed to be present or absent from the universe, and upon this there is much difference of opinion among thinkers. Although Voltaire appears generally to accept the argument from design as the most potent argument for the existence of God,[5] he here disagrees sharply with

---

[4] M. indicates the critical edition of the *Vicaire savoyard* by Pierre-Maurice Masson published by Hachette in 1914.
[5] Moland, L. 75 (*Correspondance*, 1776).

LE VICAIRE SAVOYARD   95

Rousseau on making man a supreme object of this design in the universe.

ROUSSEAU (III, 60; H. II, 248; M. 159)   VOLTAIRE
Il est donc vrai que l'homme est le Roi
de la terre qu'il habite; car non-seulement
il dispose des élémens par son industrie;
mais lui seul sur la terre en sait disposer, &
il s'approprie encore, par la contemplation,
les astres mêmes dont il ne peut approcher.   beau domaine!

Voltaire has underlined the verb "s'approprie," no doubt in irony at the implication of proprietorship of the remote heavens. It is amusing to recall in this connection the occasion fifteen years before when, according to Longchamp,[6] a broken axle tumbled Voltaire and Mme du Châtelet out into the snow and forced upon them this very contemplation of the stars to which, in spite of Voltaire's satire of Rousseau's language, the "divine Emilie" and her companion were most enthusiastically devoted.

ROUSSEAU (III, 60-61; H. II, 248-49;   VOLTAIRE
    M. 159, 161, 163)
Quoi! je puis observer, connoître les
:tres & leurs rapports; je puis sentir ce que
c'est qu'ordre, beauté, vertu; je puis contempler l'Univers, m'élever à la main qui
le gouverne; je puis aimer le bien, le faire;
& je me comparerois aux bêtes! Ame abjecte, c'est ta triste philosophie qui te rend
semblable à elles! ou plutôt tu veux en vain
t'avilir, ton génie dépose contre tes principes, ton cœur bienfaisant dément ta doctrine, & l'abus même de tes facultés prouve   cela empêche t'il que la bete
leur excellence en dépit de toi.   ne soit organisée comme toy?

[6] Longchamp et Wagnière, *Mémoires sur Voltaire*, Paris, 1826, II, 168. "M. *de Voltaire* et madame *du Châtelet* s'étaient assis à côté l'un de l'autre sur les coussins du carrosse, qu'on avait retirés et posés sur le chemin couvert de neige; là, presque transis de froid malgré leurs fourrures, ils admiraient la beauté du ciel. . . . On sait que l'astronomie a toujours été une des études favorites de nos deux philosophes. Ravis du magnifique spectacle déployé au-dessus et autour d'eux, ils dissertaient, en grelottant, sur la nature et le cours des astres, sur la destination de tant de globes immenses répandus dans l'espace. Il ne leur manquait que des télescopes pour être parfaitement heureux." Of course such interest and admiration are entirely natural and possible without adopting Rousseau's conclusions.

Here appears a fundamental point of cleavage between the two men. Pushing aside rhetoric, Voltaire drives straight at the heart of the question. While Rousseau emphasizes the uniqueness of man, his critic stresses the essential unity of the whole animal kingdom, the differences being of degree, but not of kind. Modern science tends to support Voltaire's position[7] in this respect. Differences of degree still remain differences, however, and must not be too greatly minimized whatever their origin. A realistic view toward biology, physiology, and psychology need not obscure the fact that the question of philosophical interpretation, whether in Pascalian terms of human baseness and grandeur or otherwise, still remains important in shaping the attitude of mankind toward life. Rousseau's effort here, however inadequate, is to stress human dignity against tendencies toward cynicism not infrequent among his eighteenth-century "philosophic" opponents.

ROUSSEAU (III, 62; H. II, 249; M. 167)   VOLTAIRE
Le tableau de la nature ne m'offroit qu'harmonie & proportions, celui du genre humain ne m'offre que confusion, désordre! Le concert règne entre les élémens, & les hommes sont dans le chaos!

quel concert que des inondations, des tremblements des goufres?

The reading of the last word as "goufres" is not quite certain. Ironically Voltaire underlined "concert" in his attack upon the popular idea of the "harmony of the universe" which Rousseau adopted from Pluche and other similar predecessors. Voltaire no doubt had in mind catastrophes similar to the Lisbon earthquake and tidal wave of 1755, which so profoundly impressed him and left such important traces in his correspondence and in works like *Le Poème sur le Désastre de Lisbonne* of 1756 and *Candide* of 1759. Rousseau's letter to Voltaire on Providence in refutation of the Poem on Lisbon had shown as early as August 18, 1756, the profound difference in attitude of the two men on this point. In fact Rousseau always maintained, no doubt

---

[7] As early as 1733, Voltaire is concerned with this question of the unity of matter. Is thought one of the properties of matter? Should the old duality between spirit and matter disappear in favor of a broader concept of matter alone? Already Voltaire is inclined to answer these questions in the affirmative. Cf. Moland, XXXIII, 373; XXXIV, 8.

with considerable exaggeration, that *Candide* was Voltaire's real reply to his letter.[8]

Very important also is the difference in viewpoint shown by the following passage in which Rousseau expresses his well-known belief in freedom of the will.

ROUSSEAU (III, 64; H. II, 249; M. 167, 169)   VOLTAIRE

Je suis actif quand j'écoute la raison, passif quand mes passions m'entraînent; & mon pire tourment, quand je succombe, est de sentir que j'ai pu résister.

           déclamation
           non tu nelaspas
           pu

This, like a passage commented on a short distance below, shows Voltaire in contrast to Rousseau a determinist. In his youth the former had defended against Frederick an already somewhat attenuated doctrine of free will;[9] in his old age he tended more and more toward determinism, admitting with praiseworthy candor that "l'ignorant qui pense ainsi n'a pas toujours pensé de même, mais il est enfin contraint de se rendre."[10]

ROUSSEAU (III, 65-66; H. II, 250; M. 173, 175, 177)   VOLTAIRE

Quand un philosophe viendra me dire que les arbres sentent & que les rochers pensent, il aura beau m'embarrasser dans ses argumens subtils, je ne puis voir en lui qu'un sophiste de mauvaise foi, qui aime mieux donner le sentiment aux pierres que d'accorder une âme à l'homme.

           mais on ne le dit point

Rousseau strikes out directly at the tendency of members of the philosophic party to wipe out the traditional distinction between matter and spirit. While it appears that Voltaire did not himself categorically attribute thought to matter, he early asserted this as a possibility,[11] thus tending toward a materialistic monism in contrast to the dualism of Rousseau. As to the inaccuracy of Voltaire's note here,

---

[8] Hachette, VIII, 308 *(Confessions)*; XI, 123-24 *(Correspondance)*. See my forthcoming edition of *Candide*, N. Y., Holt, 1933 or 1934 (Introduction), for a more extended discussion of this question.

[9] Moland, XXXIV, 320-23, 368-71, 394-97. Cf. also *Le Traité de métaphysique* of 1734.

[10] Moland, XXVI, 57 *(Le Philosophe ignorant*, 1766). Cf. *ibid.*, 55-57.

[11] *Ibid.*, XXII, 422-23; XXXIII, 373, 518, 599; XXXIV, 8-9. Cf. above, p. 96, n.

we need only refer to Pierre-Maurice Masson's critical edition to discover that Rousseau might have found examples to justify his contention in Campanella, Hobbes, La Mettrie, and Bayle.[12] Either Voltaire was unwilling himself to go so far in his opinion on this question, or else his comment is an evidence of bad faith.

In the next paragraph Rousseau, probably following Clarke,[13] imagines a dialogue between himself and a deaf man who denies the existence of sounds because he has never heard them, the other speaker awkwardly explaining the vibrating cords of a musical instrument as due to these same sounds. The deaf man replies:

Rousseau (III, 67; H. II, 251; M. 181)	Voltaire
Parce que je ne conçois pas comment frémit cette corde, pourquoi faut-il que j'aille expliquer cela par vos sons, dont je n'ai pas la moindre idée? C'est expliquer un fait obscur, par une cause encore plus obscure. Ou rendez-moi vos sons sensibles, ou je dis qu'ils n'existent pas.	le sourd a raison et son antagoniste s'explique fort mal

Voltaire remains true to the sensationalism of Locke, followed by Diderot in his *Lettre sur les aveugles* and in his *Lettre sur les sourds et muets*, from which works Rousseau may also have taken his cue. It is interesting to recall, however, that Voltaire himself took issue with Diderot's conclusions in June of 1749 on receipt of the first of the works mentioned.[14] Had he changed in the meantime or is his remark applicable only to this brief passage itself and not to the argument as a whole? It seems probable that the important decade intervening had made Voltaire bolder and ready to go farther in his thinking than before the turn of the century in 1750. In any case his hostility to all this part of the *Vicaire savoyard* remains consistent as he comments on passage after passage.

Rousseau continues his argument for separation of matter and spirit.

Rousseau (III, 68-69; H. II, 251; M. 183, 185)	Voltaire
J'ai un corps sur lequel les autres agissent & qui agit sur eux; cette action réciproque	

[12] *Op. cit.*, 173, 175.
[13] *Ibid.*, 181.
[14] Moland, XXXVII, 22-23.

LE VICAIRE SAVOYARD

n'est pas douteuse; mais ma volonté est
indépendante de mes sens; je consens ou
je résiste, je succombe ou je suis vainqueur,
& je sens parfaitement en moi-même quand
je fais ce que j'ai voulu faire, ou quand   on en peut dire autant du
je ne fais que céder à mes passions.   chien qui craint son maitre.

Voltaire again insists upon the essential identity of man and animal, to which Rousseau is opposed. In the rest of the paragraph Rousseau returns once more to the question of free will.

ROUSSEAU (III, 69; H. II, 251; M. 185)   VOLTAIRE
Je suis esclave par mes vices, & libre par
mes remords: le sentiment de ma liberté ne
s'efface en moi que quand je me déprave,
& que j'empêche enfin la voix de l'âme de
s'élever contre la loi du corps.   déclamation

This is the second time Voltaire has used in commenting on Rousseau the single word "déclamation," which is frequently most apt. It occurs more and more often in comment upon later passages. Voltaire seeks a more exact and scientific discussion of the question.[15]

ROUSSEAU (III, 69-70; H. II, 251;   VOLTAIRE
           M. 187)
Si l'on comprend bien que l'homme est
actif dans ses jugemens, que son entende-   passif
ment n'est que le pouvoir de comparer &
de juger, on verra que sa liberté n'est qu'un
pouvoir semblable, ou dérivé de celui-là.[16]

This is a question which had occupied Voltaire's thought for many years and in regard to which he had come at length to a definite conclusion. His underlining of the key word "actif" and his substitution of the opposite word "passif" link this comment with the one mentioned a few pages back and show him as a determinist in contrast to Rousseau's position in favor of free will. "Mes idées entrent nécessairement dans mon cerveau," wrote Voltaire a few years later in the *Philosophe ignorant*, "comment ma volonté, qui en dépend, serait-elle

---
[15] Note that there is much in common here between Rousseau's attitude and that which Voltaire had expressed in his *Poème sur la Loi naturelle* (1752-56), a poem admired indeed by Rousseau as he tells us at the beginning of his *Lettre sur la Providence*. Probably, however, this poem by no means expressed Voltaire's whole thought on the subject, but was influenced by considerations of prudence.
[16] Cf. Hachette, XII, 304.

à la fois nécessitée, et absolument libre?"¹⁷ The comments on the next few passages are likewise closely linked to this same question.

Rousseau (III, 70; H. II, 251; M. 187, 189)	Voltaire
Et quelle est la cause qui détermine son jugement? C'est sa faculté intelligente, c'est sa puissance de juger.	oui mais son jugement est necessaire.
Ma liberté consiste en cela même, que je ne puis vouloir que ce qui m'est convenable, ou que j'estime tel, sans que rien d'étranger à moi me détermine. (*Ibid.*) (M. 189)	sophisme
Le principe de toute action est dans la volonté d'un être libre. (*Ibid.*)	et la vegetation! la gravitation!
Il n'y a point de véritable volonté sans liberté. (III, 71; H. II, 252; M. 191)	la liberté ne consiste qua faire ce quon veut.

Voltaire underlined the words *liberté* and *sans liberté*. In this last comment he has given us his final definition of the limited free will which he was willing to admit. In *Le Philosophe ignorant* four years later he used almost the same expression as here. It had evidently crystallized in his mind as his best thought on the subject: "Etre véritablement libre, c'est pouvoir. *Quand je peux faire ce que je veux, voilà ma liberté;* mais je veux nécessairement ce que je veux."¹⁸

Rousseau (III, 71; H. II, 252; M. 191)	Voltaire
L'homme est donc libre dans ses actions, &, comme tel animé d'une substance immatérielle;ˣ	ˣ quelle conséquence? et mon chien ne fait-il pas ce quil veut.
Si l'homme est actif & libre, il agit de lui-même; tout ce qu'il fait librement n'entre point dans le système ordonnéˣ de la Providence, & ne peut lui être imputé. (*Ibid.*)	ˣ et comment quelque chose peut il etre hors de la providence
Elle [la Providence] ne veut point le mal que fait l'homme, en abusant de la liberté qu'elle lui donne, mais elle ne l'em-	

¹⁷ Moland, XXVI, 56.
¹⁸ *Ibid.* The italics are mine.

pêche pas de le faire; soit que de la part d'un être si foible ce mal soit nul à ses yeux; soit qu'elle ne pût l'empêcher sans gêner sa liberté, & faire un mal plus grand en dégradant sa nature. Elle l'a fait libre afin qu'il fît, non le mal, mais le bien par choix. Elle l'a mis en état de faire ce choix, en usant bien des facultés dont elle l'a doué; mais elle a tellement borné ses forces, que l'abus de la liberté qu'elle lui laisse, ne peut troubler l'ordre général. Le mal que l'homme fait, retombe sur lui, sans rien changer au système du monde. (III, 71-72; H. II, 252; M. 191)

tout cela est bien peu philosophiq:

Murmurer de ce que Dieu ne l'empêche pas de faire le mal, c'est murmurer de ce qu'il l'a fait d'une nature excellente, de ce qu'il mit à ses actions la moralité qui les ennoblit de ce qu'il lui donna droit à la vertu. La suprême jouissance est dans le contentement de soi-même; c'est pour <u>mériter ce contentement</u> que nous sommes placés sur la terre & doués de la liberté. (III, 72; H. II, 252; M. 191, 193)

beau but!

To these closely succeeding passages dealing with free will and Providence, Voltaire has made many objections. Rousseau now two pages later turns to a discussion of death in its bearing upon the goodness of God.

Rousseau (III, 74; H. II, 252-53; M. 195)

Voltaire

Combien l'homme vivant dans la simplicité primitive est sujet à <u>peu de maux</u>! Il vit presque sans maladies ainsi que sans passions, & ne prévoit ni ne sent la mort, quand il la sent, <u>ses misères</u> la lui rendent désirable.

contradiction evidente

Here Voltaire has evidently caught Rousseau in a contradiction. Three pages further on the latter expresses his belief in immortality as the necessary compensation for what he is after all constrained to admit are the ills of this life.

VOLTAIRE ON ROUSSEAU

ROUSSEAU (III, 77; H. II,254; M.203)　　　　VOLTAIRE
Tu vas mourir, penses-tu; non, tu vas
vivre.　　　　　　　　　　　　　　　　　　　qui te la dit?

So Voltaire questions Rousseau's categorical assertion unsupported, as it is, by argument. Voltaire's final point of view is doubtless most clearly expressed in his *Lettres de Memmius à Cicéron* of 1771. "Que le grand Etre veuille persévérer à nous continuer les mêmes dons après notre mort; qu'il puisse attacher la faculté de penser à quelque partie de nous-mêmes qui subsistera encore, à la bonne heure: je ne veux ni l'affirmer ni le nier; je n'ai de preuve ni pour ni contre. Mais c'est à celui qui affirme une chose si étrange à la prouver clairement; et comme jusqu'ici personne ne l'a fait, on me permettra de douter."[19] This is confirmed by the recently published testimony of Boswell giving his interview with Voltaire at the end of December, 1764. Boswell wrote to Temple: "He [Voltaire] does not inflame his mind with grand hopes of the immortality of the Soul. He says it may be; but he knows nothing of it. And his mind is in perfect tranquillity. I was moved; I was sorry. I doubted his sincerity. I called to him with emotion, 'Are you sincere? are you realy [sic] sincere?' He answered, 'Before God I am.' "[20]

Continuing his argument for immortality, Rousseau says:

ROUSSEAU　　　　　　　　　　　　　　　　　VOLTAIRE
(III, 78; H. II, 254; M. 205)
O! soyons bons premièrement, & puis　　　　décla
nous serons heureux.

Il est très-simple que durant ma vie
corporelle, n'apercevant rien que par mes
sens, ce qui ne leur est point soumis　　　　-mation
m'échappe. (III, 79; H. II, 254; M. 207)

Je crois que l'âme survit au corps assez
pour le maintien de l'ordre; qui sait si c'est　　　pué
assez pour durer toujours? (III, 80; H.
II, 254; M. 207)

Or je ne saurois me rappeler, après ma
mort ce que j'ai été durant ma vie, que je
ne me rappelle aussi ce que j'ai senti, par

---
[19] *Ibid.*, XXVIII, 459-60.
[20] Boswell to Temple. Dec. 28, 1764. Ralph H. Isham, *The Unpublished Papers of James Boswell*, N. Y., 1929, IV, 19.

conséquent ce que j'ai fait, & je ne doute 　　　　　　　　rile
point que ce souvenir ne fasse un jour la
félicité des bons & le tourment des méchans.
(III, 81; H. II, 255; M. 209)

The reading of the comment on the last two passages is not quite certain, but, just as above Voltaire has carried his word "déclamation" over two pages and thus made it apply to the whole long passage on the spirituality of the soul, so here he seems to have written "puérile" and used it similarly to express his contempt for Rousseau's exposition of immortality.

ROUSSEAU (III, 82; H. II, 255;　　　　　　VOLTAIRE
　　　M. 211, 213)
Je ne dis point que les <u>bons seront ré-</u>　　et tu las dit tout a l'heure
<u>compensés;</u>　　　　　　　　　　　　　　　pauvre homme

Rousseau goes on to explain that he means no tangible recompense except the joy of existing under perfect conditions, but Voltaire is content to catch him in a seemingly direct verbal contradiction and to note it accordingly. Perhaps, in his impetuosity, he made his notation the moment this sentence caught his eye without waiting to read Rousseau's qualification of his position.

On the next page[21] Rousseau raises the question of whether the wicked receive eternal punishment and concludes: "Toutefois j'ai peine à croire qu'ils soient condamnés à des tourmens sans fin. Si la suprême justice se venge, elle se venge dès cette vie. Vous & vos erreurs, ô nations! êtes ses ministres. Elle emploie les maux que vous vous faites, à punir les crimes qui les ont attirés. C'est dans vos cœurs insatiables, rongés d'envie, d'avarice & d'ambition, qu'au sein de vos fausses prospérités les passions vengeresses punissent vos forfaits." This passage has been marked with a vertical line in the right margin, but there is no comment. On the same page,[22] however, opposite Rousseau's citation of Psalm 115[23] in a footnote, Voltaire wrote in the margin: "quoi cest ce coquin insensé qui cite des psaumes!"—which gives sufficient indication of his general attitude at this moment.

On the preceding page Rousseau had said of the wicked: "Que m'importe ce que deviendront les méchans? Je prends peu d'intérêt

[21] III, 83; H. II, 255; M. 215, 217.
[22] M. 213.
[23] 113 in the Vulgate, Masson, *ibid*.

à leur sort." Now, with a revulsion of warm-hearted feeling, he contradicts himself on the page following. This contradiction has been often mentioned by students of Rousseau and it is no matter for surprise that Voltaire should pounce upon it at once for a characteristic comment.

Rousseau (III, 84; H. II, 256; M. 219)	Voltaire
Le méchant n'est-il pas mon frère?	et tu viens de dire que tu ne prends nul interest a eux

To bring out the contradiction more strongly, Voltaire exaggerates what Rousseau had actually written in the former passage, which reads "peu d'intérêt" rather than "nul intérêt." He could not have known that Rousseau had first written "aucun intérêt," but revised it before publication.[24] As a matter of fact, the lack of complete harmony between the different parts of Rousseau's discussion of the fate of the wicked is partly due, as Masson has shown,[25] to its having been composed at different times without having ever been completely welded together into a uniform whole.

Rousseau (III, 86; H. II, 256; M. 223, 225)	Voltaire
Nous ne sommes libres que parce qu'il [Dieu] veut que nous le soyons, & sa substance inexplicable est à nos âmes ce que nos âmes sont à nos corps. S'il a créé la matière, les corps, les esprits, le monde, je n'en sais rien. L'idée de création me confond & passe ma portée; je la crois autant que je la puis concevoir; mais je sais qu'il a formé l'univers & tout ce qui existe, qu'il a tout fait, tout ordonné.	contradiction

This passage has been marked with a vertical line in the margin. Evidently Voltaire thinks that Rousseau's scepticism about creation is in contradiction with his certainty that God formed the universe and everything which exists. In fact, Rousseau in harmony with some of his contemporaries and immediate predecessors attempts to distinguish between creation of matter out of nothing and its organization into a universe,[26] but, whether valid or not, the distinction is not expressed in clear-cut fashion.

[24] Masson, *op. cit.*, p. 215, n. 1.
[25] *Ibid.*, 219, n. 1
[26] Cf. *Ibid.*, 225, n. 3.

LE VICAIRE SAVOYARD

ROUSSEAU (III, 87; H. II, 256; M. 225)　　VOLTAIRE
Qu'un être que je ne conçois pas donne l'existence à d'autres êtres, cela n'est qu'obscur & incompréhensible; mais que l'être & le néant se convertissent d'eux-mêmes l'un dans l'autre, c'est une contradiction palpable, c'est une claire absurdité.　　galimatias

So Voltaire indicates his contempt for the vagueness of Rousseau's thought.

ROUSSEAU (III, 87; H. II, 257; M. 227)　　VOLTAIRE
Toutes les vérités ne sont pour elle [la suprême intelligence] qu'une seule idée.　　qui te l'a dit?

With characteristic scepticism about the certainty of metaphysical knowledge, Voltaire returns to his embarrassing query, already previously used:[27] "Qui te l'a dit?", which brings out with clear-cut directness the necessarily speculative character of Rousseau's statement.

On the next ten pages there are no comments and when Voltaire next writes down a note, it is on a subject different, but no less characteristic. Rousseau, holding the moral instinct innate, contrasts the presence of esteem for virtue among the ancients with the low standards of conduct represented by the Greek and Roman gods.

ROUSSEAU (III, 98; H. II, 260; M. 255)　　VOLTAIRE
La chaste Lucrèce adoroit l'impudique Vénus.　　cela nest pas vrai il ny avait point de temple dédié a Vénus la putain.

Masson has shown that this contrast was a commonplace in the sources upon which Rousseau drew.[28] Voltaire willfully misinterprets Rousseau's reference to the worship of the corrupt Aphrodite and criticizes him unfairly, though he may have had in mind here an idea expressed much later in his correspondence of 1776: "Je crois fermement qu'il n'y a jamais eu de culte contre les mœurs, c'est-à-dire contre la décence établie chez une nation. . . . Je sais bien que partout les fêtes, les processions nocturnes, dégénérèrent en parties de plaisir. . . . Mais, dans l'origine, les fêtes n'étaient que sacrées."[29] However that may be, he has none the less twisted Rousseau's thought into a grotesque exaggeration.

[27] Cf. above, p. 102.
[28] Cf. Masson, *op. cit.*, 253, n. 2.
[29] Moland, XLIX, 562.

ROUSSEAU (III, 100; H. II, 260; M. 259, 261)

VOLTAIRE

Cet accord évident & universel de toutes les nations, ils [les philosophes] l'osent rejetter: &, contre l'éclatante uniformité du jugement des hommes, ils vont chercher dans les ténèbres quelque exemple obscur & connu d'eux seuls; comme si tous les penchans de la nature étoient anéantis par la dépravation d'un peuple, & que, sitôt qu'il est des monstres, l'espèce ne fût plus rien. Mais que servent au sceptique Montaigne les tourmens qu'il se donne pour déterrer en un coin du monde une coutume opposée aux notions de la justice?

jay dit tout cela vingt fois en vers et en prose

Here at length we find Voltaire again in agreement with Rousseau, but only to claim primacy over him in expressing this idea so common in the eighteenth century of the similarity of moral principles throughout mankind. If Voltaire has perhaps not said this "vingt fois," the thought is at any rate to be found in the *Poème sur la Loi naturelle*, the *Essai sur les mœurs*, and elsewhere.[30]

Following immediately in Rousseau's text is another reference to Montaigne.

ROUSSEAU (III, 100-101; H. II, 260; M. 261)

VOLTAIRE

O Montaigne! toi qui te piques de franchise & de vérité, sois sincère & vrai, <u>si un Philosophe peut l'être</u>.

Rousseau's characteristic dig at the philosophic school has been underlined, but strange to say, Voltaire made no comment on this deliberate thrust which he ordinarily and quite naturally was quick to resent.

Eight pages later Rousseau develops his idea that the moral law must have theistic sanctions.

ROUSSEAU (III, 109-10; H. II, 263; M. 279, 281, 283)

VOLTAIRE

On a beau vouloir établir la vertu par la raison seule, quelle solide base peut-on lui

[30] *Ibid.*, IX, 444; XI, 54; XV. 15.

LE VICAIRE SAVOYARD

donner? La vertu, disent-ils, est l'amour de l'ordre; mais cet amour peut-il donc & doit-il l'emporter en moi sur celui de mon bien-être? Qu'ils me donnent une raison claire & suffisante pour le préférer. Dans le fond, leur prétendu principe est un pur jeu de mots; car je dis aussi, moi, que le vice est l'amour de l'ordre, pris dans un sens différent. Il y a quelque ordre moral partout où il y a sentiment & intelligence. La différence est, que le bon s'ordonne par rapport au tout, & que le méchant ordonne le tout par rapport à lui. Celui-ci se fait le centre de toutes choses; l'autre mesure son rayon & se tient à la circonférence. Alors il est ordonné, par rapport au centre commun, qui est Dieu, & par rapport à tous les cercles concentriques, qui sont les créatures. Si la Divinité n'est pas, il n'y a que le méchant qui raisonne, le bon n'est qu'un insensé.

il ne faut jamais decouvrir ces horreurs au public

In addition to the comment above, the last sentence is marked with a vertical line in the margin. It would seem that the advocate of the necessity of a "Dieu rémunérateur et vengeur"[31] and the author of the line, "Si Dieu n'existait pas, il faudrait l'inventer"[32] feared the moral consequences of giving to the public the suggestion that virtue is madness unless God exists. In 1769 Voltaire wrote to D'Argental, rather cynically it seems: "Toutefois il est fort bon de faire accroire aux hommes qu'ils ont une âme immortelle, et qu'il y a un Dieu vengeur qui punira mes paysans s'ils me volent mon blé et mon vin, qui fera rouer là-bas ou là-haut les juges des Calas, et brûler ceux d'Abbeville."[33]

Why is man's spirit held in bondage by the limitations of his body, asks Rousseau?

ROUSSEAU (III, 112; H. II, 264; M. 287)
Je me dis: "Si l'esprit de l'homme fût restée libre & pur, quel mérite auroit-il d'aimer & suivre l'ordre qu'il verroit établi

VOLTAIRE

---

[31] *Ibid.*, XVII, 462. Cf. XXVII, 399-400; L. 454.
[32] *Ibid.*, X, 403 (1769). Cf. XXIX, 10.
[33] *Ibid.*, L, 454.

& qu'il n'auroit nul intérêt à troubler?" Il seroit heureux, il est vrai; mais il manqueroit à son bonheur le degré le plus sublime, la <u>gloire</u> de la vertu & le bon témoignage de soi; il ne seroit que comme <u>les Anges</u>; & sans doute l'homme vertueux sera plus qu'eux.

ou est la gloire?

qu'est-ce quun incredule qui parle d'anges?

Where is the glory in connection with being virtuous? asks Voltaire. But Rousseau's idea is clear to one familiar with his work. Contrary to the misconception of "natural goodness" dear to many of the adversaries of Rousseau, the latter holds a quite conventional idea of virtue. However *natural* goodness might be under ideal conditions, in modern society virtue is necessary. "Il n'y a point de bonheur sans courage, ni de vertu sans combat," writes Rousseau elsewhere in *Emile*. "Le mot de *vertu* vient de *force*; la force est la base de toute vertu. La vertu n'appartient qu'à un être foible par sa nature, et fort par sa volonté. . . . L'homme qui n'est que bon n'est bon que pour lui. . . . Apprends à devenir ton propre maître: commande à ton cœur, ô Emile, et tu seras vertueux."[34] So it is that the natural man, "né dans le fond d'un bois . . . , eût vécu plus heureux et plus libre; mais n'ayant rien à combattre pour suivre ses penchans, il eût été bon sans mérite, il n'eût point été vertueux, et maintenant il sait l'être malgré ses passions."[35] Thus the merit, the *glory*, of virtue are but too well understood by Rousseau in the midst of his struggle-filled life, too seldom crowned with the complete victory over temptation which he vainly sought. As to the *Angels* underlined and commented upon by Voltaire, it is not clear whether Rousseau uses the word merely as a means of quickly expressing his meaning without seriously raising the philosophic question of the existence of such beings, or whether he does believe in them. Masson has pointed out Rousseau's hesitation on this point.[36] In any case, Voltaire's comment effectively calls attention to the anomalous position of his adversary in this respect. Rousseau's mingling of rationalism and mysticism is entirely outside of Voltaire's comprehension.

[34] Rousseau, *Œuvres* (Hachette), II, 416-17.
[35] *Ibid.*, 445. Cf. my articles on "La théorie de la bonté naturelle de l'homme chez J.-J. Rousseau," RHL., 1924-25.
[36] Masson, *op. cit.*, 287, n. 2.

LE VICAIRE SAVOYARD

Rousseau (III, 116; H. II, 265; M. 291)

J'aspire au moment où, délivré des entraves du corps, je serai *moi* sans contradiction, sans partage, & n'aurai besoin que de moi pour être heureux.

Voltaire

jean jaques incredule débauché fait icy le St. augustin

Rousseau's mingling of rationalism and mysticism is entirely incomprehensible to Voltaire and provokes in him exasperated remarks like this last, which nevertheless amuses by the form of expression. The charge of "debauch" against Rousseau suggests the ugly rumors about his bodily infirmities, his relations with Thérèse Le Vasseur, and his abandonment of his children, which, through the unprofessional loquacity of Dr. Tronchin or otherwise, were being circulated about Geneva[37] and were maliciously utilized by Voltaire in his *Sentiment des citoyens* of 1764.

Rousseau (III,118-19; H. II,266; M. 299-301)

LE BON PRÊTRE avoit parlé avec véhémence; il étoit ému, je l'étois aussi. Je croyois entendre le divin Orphée chanter les premiers Hymnes.

Voltaire

ton vicaire Savoiard orphée! quel fou?

Masson tells us that this none too happy comparison of the Vicar with Orpheus was absent from the original manuscript, but was inserted by Rousseau at the request of his Paris publisher, Duchesne, in order to furnish a subject for an additional engraving.[38] Unaware of this, Voltaire has nevertheless put his finger unerringly on a detail of doubtful literary taste.

Rousseau (III, 122; H. II, 267; M. 307)

Montrez-moi ce qu'on peut ajouter pour la gloire de Dieu, pour le bien de la société, & pour mon propre avantage, aux devoirs de la loi naturelle.

Voltaire

toujours dieu glorieux

In his criticism Voltaire probably had in mind the same objection to anthropomorphism evident in his article *Athéisme* in the *Dictionnaire philosophique*. "Les philosophes, sans y penser, tombent presque

---
[37] Louis Ducros, *Rousseau*, III (1918), 134-36.
[38] Masson, *op. cit.*, 299, n. 2.

toujours dans les idées du vulgaire, en supposant que Dieu est jaloux de sa gloire."[39] Except for this phrase, Rousseau's passage would probably have pleased Voltaire.

Emphasizing, like Diderot,[40] the sufficiency of natural religion, Rousseau insists upon the confusing diversity of sects: "Je considérois cette diversité de sectes qui règnent sur la terre & qui s'accusent mutuellement de mensonge & d'erreur; je demandois, *Quelle est la bonne?*"[41] Of this argument, which tended to give the preference to natural, over revealed, religion, Voltaire probably approved. In any case the passage is marked in the margin without comment. Likewise the whole long passage on the four pages beginning with p. 128 at the sentence, "S'il étoit une religion sur la terre," and ending on p. 131, "pour juger quel poids doit avoir le silence des adversaires,"[42] is marked with long lines in the margin from top to bottom of each page. Rousseau argues that, if there were in the world any one religion ignorance of which would subject to eternal punishment any man of good faith, the God guilty of such a requirement would be the worst of tyrants. Since such a situation cannot exist, let each man judge in the light of his own conscience and reason how much religion and theology he can accept. The testimony and the authority of other men can carry no weight except in so far as their statements are valid in the light of reason. All of this would certainly be most acceptable to Voltaire.

There now follow on pp. 132-64[43] twenty other passages which are likewise marked in the margin without comment. These contain Rousseau's attacks upon prophecy and miracle as proofs of revealed religion and his refusal to believe a just God capable of condemning a majority of the world to eternal damnation for not having accepted a single particular religion of which they have perhaps not even heard. We could be sure on the basis of the ideas expressed that the author of the *Epître à Uranie*[44] would approve of such passages.

---

[39] Moland, XVII, 462.

[40] Diderot, *De la suffisance de la religion naturelle*, written in 1747, published in 1770. Assézat edition, I, 259-73.

[41] III, 126; H. II, 268; M. 315.

[42] H. II, 269, line 3, to 270, line 3: M. 319, line 6, to 325, line 11.

[43] H. II, 270-79; M. 325-99.

[44] Cf. Moland, IX, 360-61. Cf. also the famous "note des damnés" added to the *Henriade* in 1746, Moland, VIII, 175, n. 1. On the *Epître à Uranie*, later known as *Le Pour et le Contre*, the reader should consult the important study by Ira O. Wade in PMLA., XLVII (Dec., 1932), pp. 1066-1112.

LE VICAIRE SAVOYARD

His favorable attitude is shown conclusively by the fact that here he took up his pen again for some of the comments in the edition at Geneva studied by M. Bouvier and that these marginal notes on this particular section of the *Vicaire savoyard* stand out above all the others in showing regularly an unqualified approval which is most exceptional elsewhere. We shall reproduce the marked passages from the Leningrad *Emile* with the minimum of commentary.

> Tous ces monumens reconnus pour incontestables, il faut passer ensuite aux preuves de la mission de leurs auteurs; il faut bien savoir les lois des sorts, les probabilités éventives, pour juger quelle prédiction ne peut s'accomplir sans miracle; le génie des langues originales pour distinguer ce qui est prédiction dans ces langues, & ce qui n'est que figure oratoire; quels faits sont dans l'ordre de la nature, & quels autres faits n'y sont pas. (III, 132; H. II, 270; M. 325, 327.)

> (Il faut) dire enfin pourquoi Dieu choisit, pour attester sa parole, des moyens qui ont eux-mêmes si grand besoin d'attestation, comme s'il se jouoit de la crédulité des hommes, & qu'il évitât à dessein les vrais moyens de les persuader. (III, 133; H. II, 270; M. 327.)

C'est l'ordre inaltérable de la nature qui montre le mieux l'Etre suprême; s'il arrivoit beaucoup d'exceptions, je ne saurois plus qu'en penser; & pour soi, je crois trop en Dieu pour croire à tant de miracles si peu dignes de lui. (III, 134; H. II, 270; M. 329.)

Here, as might be expected, Voltaire noted in the Geneva *Emile* opposite the end of this last passage the word "excellent,"[45] thus indicating an enthusiastic agreement which is most rare in his attitude toward Rousseau. The presence of this marginal comment, and of others under similar circumstances elsewhere, offers further evidence that the unannotated passages which have been marked were actually marked by Voltaire and not by another.

[45] *Annales Jean-Jacques Rousseau*, I, 278.

> Si vos miracles, faits pour prouver votre
> doctrine, ont eux-mêmes besoin d'être
> prouvés, de quoi servent-ils? Autant valoit
> n'en point faire. (III, 135; H. II, 270-71;
> M. 331.)

In the following paragraph, Rousseau wrote: "Et puisque les magiciens de Pharaon osoient, en présence même de Moïse, faire les mêmes signes qu'il faisoit par l'ordre exprès de Dieu, pourquoi, dans son absence, n'eussent-ils pas, aux mêmes titres, prétendu la même autorité?" upon which, in the Geneva *Emile*, Voltaire commented: "bon."[46]

> Quand donc les Païens mettoient à mort
> les Apôtres leur annonçant un Dieu étranger,
> & prouvant leur mission par des prédictions
> & des miracles, je ne vois pas ce qu'on avoit
> à leur objecter de solide, qu'ils ne pussent à
> l'instant rétorquer contre nous. Or que faire
> en pareil cas? Une seule chose: Revenir au
> raisonnement, & laisser là les miracles. (III,
> 136, n.12; H. II, 271, n.1; M. 337, n.)

This is the second case in which Voltaire commented in the Geneva *Emile* upon a passage marked without comment in the copy at Leningrad. Again he recorded his approval in a succinct "bon."[47]

> Celui qui commence par se choisir un
> seul peuple & proscrire le reste du genre
> humain, n'est pas le père commun des
> hommes; celui qui destine au supplice
> éternel le plus grand nombre de ses
> créatures, n'est pas le Dieu clément & bon
> que ma raison m'a montré.
> A l'égard des dogmes, elle me dit qu'ils
> doivent être clairs, lumineux, frappans par
> leur évidence. (III, 138; H. II, 271-72;
> M. 341, 343.)

Upon the first part of this passage the Geneva *Emile* contains the comment: "très bon."[48]

There follows in Rousseau's text a supposed dialogue in which *L'Inspiré* endeavors to convince *Le Raisonneur* that he should bow to

[46] *Ibid.*
[47] *Ibid.*
[48] *Ibid.*

the religious authority of the former and accept his theological teaching even though it is absurd and contrary to reason.

> LE RAISONNEUR.—Et qui êtes-vous, pour m'oser dire que Dieu se contredit? et à qui croirai-je par préférence, de lui qui m'apprend par la raison les vérités éternelles, ou de vous qui m'annoncez de sa part une absurdité?
> L'INSPIRÉ.—A moi, car mon instruction est plus positive; & je vais vous prouver invinciblement que c'est lui qui m'envoie.
> LE RAISONNEUR.—Comment? vous me prouverez que c'est Dieu qui vous envoie déposer contre lui? Et de quel genre seront vos preuves pour me convaincre qu'il est plus certain que Dieu me parle par votre bouche que par l'entendement qu'il m'a donné? (III, 140; H. II, 272; M. 349, 351.)
> LE RAISONNEUR.—. . . Car, supposant qu'en raisonnant vous m'avez convaincu, comment saurai-je si ce n'est point ma raison corrompue par le péché qui me fait acquiescer à ce que vous me dites? D'ailleurs, quelle preuve, quelle demonstration pourrez-vous jamais employer plus évidente que l'axiome qu'elle doit détruire? Il est tout aussi croyable qu'un bon syllogisme est un mensonge, qu'il l'est que la partie est plus grande que le tout.
> (III, 142; H. II, 273; M. 353.)
> L'INSPIRÉ.—. . . Mais que dites-vous des prophéties?
> LE RAISONNEUR.—Je dis premièrement que je n'ai pas plus entendu de prophéties que je n'ai vu de miracles. Je dis de plus qu'aucune prophétie ne sauroit faire autorité pour moi. (III, 144; H. II, 273; M.357.)
> Parmi tant de religions diverses qui se proscrivent & s'excluent mutuellement, une seule est la bonne, si tant est qu'une le soit.
> (III, 146; H. II, 274; M. 359.)

This significant parenthetical phrase with its strongly sceptical note about the validity of any revealed religion has been underlined. It would quite naturally appeal to Voltaire. The next passage marked follows immediately after the preceding.

> Pour la reconnoître [la bonne religion], il ne suffit pas d'en examiner une, il faut les examiner toutes; &, dans quelque matière que ce soit, on ne doit pas condamner sans entendre; il faut comparer les objections aux preuves; il faut savoir ce que chacun oppose aux autres, & ce qu'il leur répond. (III, 146; H. II, 274; M. 359.)

> Quand vous avez voulu juger de la Foi Catholique sur le livre de Bossuet, vous vous êtes trouvé loin de compte après avoir vécu parmi nous. Vous avez vu que la doctrine avec laquelle on répond aux Protestans n'est point celle qu'on enseigne au peuple, & que le livre de Bossuet ne ressemble guère aux instructions du prône. (III, 148; H. II, 274; M. 361, 363.)

> Nous avons trois principales religions en Europe. . . . Celle qui n'admet qu'une révélation est la plus ancienne, & paroît la plus sûre; celle qui en admet trois est la plus moderne, & paroît la plus conséquente; celle qui en admet deux, & rejette la troisième, peut bien être la meilleure, mais elle a certainement tous les préjugés contre elle, l'inconséquence saute aux yeux.

> Dans les trois révélations, les Livres sacrés sont écrits en des langues inconnues aux peuples qui les suivent. Les Juifs n'entendent plus l'Hébreu, les Chrétiens n'entendent ni l'Hébreu ni le Grec. (III, 149-50; H. II, 275; M. 365, 367.)

> Connoissez-vous beaucoup de Chrétiens qui aient pris la peine d'examiner avec soin ce que le Judaïsme allègue contr'eux? Si quelques-uns en ont vu quelque chose, c'est dans les livres des Chrétiens. (III, 152; H. II, 276; M. 369, 371.)

> Je ne croirai jamais avoir bien entendu
> les raisons des Juifs, qu'ils n'aient un Etat
> libre, des écoles, des universités, où ils
> puissent parler & disputer sans risque. (III,
> 154; H. II, 276; M. 375.)

The orthodox argue that ignorance of Christianity is no longer an excuse for not accepting it since missionaries have gone all over the world. Rousseau, however, questions the truth of this contention.

> Cela est bientôt dit. Mais vont-ils dans
> le cœur de l'Afrique encore inconnue, & où
> jamais Européen n'a pénétré jusqu'à présent? Vont-ils dans la Tartarie méditerranée suivre à cheval les Hordes ambulantes,
> dont jamais étranger n'approche, & qui loin
> d'avoir ouï parler du Pape, connoissent à
> peine le grand Lama? (III, 155; H. II,
> 277; M. 379, 381.)

> Qu'ont fait les femmes de cette partie
> du monde pour qu'aucun missionnaire ne
> puisse leur prêcher la foi? Iront-elles toutes
> en enfer pour avoir été recluses?
> Quand il seroit vrai que l'Evangile est
> annoncé par toute la terre, qu'y gagneroit-on? La veille du jour que le premier Missionnaire est arrivé dans un pays, il y est
> sûrement mort quelqu'un qui n'a pu l'entendre. (III, 156; H. II, 277; M. 381.)

> Voyez si je dois, sur votre seul témoignage, croire toutes les choses incroyables
> que vous me dites, & concilier tant d'injustices avec le Dieu juste que vous m'annoncez. Laissez-moi, de grâce, aller voir
> ce pays lointain, où s'opérèrent tant de
> merveilles inouïes dans celui-ci; que j'aille
> savoir pourquoi les habitans de cette Jérusalem ont traité Dieu comme un brigand.
> (III, 158; H. II, 277-78; M. 385.)

> Or je soutiens qu'il n'y a pas de révélation contre laquelle les mêmes objections
> n'ayent autant & plus de force que contre
> le Christianisme. D'où il suit que s'il n'y

> a qu'une religion véritable, & que tout homme soit obligé de la suivre sous peine de damnation, il faut passer sa vie à les étudier toutes. (III, 160; H. II, 278; M. 387, 389.)

The sentence immediately preceding this last passage expresses Rousseau's conviction that any one would be justified in requiring a missionary to answer successfully the objections just presented before allowing him to carry on his mission. Voltaire commented on this sentence in the copy of *Emile* at Geneva: "tout ce discours se trouve mot à mot dans le poème de la religion naturelle et dans l'épître à Uranie."[49] In this connection Masson observes: "La remarque de Voltaire est exacte, à condition de ne pas la prendre à la lettre. On ne peut pas dire que 'tout ce discours' du païen au Missionnaire 'se trouve mot à mot' dans Voltaire, mais, du moins, l'esprit s'y trouve. . . . Partout où le déisme du Vicaire devient franchement rationaliste, ce sont les arguments et souvent les formules de Voltaire qui s'imposent à lui. . . . Cette note marginale montre que Voltaire a bien senti cette dépendance intellectuelle du déisme de Jean-Jacques à l'égard du sien. Il n'en est que plus violemment irrité, lorsque le Vicaire fait bon marché de la 'raison,' et s'abandonne aux appels du 'cœur.' "[50]

Still pursuing the question of the fate of the heathen, Rousseau mentions the arguments by which theologians try to dispose of the problem.

> Pressés par ces raisons, les uns aiment mieux faire Dieu injuste, & punir les innocens du péché de leur père, que de renoncer à leur barbare dogme. Les autres se tirent d'affaire, en envoyant obligeamment un ange instruire quiconque, dans une ignorance invincible, auroit vécu moralement bien. La belle invention que cet ange! Non contens de nous asservir à leurs machines, ils mettent Dieu lui-même dans la nécessité d'en employer. (III, 162; H. II, 279; M. 391, 393.)

[49] *Annales Jean-Jacques Rousseau*, I, 279.
[50] Masson, *op. cit.*, 387, n. 1.

LE VICAIRE SAVOYARD

The scant respect paid to angels when introduced in lieu of convincing theological argument shows Rousseau's rationalism here very much in the foreground. The passage contrasts sharply with his mention of angels on a previous occasion.[51]

> Il y a tant de raisons solides pour & contre [la révélation], que, ne sachant à quoi me déterminer, je ne l'admets ni ne la rejette; je rejette seulement l'obligation de la reconnoître, parce que cette obligation prétendue est incompatible avec la justice de Dieu. (III, 164; H. II, 279; M. 399.)

This completes the group of passages merely marked in the margin without comment. All of them represent the destructive, rationalistic side of Rousseau's position and with them Voltaire naturally agrees, as is clearly shown by his occasional comments in the Geneva edition of *Emile*. When Rousseau begins to develop the constructive side of his religious ideas, however, Voltaire's hostility manifests itself again in concrete fashion. On the succeeding pages the marginal comments abound both in the Geneva and the Leningrad copies, in a number of cases overlapping.

ROUSSEAU (III, 166; H. II, 280; M. 407, 409) | VOLTAIRE

Socrate . . . inventa, dit-on, la morale; d'autres avant lui l'avoient mise en pratique: il ne fit que dire ce qu'ils avoient fait, il ne fit que mettre en leçons leurs exemples. | et Zaleucus! confusé!

Inventa and *dit-on* have been underlined. In his other copy of *Emile*, now at Geneva, Voltaire had commented: "qui jamais a dit cela?"[52] thus ignoring, as Masson indicates,[53] the presence of such a statement in Legendre de Saint-Aubin's *Traité de l'opinion*, upon which Rousseau often drew. Voltaire mentioned Zaleucus in the Introduction to the *Essai sur les mœurs* in a part first published in 1765.[54] On September 19, 1766, Voltaire praised the translation of *L'Exorde des Lois de Zaleucus* recently received.[55] In the *Philosophe*

[51] Cf. above, p. 108.
[52] *Annales Jean-Jacques Rousseau*, I, 279.
[53] Masson, *op. cit.*, 409, n. 2.
[54] Moland, XI, 78. Cf. *ibid.*, p. viii.
[55] *Ibid.*, XLIV, 440.

ignorant, which appeared at the end of 1766,[56] a brief paragraph accords high praise to Zaleucus,[57] at the same time citing the *Exorde*. This interesting juxtaposition of dates, coupled with the fact that, so far as I have been able to discover, Voltaire had apparently not mentioned Zaleucus previously, raises the question as to whether this marginal note may not also date from 1765 or 1766 rather than from 1762, when *Emile* first appeared. Confucius, of course, is often referred to in Voltaire's works, and his being mentioned here is no matter for surprise. A note in the Geneva *Emile* on a passage immediately below dealing with predecessors of Jesus' moral teaching reads: "Epictete porphire confutzé pitagore: tant d'autres,"[58] but there is no mention of Zaleucus. It is evident that several of these names are closely associated in Voltaire's mind and come readily under his pen together. Thus in the *Philosophe ignorant*, Confucius, Pythagoras, and Zaleucus are discussed on successive pages.[59] No positive conclusion about the date of these marginal comments is possible without further evidence. Indeed they may have been made, some at one time and some at another, during repeated readings of the same book.

ROUSSEAU (III, 168; H. II, 280; M. 411)
Oui, si la vie & la mort de Socrate sont d'un Sage, la vie & la mort de Jésus sont d'un Dieu.

VOLTAIRE
quelle extravagante absurdité as tu vu mourir des dieux pauvre fou!

In the Geneva *Emile* the above passage is annotated in the same spirit: "quesce que la mort d'un dieu!"[60]

ROUSSEAU (III, 169-70; H. II, 281; M. 417, 419)
Je regarde toutes les religions particuliéres comme autant d'institutions salutaires. . . . Je les crois toutes bonnes quand on y sert Dieu convenablement: Le culte essentiel est celui du cœur. Dieu n'en rejette point l'hommage, quand il est sincère, sous quelque forme qu'il lui soit offert. Appellé

VOLTAIRE

voila donc un incrédule dévot

---

[56] *Ibid.*, XXVI, 47, n.
[57] *Ibid.*, XXVI, 89.
[58] *Annales Jean-Jacques Rousseau*, I, 280.
[59] Moland, XXVI, 88-89.
[60] *Annales Jean-Jacques Rousseau*, I, 280.

dans celle que je professe au service de
l'Eglise, j'y remplis, avec toute l'exactitude
possible, les soins qui me sont prescrits, &
ma conscience me reprocheroit d'y manquer volontairement en quelque point.

Here is a characteristic and illuminating comment by Voltaire which shows clearly the fundamental disaccord between him and Rousseau. Voltaire wants all one thing, or all the other. He cannot understand Rousseau's combination of a modified rationalism with faith, though there is much in this passage not out of harmony with what Voltaire himself, perhaps from prudence, had many times written.[61] It appears to aggravate him, however, to see Rousseau manifest any friendliness toward the Church.

ROUSSEAU (III, 171; H. II, 281; M. 419)　　　VOLTAIRE
Je suis avec soin tous les Rites; je récite
attentivement: je m'applique à n'omettre
jamais ni le moindre <u>mot ni la moindre</u>　　et pourquoi?
cérémonie.　　　　　　　　　　　　　　　　misérable!

On the rest of this passage dealing with the Vicar's reverent attitude toward the mass, Voltaire commented also in the *Emile* now at Geneva: "ridicule car tu ne crois pas à ta messe." On the cultivation beforehand of an attitude of pious meditation, Voltaire in the same copy wrote simply: "impertinent."[62] In the Leningrad *Emile* he gave expression to the same viewpoint.

ROUSSEAU (III, 171; H. II, 282; M. 419)　　　VOLTAIRE
Quoi qu'il en soit de ce mystère incon-
cevable, je ne crains pas qu'au jour de
jugement je sois puni pour l'avoir jamais　　et tu ny crois pas!
profané dans mon cœur.

The fundamental antinomy in Rousseau's position is evident to Voltaire. It annoys him as a thinker, because it is a sincere concession to contemporary opinion. Had it been a mere ruse on the part of Rousseau, Voltaire would probably have applauded it as a necessary stratagem in the warfare against established powers. Was not he himself constantly ready to practice such tricks? Did he not in fact later censure Rousseau's very honesty in signing his name to danger-

[61] Cf. Moland, IX, 362 456, to mention but two cases antedating Rousseau's *Emile*.
[62] *Annales Jean-Jacques Rousseau*, I, 280.

ous works instead of following the frequent practice of prudent anonymity?[63] Rousseau's justification of his attitude in this passage is made clear by Masson in a quotation from his correspondence.[64]

The phrase in the next sentence "les sublimes devoirs"[65] in reference to the duties of the priesthood is underlined doubtless in the same hostile spirit. While Voltaire approved of the Vicar's program of preaching good conduct rather than theology and wrote in the margin of the Geneva copy: "bon cela,"[66] these are his last favorable words, and he quickly found matter to object to at the end of the very same paragraph.

ROUSSEAU (III, 173; H. II, 282; M. 425)   VOLTAIRE
Quoiqu'il arrive, je ne blasphémerai point contre la justice Divine, & ne mentirai point contre le Saint-Esprit.   c'est bien a toy a parler du St. esprit!

On the same passage in his other copy, Voltaire commented: "Que veux tu dire?"[67]

ROUSSEAU (III, 173; H. II, 282; M. 425)   VOLTAIRE
Mon bon ami, je ne trouve rien de si beau que d'être Curé.   le fat

Thinking of the personal and social mission of the devoted, upright priest, Rousseau is filled with admiration and respect. Philosophical and theological considerations fall into a subordinate position by comparison. Voltaire too in calmer moments had expressed a similar viewpoint: "Un sot prêtre excite le mépris; un mauvais prêtre inspire l'horreur; un bon prêtre, doux, pieux, sans superstition, charitable, tolérant, est un homme qu'on doit chérir et respecter."[68] Likewise in another place Voltaire wrote: "Un bon prêtre doit être le médecin des âmes."[69] Probably the essential difference between the two men on this point lies in the fact that with Voltaire such statements appear to be intellectual admissions calculated to strengthen his propaganda against priestly abuses; with Rousseau they are the outcome of warm, emotional feeling.

[63] Cf. below, pp. 136, 139.
[64] Masson, *op. cit.*, 419, 421, n. 3.
[65] III, 172; H. II, 282; M. 421.
[66] *Annales Jean-Jacques Rousseau*, I, 280.
[67] *Ibid.*
[68] Moland, XVIII, 379.
[69] *Ibid.*, XX, 273.

LE VICAIRE SAVOYARD

ROUSSEAU (III, 173-74; H. II, 282; M. 427)

O si jamais dans nos montagnes j'avois quelque pauvre Cure de bonnes gens à desservir, je serois heureux; car il me semble que je ferois le bonheur de mes Paroissiens! Je ne les rendrois pas riches, mais je partagerois leur pauvreté; j'en ôterois la <u>flétrissure & le mépris</u> plus insupportable que l'indigence.

VOLTAIRE

comment?

Rousseau stresses the power of comradeship and sympathy to relieve the burden of contempt and social ostracism. Voltaire with his query seeks more tangible relief.

ROUSSEAU (III, 181; H. II, 284; M. 443)
<u>Sans la foi nulle véritable vertu n'existe.</u>

VOLTAIRE
un incrédule recommander la foy

This resembles Voltaire's comment above: "voila donc un incrédule dévot."[70] On a passage in the preceding paragraph in which Rousseau had said: "C'est une inexcusable présomption de professer une autre religion que celle où l'on est né," Voltaire commented in the Geneva *Emile:* "pourquoy professer des sottises? il n'y a qua se taire et ne rien professer!"[71] Thus again the essential difference between the two men appears. Rousseau's Protestantism has marked him to the core. Abandoning some of the externals of the religion in which he was born, he has kept the essential. Voltaire, on the other hand, from a nominal Catholic became quickly a freethinker making war on the Church. M. Lanson has well expressed this contrast: "Le protestant qui cesse de croire peut se chamailler avec quelques ministres, il ne se heurte point au même dogme compact, à la même autorité intraitable: il n'est pas mis hors de son Eglise; il fait un parti avancé, il peut faire une nouvelle Eglise, en restant membre de la grande et multiple Eglise chrétienne. Nous voyons tous les jours le libre penseur catholique en vouloir à mort aux prêtres et aux dévots catholiques; le libre penseur protestant, sauf exception, garde le respect de Calvin et des sympathies étroites pour l'Eglise de Calvin. Rousseau, déiste, en guerre avec les pasteurs, incrédule à la révélation, est tout simplement un protestant libéral."[72]

---

[70] Cf. above, p. 118.
[71] *Annales Jean-Jacques Rousseau*, I, 280.
[72] G. Lanson, *Histoire de la littérature française*, 12th ed., Paris, 1912, p. 789.

This brings to an end our discussion of Voltaire's attitude toward the *Vicaire savoyard* on which there are a few more comments, all hostile, in the Geneva *Emile*, but none in the copy at Leningrad. Voltaire now passes over the next eighty pages without comment.

III. *Emile* after *Le Vicaire savoyard*

Having left the *Vicaire savoyard* behind him and returned to Rousseau's discussion of secular education, Voltaire seems to have hurried on rapidly in his reading of the copy now at Leningrad, until perhaps the name of Montaigne caught his eye and led him to pause and comment upon a passage of which he was to make later use in his satire of Rousseau. A marker still rests between pp. 260-261 and on it is noted for quick reference: "précepteur au bordel." The passage is also marked with a vertical line in the margin.

> Montaigne dit qu'il demandoit un jour au Seigneur de Langey combien de fois, dans ses négociations d'Allemagne, il s'étoit enivré pour le service du Roi. Je demanderois volontiers au gouverneur de certain jeune homme combien de fois il est entré dans un mauvais lieu pour le service de son élève. (III, 261; H. II, 308.)

While this edition contains no comment in the margin, but only the notation on the marker for ready reference, Voltaire did enter in the Geneva *Emile* the following note: "quelle plate indécence! tu n'as de lesprit que contre le christianisme."[1] The use he made of this passage appears in 1770 in the article *Assassinat*, incorporated finally into the *Dictionnaire philosophique*, where Voltaire gleefully says of Rousseau: "Le même esprit de sagesse et de décence qui lui fait prononcer qu'un précepteur doit souvent accompagner son disciple dans un lieu de prostitution, le fait décider que ce disciple doit être un assassin."[2] The reference to assassination has already been discussed in connection with Rousseau's attack upon duelling.[3] In the *Dialogues d'Evhémère* of 1777 Voltaire returned to both subjects. In this instance, however, he used in abbreviation the gross word *bordel*,

---
[1] *Annales Jean-Jacques Rousseau*, I, 282.
[2] Moland, XVII, 444.
[3] Cf. above, pp. 91-92.

EMILE

which he had written on his marker, instead of the suaver expression *lieu de prostitution*.[4] In his correspondence of 1761 he had already made a similar reference to a like situation in the *Nouvelle Héloïse*,[5] so that he was well prepared to note its repetition in *Emile*. While Rousseau's language in such cases as this, when torn from its context, obviously lends itself readily to Voltaire's not overscrupulous mockery, the latter's use of *souvent* is distinctly belied by the rest of Rousseau's passage, which, open to criticism as it may be, is by no means so ridiculous as Voltaire implies. It must be approached in the light of the author's real aim and meaning. Rousseau distinctly speaks of an extreme expedient to be used once and then abandoned along with the pupil himself if the latter is too brutish to be cured.

Voltaire passed over the next seventeen pages in this edition without comment, though in the text at Geneva there is a single marginal note of little importance. On p. 288[6] of the Leningrad edition he found Rousseau citing in praise of ancient inscriptions a line applied to the legendary Sardanapalus:

"J'ai bâti Tarse et Anchiale en un jour, et maintenant je suis mort."

A marker has been inserted between the pages and on it Voltaire wrote: "jai bati tarse et ankiale en un jour," probably in mockery of this impossible feat.

Occasionally in his books, as has been noted elsewhere,[7] Voltaire followed a curious practice in marking passages. He tore off a tiny bit of paper from the corner of one of his paper bookmarkers and stuck it down over or near part of the passage in question. It was in this way that he marked on p. 301[8] the sentence: "Je n'enverrois pas chez les Marchands, j'irois moi-même," which, as it happens, follows immediately after the phrase "comme qu'on s'y prenne" underlined, probably in censure, in the Geneva *Emile*.[9] No doubt Voltaire, practical man of affairs that he was, appreciated the advantages of personal negotiation.

We have now reached Book V of *Emile* dealing with the educa-

[4] Moland, XXX, 529.
[5] *Ibid.*, XLI, 240.
[6] Hachette, II, 316.
[7] G. R. Havens and N. L. Torrey, "The Private Library of Voltaire at Leningrad," PMLA., XLIII (Dec., 1928), 995.
[8] Hachette, II, 320.
[9] *Annales Jean-Jacques Rousseau*, I, 281-82.

tion of Sophie, Rousseau's ideal woman. In the original edition this section is contained in Volume IV. Here there are no marginal comments by Voltaire, but there are four passages marked in one way or another. Between pp. 76-77[10] of Volume IV there are two paper slips as bookmarkers. Both are blank and presumably one of them (being unneeded) is now misplaced. These pages deal with the method of teaching religion to young girls by making it agreeable rather than forbidding. They also attack the catechism as only partially intelligible to adults and consequently far beyond the comprehension of children. It is entirely likely that Voltaire was interested in Rousseau's criticism of the catechism. In fact, the probability that this passage was originally marked by Voltaire himself is increased by the presence of a similar bookmark between pp. 86-87,[11] which deal with a detailed application of the same criticism to the question of the nature of God, the Virgin birth, and other dogmas of the catechism, pushing these questions aside in favor of good conduct as alone important. It is a doctrine to which Voltaire could readily have subscribed.

The master of Ferney now passed the next ninety pages without leaving a sign behind him. The following passage, however, offered grist to his mill. He liked to use it in his warfare against Rousseau later. So he marked it in the margin and in addition inserted an annotated bookmark between the pages.

Je ne dis pas que les rapports conventionnels soient indifférens dans le mariage, mais je dis que l'influence des rapports naturels l'emporte tellement sur la leur, que c'est elle seule qui décide du sort de la vie, & qu'il y a telle convenance de goûts, d'humeurs, de sentimens, de caractères, qui devroient engager un père sage, fût-il Prince, fût-il Monarque, à donner sans balancer à son fils la fille avec laquelle il auroit toutes ces convenances, fût-elle née dans une famille déshonnête, fût-elle la fille du Bourreau. Oui, je soutiens que,

---

[10] The passage begins with "demandant" (Hachette, II, 349, line 33) and ends with "jamais écrit, et" (*Ibid.*, 350, line 12).
[11] Beginning with "à résoudre" (Hachette, II, 352, line 17) and ending with "d' être bien -(faisans)" (*ibid.*, 352, end).

EMILE

tous les malheurs imaginables dussent-ils tomber sur deux époux bien unis, ils jouiront d'un plus vrai bonheur à pleurer ensemble, qu'ils n'en auroient dans toutes les fortunes de la terre, empoisonnées par la désunion des cœurs. (IV, 177-78; H. II, 378.)

Having marked the latter part of this passage with a vertical line in the margin, Voltaire also left behind him a slip of paper as a marker on which is written the key phrase: "la fille du bourreau." This reference to marriage with "la fille du bourreau" became a stock joke with Voltaire, sharing honors of frequent repetition with his description of Emile as a "gentilhomme menuisier."[12] In fact, the former phrase was used five times in the years 1768 to 1777.[13] Since it occurs so frequently in Voltaire's works after 1768 and apparently not at all before, one wonders whether the discovery of this passage and the placing of the marker there did not perhaps occur five or six years after the appearance of the original edition of *Emile* in 1762. As in the case of the attempt to date any of the other marginalia, one can only speculate and surmise, however, for there is no evidence permitting a positive conclusion. Voltaire's mockery of Rousseau in this instance is obviously that of a man determined to find fault and eager to seize upon any pretext. Rousseau has expressed himself in striking form, and for emphasis has intentionally taken an extreme case. No just criticism can be attached, however, to his fundamental idea. With more *nuance* than usual he admits that conventional associations of social status are not without their bearing upon a successful marriage, but insists rightly that these are of far less significance than natural harmonies of character and inclination.

Passing over nearly two hundred pages, we find between pp. 360-61 a marker and on it written the word "puissance."[14] These pages give a résumé of part of Rousseau's political principles as expounded in the *Contrat social*. The word "puissance" on the marker can seemingly refer to nothing specific on these pages. It does occur,

[12] Moland, X, 160; XVII, 444; XXIV, 420-21; XXVI, 40; XXX, 529, 573; XLII, 457.
[13] *Ibid.*, X, 160; XV, 434; XVIII, 31-32; XXX, 529, 573.
[14] Beginning with: "Si donc les matières" (Hachette, II, 430, line 36) and ending with "quand même on pour -(roit)" (*ibid.*, 431, line 17).

however, at the top of the very next page. Rousseau says: "Nous examinerons encore si l'on est obligé en conscience de donner sa bourse à un bandit qui nous la demande sur le grand chemin, quand même on pourroit la lui cacher, car enfin le pistolet qu'il tient est aussi une *puissance*." Probably Voltaire slipped his marker between the pages where the beginning of the passage which interested him occurs. The reason for marking it is not clear. Perhaps this also was intended to furnish material for mockery similar to that in the passages just mentioned previously, but so far as we know it was never used.

IV. Summary of Voltaire's Attitude toward *Emile*

We have now studied all the passages in any way marked by Voltaire in the copy of *Emile* found in his library at Leningrad. Obviously these passages with their comments are of very unequal value, but neither the student of Voltaire nor of Rousseau would want us in this case to pick and choose. Completeness here is of first importance. Voltaire's comments on *Emile* present the double interest attaching to his attitude toward Rousseau's ideas on education and on religion. At the same time they illuminate in detail the points of resemblance and the numerous points of difference between the two men. The fact that there are seventy-three passages in *Emile* upon which Voltaire wrote comments in the edition at Leningrad and sixty-three other passages marked in some fashion or other without comment offers very concrete evidence of the great importance Voltaire attached to the book in spite of his violent hostility to the author and to most of his ideas.

Towards Rousseau's educational theories Voltaire's notes indicate, as might be expected, nothing but contempt. As in the case of the *Discours sur l'inégalité*, he ridicules the preference given to the primitive over the civilized. Rousseau had written: "Il y a plus d'erreurs dans l'Académie des Sciences que dans tout un Peuple de Hurons." Voltaire's comment is scathing: "Quelle impertinence absurde!" Several of the latter's marginal notes show his contempt for Rousseau's emphasis on non-intellectual education. Speaking of the progress of his pupil, the author of *Emile* said: "Je ne lui permets jamais d'aller loin," upon which Voltaire commented succinctly:

SUMMARY ON EMILE

"Je le crois." Likewise, when Rousseau observed: "Pour avoir aussi les vertus sociales, il lui manque uniquement de connoître les relations qui les exigent," Voltaire noted in the margin: "Il lui manque tout." When Rousseau asked: "Trouvez-vous qu'un enfant ainsi parvenu à sa quinzième année ait perdu les précédentes?" Voltaire was ready with his answer: "Oui, car c'est une brute qui ne connais [sic] pas une seulle vertu socialle." Rousseau's feeling that one is justified in taking the law into one's own hands to avenge an unmerited affront instead of fighting a duel was qualified by Voltaire as "assassination." Marriage for love without regard to social station even with "la fille du bourreau" aroused the irony of Voltaire. Likewise the "précepteur au bordel," as the latter called him, seemed almost to invite his satire, unjust as it was.

In the *Vicaire savoyard*, Rousseau expressed his religious ideas boldly. His position was unfortunate for his own comfort. He was too heretical for the Church, either Catholic or Protestant, not heretical enough for the philosophic party, to which Voltaire belonged. Thus he thoroughly displeased both of these influential groups. In the Leningrad copy of *Emile* Voltaire's comments on the *Vicaire savoyard* are entirely unfavorable, ironical, or critical, but many of the passages merely marked for reference show the favor with which Voltaire viewed the destructive side of Rousseau's position, his attacks upon the validity of prophecy and miracles, his undermining of revelation, and his rejection of religious authority outside of the individual conscience. The Voltaire notes studied by M. Bouvier in the copy of *Emile* now at Geneva bring definite confirmation of his position on these points. On the other hand, the notes in the Leningrad copy refute M. Bouvier's inference, entirely justified on the basis of the evidence before him, that Voltaire hurried over without comment Rousseau's important development of his position as contained in the nearly one hundred pages between pp. 39 and 134. As a matter of fact, we have seen that, beginning with p. 59 in the Leningrad edition, important notes follow one another in quick succession. Thus these two sets of notes supplement one another in interesting and instructive fashion.

In his notes on the Leningrad copy of the *Vicaire savoyard*, Voltaire showed himself opposed to Rousseau's anthropocentric idea of the universe, his attribution of personality to divinity, his differentiation between man and animal in the interest of the spirituality of the soul, his belief in the harmony of nature so dear later to the romanticists, his confident acceptance of free will instead of determinism, his dogmatic assertion of the truth of immortality, and in general all in his position which was not destructive of orthodox ideas in theology and metaphysics. Voltaire's "qui te l'a dit" might be taken as his typical query to all attempts at a speculative solution of these problems. That Rousseau's mingling of rationalism and faith was incomprehensible to Voltaire appears in such comments as "Voilà donc un incrédule dévot" and "un incrédule recommander la foy." In sum, it comes down to the fact that Rousseau was mystical and Voltaire in general was not. Voltaire was entirely incapable of appreciating the spirit of worship and reverence which formed an important part of Rousseau's personality. To this we must attribute the fact that Voltaire, right as he often was in his criticisms, was nevertheless too apt, in his hostility toward Rousseau and in his quibbling over details, to miss the spirit of a given passage taken as a whole. He certainly failed to appreciate the significance and value of Rousseau's suggestive approach to the problem of education. He could tolerate only the negative, destructive side of Rousseau's religious ideas in the *Vicaire savoyard*.

CHAPTER V

VOLTAIRE'S COMMENTS ON ROUSSEAU'S *Lettre à M. de Beaumont*

In his first opinion expressed after reading *Emile*, Voltaire wrote that it contained "une quarantaine de pages contre le christianisme, des plus hardies qu'on ait jamais écrites,"[1] thus paying involuntary tribute to Rousseau's straightforward sincerity and courage. That Voltaire's estimate was no idle phrase is proved by the prompt condemnation and burning of *Emile* and by Rousseau's forced flight from Montmorency. Further evidence was furnished by the *Mandement* against *Emile* of the Archbishop of Paris, Christophe de Beaumont, under date of August 20, 1762.[2] Rousseau probably first learned of the *Mandement* early in September[3] and after some delay obtained a copy of it during the latter half of the same month.[4] Through October, November, and December,[5] he worked secretly on his reply and was able to send the manuscript to his printer Rey at Amsterdam on January 1, 1763.[6] On February 23 Rey sent the author some first copies for private circulation[7] and during the latter half of March Rousseau's correspondence shows him actively distributing some of them among his friends.[8] Although it is possible that some copies of his reply to the Archbishop may have been put on sale at this time in and about Geneva,[9] the statements of Moultou and of Rousseau himself[10] are against this conclusion and in any case the

[1] Moland, XLII, 136.

[2] This is the date given at the end of the *Mandement*. Cf. Hachette, III, 57.

[3] Rousseau, *Correspondance*, VIII (Colin, 1927), 89, a letter from Paris of August 30, 1762. Cf. *ibid.*, IX, 218.

[4] *Ibid.*, VIII, 161.

[5] On December 1, Rousseau says he has been working on it for two months and hopes to have it ready by Twelfth Night (January 6) or at the latest within six weeks. He hopes it may be published before Easter. *Ibid.*, VIII, 294-95.

[6] *Ibid.*, VIII, 344.

[7] *Ibid.*, IX, 154. Rey's letter, however, was not written till March 7.

[8] *Ibid.*, IX, 153, 154, 165, 171-72, 178, 191, 194-95.

[9] This is the statement of Louis Ducros, *J.-J. Rousseau de Montmorency au Val de Travers* (1917), p. 259, and might be implied by Rey (Rousseau, *Corr.*, IX, 220), though the next sentence suggests that Rey is referring only to the copies distributed privately by Rousseau.

[10] Rousseau, *Corr.*, IX, 230-31 (April 13); *ibid.*, 238 (April 16). Rousseau even fears his reply may have been suppressed.

book seems to have been difficult to obtain there for another month.[11] As for the situation at Paris, while some copies are mentioned as circulating by April 23,[12] even as much as four weeks later Le Nieps writes Rousseau about the *Lettre à Beaumont*: "On ne la trouve que difficilement, et je crois même que ce sont des Lettres d'une autre édition."[13] Even on June 9 he reiterates: "On la trouve difficilement."[14] Rey was right in saying of the Archbishop, "cet homme a les bras longs en France pour se venger du libraire qui auroit osé vendre cet ouvrage,"[15] and Rousseau's reply could at first appear there only under cover.[16]

The edition in Voltaire's library at Leningrad is entitled: *A Christophe de Beaumont. Œuvres*, t. III, 2-me Partie. Amsterdam, Marc-Michel Rey, 1763, in-12. 134 pp. It is followed by 45 pp. of the *Mandement*, printed in Paris, 1762. This is the second edition mentioned by Théophile Dufour,[17] but it appears to have been printed very promptly after the first and distributed almost at the same time, for Rey published at least five editions during the single year 1763.[18]

Voltaire procured his copy probably during the first part of April. His letter to Helvétius signed with the pseudonym "De Mitèle" and headed "Mars," in which he praised parts of the *Lettre à Beaumont*,[19] must be misdated, unless the letter to Vernes of April 2 is wrongly classified or its testimony to be rejected as feigned, a procedure on the part of Voltaire for which there would seem to be no motive of prudence necessary in this case. In this letter of early April he wrote: "La *Lettre à Christophe* me donne la pépie. Je ne dormirai point que je n'aie vu la *Lettre à Christophe*: avez-vous vu la *Lettre à Christophe?* pouvez-vous me faire avoir la *Lettre*

---

[11] On April 26, Moultou writes that more than 150 copies have been sold in one day and more than 250 altogether up to that time, which implies that it has only very recently become available. *Ibid.*, IX, 255.

[12] *Ibid.*, IX, 247.

[13] *Ibid.*, 307.

[14] *Ibid.*, 338.

[15] *Ibid.*, 29.

[16] Rey tried to sell copies to dealers in Paris, Lyons, and Rouen, but Rouen alone was willing to take the risk, and Rey sent 500 copies. *Ibid.*, IX, 219. Cf. *ibid.*, 29.

[17] *Op. cit.*, pp. 185-86 (No. 215). Cf. the parenthetical note under No. 215 on p. 186: "A l'exemplaire Bc 3258 est joint le *Mandement*," etc.

[18] *Ibid.*

[19] Moland, XLII, 446-47.

à Christophe? où trouve-t-on la *Lettre à Christophe?*"[20] This sounds as though Voltaire's appetite had been whetted by the conversation of his friends. Perhaps he had been allowed to glance through a borrowed copy,[21] but had not yet procured one which he could examine thoroughly for himself. Rousseau and Moultou had been careful to distribute the work in confidence only to the friends of the author[22] among whom Voltaire at this time could certainly not be included. Even on the 22nd of April, Voltaire wrote to the Marquis de Dirac: "Il est fort difficile d'en avoir des exemplaires: s'il m'en tombe entre les mains, je tâcherai de vous les faire parvenir contresignés."[23] On the 25th, however, a date which corresponds strikingly with the time when Moultou's letter of the 26th indicates that the work was at length being sold,[24] Voltaire wrote to his close friend D'Argental at Paris: "Vous aurez incessamment la Lettre de *Jean-Jacques à Christophe*,"[25] thus showing definitely that copies were finally obtainable.

Voltaire's opinion of the work was expressed in several letters of this period. In the letter to Helvétius referred to above as probably misdated, the master of Ferney wrote: "Il y a cinq ou six pages excellentes, et de la plus grande force, dans une petite brochure qui paraît depuis peu, qui perce avec peine à Paris, et que vous aurez vue sans doute.[26] C'est un grand dommage que l'auteur y parle sans cesse de lui-même, quand il ne doit parler que de choses utiles. Son titre est d'une indécence impertinente, son ridicule amour-propre révolte: c'est Diogène, mais il s'exprime quelquefois en Platon. Croiriez-vous que ses audacieuses sorties contre un monstre respecté n'ont révolté personne, et que sa philosophie a trouvé autant de partisans[27] que sa vanité cynique a eu de censeurs? Oh! si quelqu'un

---

[20] *Ibid.*, 449.
[21] Cf. the testimony of Colonel De Pury that a copy is being circulated (March 27-April 3), Rousseau, *Corr.*, IX, 192.
[22] *Ibid.*, IX, 165, 191, 192, 205.
[23] Moland, XLII, 457.
[24] Rousseau, *Corr.*, IX, 255.
[25] Moland, XLII, 460.
[26] From what has been said before about the rarity of the work in France, it would appear practically impossible that Helvétius could have seen Rousseau's *Lettre* in March. This fact offers an additional argument in favor of the conclusion that Voltaire's letter to Helvétius is misdated.
[27] Note Voltaire's surprise and encouragement at the favorable reception accorded Rousseau's attacks upon the Church. This offers evidence in favor of the theory that Rousseau definitely influenced Voltaire in the direction of greater boldness.

pouvait rendre aux hommes le service de leur montrer les mêmes vérités, dépouillées de tout ce qui les défigure et les avilit chez cet écrivain, que je le bénirais!"[28] Thus Voltaire mingled his praise for Rousseau's attack upon orthodoxy with contempt for the author's references to himself, a criticism which Voltaire's hostility caused him to exaggerate out of all proportion. Jean-Jacques himself was conscious of this danger of inviting censure and talked of withdrawing his work from the press: "Je persiste à trouver cet écrit foible et mauvais. Quand on parle de soi il n'est pas permis de s'animer et de s'emporter comme quand on défend en général la cause des mœurs et de la justice. Cela fait aussi qu'on est froid en voulant être modéré."[29]

In his letter to D'Argental of April 25, Voltaire also expressed an opinion with characteristic mingling of blame and praise. He wrote: "Vous aurez incessamment la Lettre de *Jean-Jacques à Christophe*. Il n'a point fait de cartons, comme on le croyait: il persiste toujours à dire qu'il fallait lui élever des statues au lieu de le brûler; il assure que si on trouve quelques traits voluptueux dans son *Héloïse*, il y en a davantage dans l'*Aloïsia*,[30] que tous les prêtres ont à Paris dans leurs bibliothèques. Il proteste à Christophe qu'il est chrétien; et en même temps il couvre la religion chrétienne d'opprobres et de ridicules; il y a une douzaine de pages sublimes contre cette sainte religion. Peut-être ce qu'il dit est-il trop fort; car, après tout, le christianisme n'a fait périr qu'environ cinquante millions de personnes de tout âge et de tout sexe, depuis environ quatorze cents ans, pour des querelles théologiques. J'oubliais de vous dire que Jean-Jacques, dans son épître, prouve à Omer qu'il est un sot, en quoi je suis entièrement de son avis."[31] As in the case of *Emile*, it is the destructive side of Rousseau's religious position which Voltaire appreciated. This furnishes the "douzaine de pages sublimes." For the rest, Rousseau was both too moderate and too personal to please his great rival. In addition to those just mentioned, there are also, in Voltaire's correspondence of this period, a few other references to the

---

[28] Moland, XLII, 446-47. The last sentence in this passage appears as a forecast of what Voltaire himself would like to do.
[29] Rousseau, *Corr.*, IX, 72. Cf. 57, 121, 153.
[30] A licentious novel in Latin by Chorier.
[31] Moland, XLII, 460.

Lettre à Beaumont, but they bear only on details and will be clearer if left until later. We may therefore pass now directly to Voltaire's marginal comments.

Readers of Rousseau's work will remember that in his title he made a piquant contrast between "Jean-Jacques Rousseau, Citoyen de Genève" and "Christophe de Beaumont, Archevêque de Paris, duc de Saint-Cloud, pair de France, commandeur de l'ordre du Saint-Esprit, proviseur de Sorbonne, etc." This balancing of citizenship in Geneva against the Archbishop's numerous titles of nobility, at the same time that it harmonized with Rousseau's assumption of democratic independence, was calculated also to flatter his compatriots. It was not, however, likely to appeal to him who on occasion signed himself "comte de Ferney, comte de Tournay, gentilhomme ordinaire de la chambre du Roi," and Voltaire wrote impatiently on the title page: "ce titre est une boufonerie [sic] et l'ouvrage veut être sérieux." To Helvétius, as we have seen,[32] Voltaire had written: "Son titre est d'une indécence impertinente." We agree rather with M. Ducros that it was "d'une habile hardiesse."[33] Strange that the author of *Candide* should have been so blind! But obviously he did not try to see. Perhaps, however, Voltaire really thought this sally out of place and likely to weaken the total effect.

Consistent with the striking contrast pointed out on his title page, Rousseau at the beginning of his letter dwelt upon the lack of common ground upon which to stand in a discussion with the Archbishop. How could they understand each other? However, Rousseau must reply, not because his book had been criticized, but because the attack had been extended to include himself. Thus, not without ability, he prepared the way for the personalities which he felt to be necessary, but to which Voltaire so much objected.

Rousseau (p. 1; H. III, 58)	Voltaire
Je ne puis m'empêcher, en commençant cette Lettre de réfléchir sur les bizarreries de ma destinée. Elle en a qui n'ont été que pour moi.	tu commences par parler de toy, et tu parles toujours de toy.
J'étois né avec quelque talent; le public	toy. tu n'es pas adroit

---
[32] Cf. above, p. 131.
[33] Ducros, *op. cit.*, III, 125. Cf. Rousseau, *Corr.*, IX, 255, "Ce titre est divertissant par le ridicule." (Quoted by Moultou from the Abbé Quesnel.)

l'a jugé ainsi: cependant j'ai passé ma jeunesse dans une heureuse obscurité, dont je ne cherchois point à sortir.

J'approchois de ma quarantième année, √ & j'avois au lieu d'une fortune que j'ai toujours méprisée, √ & d'un nom qu'on m'a fait payer si cher, le repos & des amis, les deux seuls biens dont mon cœur soit avide. Une misérable question d'Académie m'agitant l'esprit malgré moi me jetta dans un métier pour lequel je n'étois point fait, ✗ (p. 2; H. III, 58)

√ qu'importe
√ vanité
sotte

eh oui tu etais fait pour etre sindic!

Quelle inconstance perpétuelle n'ai-je pas éprouvée dans les jugemens du public sur √ mon compte! (pp. 2-3; H. III, 59)

√ on se soucie bien de ton compte?

Tantôt j'étois un homme noir, & tantôt un ange de lumière. (p. 3; H. III, 59)

et quimporte?

J'ai écrit sur divers sujets, mais toujours dans les mêmes principes: toujours la même morale, (p. 3; H. III, 59)

qu'importe?

Après mon premier discours, j'étois un homme à paradoxes, qui se faisoit un jeu de prouver ce qu'il ne pensoit pas: Après ma lettre sur la musique françoise, j'étois l'ennemi déclaré de la Nation; (p. 3; H. III, 59)

et toujours toy

Ainsi va flotant [sic] le sot public sur mon compte, sachant aussi peu pourquoi il m'abhorre, que pourquoi il m'aimoit auparavant. (p. 4; H. III, 59)

et toujours toy?

Enfin lassé d'une vapeur enivrant qui enfle sans rassasier, excédé du tracas des oisifs surchargés de leur tems & prodigues du mien, soupirant après un repos si cher à mon cœur & si nécessaire à mes maux, j'avois posé la plume avec joye. (pp. 4-5; H. III, 59)

et toujours toy

Thus on the first five pages Voltaire reiterated in the margins "et toujours toy," or other variant comments, directed at Rousseau's attempt at personal vindication. This attitude of Voltaire is entirely in harmony with what he wrote to Helvétius: "C'est un grand dommage que l'auteur y parle sans cesse de lui-même."[34] Remembering Voltaire's plaints over his treatment in Germany, his susceptibility to the thrusts even of inconsequential enemies who would otherwise have been long since forgotten, we may consider him as hardly justified in criticizing Rousseau's lack of objectivity in the midst of his very real persecutions and troubles. Besides, if we may well doubt whether a purely intellectual appeal would have convinced and won over any of Rousseau's enemies, is it not certain that these personal details but worked the more upon the emotions of his friends? In any case the father of Romanticism could not do otherwise.

ROUSSEAU (p. 5; H. III, 60)	VOLTAIRE
Un Genevois fait imprimer un Livre en Hollande, & par arrêt du √ Parlement de Paris ce Livre est brûlé sans respect pour le Souverain dont il porte le privilège.	√ tu raisones mal. car supposons que tu eusses écrit contre le roy ainsi que tu as ecrit contre mon bon seigneur jesu, ce parlement parisien n'aurait il pas avec raison fait pendre le genevois?

If we assume the right of the state by arbitrary means to defend itself against the appearance of sedition in any form, if we justify the censorship of ideas and consider free speech a fallacy, then only does Rousseau's argument fall to the ground. It is strange therefore to find Voltaire as *advocatus diaboli* siding with the most arrant conservatives on this question. Obviously, however, it is an intellectual agreement only. It is as a lawyer or a debater that he criticizes Rousseau's argument, merely from the technical side, not as a real sympathizer with the Parlement or with the Archbishop.

ROUSSEAU (p. 6; H. III, 60)	VOLTAIRE
Ce même Parlement, toujours si soigneux pour les François de l'ordre des procédures, les néglige toutes dès qu'il s'agit d'un pauvre Etranger. Sans savoir si cet Etranger est bien l'auteur du livre qui porte son nom, s'il le reconnoît pour sien, si c'est lui qui l'a fait imprimer, sans égard pour son triste état, sans pitié pour les maux qu'il souffre, on commence par le décréter de prise de corps;	tu verras que le parlement devoit envoier savoir des nouvelles de ta santé

[34] Cf. above, p. 131.

Going beyond the bounds of reasonable argument under the circumstances, Rousseau appears to expect the Parlement to take into account his state of health before proceeding against him. Ironically, Voltaire hits off the weakness of this argument.

ROUSSEAU (p. 6; H. III, 60)   VOLTAIRE
Je ne sai comment cela s'accorde avec le droit des gens; mais je sai bien qu'avec de pareilles procédures la liberté de tout homme, & peut-être sa vie, est à la merci du premier Imprimeur. —

— et pourquoy as tu mis ton nom? pauvre diable.

Here a fundamental difference in attitude between Voltaire and Rousseau clearly reveals itself. The former is totally unable to understand why Jean-Jacques should insist upon a scrupulous avowal of his works in spite of danger. His own practice was exactly the opposite. Regarding himself as at war with the injustices of society, he followed the age-old, established usage of war, deceit, and employed it without stint or hesitation. "Jusqu'au feu, *exclusivement*," was his motto. Lying was so simple. Why not lie, gaily, joyously, humorously, with a straight face even, if it would save one from unpleasant consequences? Besides, in most cases this lying did not even deceive. It fooled no one. It merely saved the government's face. Probably the French government was not anxious to proceed against Rousseau, but felt its authority flaunted, its hand forced, by what seemed a deliberate defiance. So Voltaire considered Rousseau an utter fool to incur personal risk by signing his works, when he could so easily have escaped all trouble by anonymity or pretense.[35] Voltaire was expedient. The problem of personal integrity did not pose itself for him. Rousseau was on higher ground. Having taken this position, however, he should logically have accepted the dangers and the consequences without complaint. Something of this feeling was perhaps in Voltaire's mind, as he taunted him with expecting sympathetic consideration from his enemy, the Parlement.

Rousseau continues the plaints about his own situation which so angered Voltaire.

ROUSSEAU (p. 7; H. III, 60)   VOLTAIRE
Il abandonne en soupirant sa chère solitude. Il n'a qu'un seul bien, mais précieux, des amis, il les fuit.

ou sont-ils?

[35] Cf. above, pp. 69, 119-20.

LETTRE À BEAUMONT

Underlining the words *des amis,* Voltaire made a puerile comment, which was contrary to the well-known fact that Rousseau had at this time many warm partisans at Geneva and elsewhere. Such a comment should have been entirely beneath a man of Voltaire's position and intelligence. Grimm was right in saying: "Quant au bon vieux patriarche, vous savez, madame, que c'est un enfant. Il a soixante-douze ans, mais il en aurait cent qu'il serait enfant."[36] Often indeed Voltaire showed himself a petulant child. Only in the fact of Rousseau's break with Diderot, D'Alembert, and other former friends of the philosophic party, was there partial truth in Voltaire's inconsequential remark, while on the other hand it was literally true that Rousseau had been obliged to tear himself away from the warm friendship of M. and Mme du Luxembourg.

Horrified, however, that his friends at Geneva were impotent to influence the government in his favor, Rousseau cried out in dismay.

Rousseau (p. 7; H. III, 60)	Voltaire
Que vais-je dire? mon cœur se serre, ma main tremble, la plume tombe; il faut se taire, & ne pas imiter le crime de Cam. Que ne puis-je dévorer en secret la plus amére de mes douleurs!	mais comment geneve, paris berne la haye se sont ils acordez a proscrire ton livre?

Unkindly and unjustly Voltaire argues against Rousseau the seeming unanimity of supposedly independent judgments against him. That the action taken in different places in opposition to *Emile* was wholly independent is, however, more than doubtful. As for the reason why it had been condemned at Paris, here is the opinion of Lord Keith, "Milord Maréchal," a man of keen and balanced judgment, the friend of men so diverse as Rousseau and Frederick the Great. His opinion was confirmed by that of D'Alembert, certainly no partisan of Rousseau. Lord Keith wrote: "M. d'Alembert m'a confirmé ce que je croyais déjà: que le parlement, ayant sévi contre les jésuites, vous a attaqué pour qu'on ne dise pas qu'il a peu de zèle pour la religion."[37] Moreover, Rousseau's publisher at Amsterdam, Rey, testified to the influence of France upon the similar action taken at Geneva and in Holland against the *Contrat social:* "Si le *Contrat*

---

[36] Grimm, *Correspondance* (Garnier, 1882), XVI, 437.
[37] Rousseau, *Corr.*, X, 2, a letter of Milord Maréchal to Rousseau of June 28, 1763.

138   VOLTAIRE ON ROUSSEAU

social a été condamné à Genève et ici, ce n'est absolument qu'à la sollicitation de la France: vous devez en être persuadé; je le tiens de différentes personnes qui prétendent le bien savoir."[38] The fact that the *Contrat social*, though it had appeared over a month earlier than *Emile*, was seized with it at Geneva only two days after the condemnation of the latter work at Paris June 9 and that both were likewise condemned in Rousseau's own city ten days after the similar action in France[39] lends strong support to the contemporary opinion of D'Alembert, Lord Keith, and Rey. Very significant also is the fact that the Comte de Choiseul took pains to testify to the Council of Geneva his approval of their action, communicated to him by their own order, a striking evidence of their lack of complete independence in the matter. On July 9 a letter from M. Sellon of July 1 was actually read to the Council and recorded in their minutes to this effect: "On a lu une lettre du sieur Sellon, datée de Paris du 1er de ce mois, par laquelle il mande qu'il a communiqué à M. le comte de Choiseul le jugement du Magnifique Conseil sur deux livres de J.-J. Rousseau, et que Son Excellence lui avait témoigné qu'elle voyait avec plaisir que ces ouvrages eussent fait à Genève la même impression qu'à Paris, et que le gouvernement y eût pourvu de la même manière que le Parlement."[40] Thus diplomatically did M. de Choiseul express his appreciation of the deference of the government at Geneva for France. After this, the marginal comment of Voltaire, so little ignorant of what went on around him, appears not only entirely unfounded, but all the more petty and discreditable.[41]

ROUSSEAU (p. 8; H. III, 61)	VOLTAIRE
J'éviterai de parler de mes contemporains; je ne veux nuire à personne. Mais l'Athée Spinosa enseignoit paisiblement sa doctrine;✕ il faisoit sans obstacle imprimer ses livres.	il ecrivait en latin et tres adroitement et ne se nommait pas.

Perhaps Rousseau, in avoiding mention of his contemporaries, had in mind Voltaire and the comparative immunity which he had won. In any case the latter returns to the idea that Jean-Jacques

[38] *Ibid.*, IX, 220-21.
[39] See above, p. 72.
[40] Rousseau, *Corr.*, VII, 379, n. 1. The text of the letter is given on pp. 378-79.
[41] It was even claimed that Voltaire himself influenced the Council. See Ducros, *op. cit.*, III, 115-18.

should not have signed his book. "Frappez et cachez votre main," was Voltaire's policy in such matters.

ROUSSEAU (pp. 8-9; H. III, 61)

Il [Rousseau] eût passé le reste de ses malheureux jours dans les fers, il eût péri, peut-être, dans les supplices, si, durant le premier vertige qui gagnoit les Gouvernemens, il se fût trouvé à la merci de ceux qui l'ont persécuté.

VOLTAIRE

pourquoy tes tu nommé?

Thus the same idea recurs.

ROUSSEAU (p. 9; H. III, 61)

Echappé aux bourreaux, il tombe dans les mains des Prêtres; ce n'est pas là ce que je donne pour étonnant; mais un homme vertueux, qui a l'âme aussi noble que la naissance, un illustre Archevêque, qui devroit réprimer leur lâcheté, l'autorise.

VOLTAIRE

cet archeveque n'a fait qu'imiter le parlement

After granting veiled praise to the Archbishop of Paris in the early editions of *Le Monde comme il va* (1746),[42] Voltaire shortly revised his judgment, doubtless under the influence of Beaumont's warfare against the Jansenists and the affair of the *billets de confession*.[43] Nevertheless, the fact that Voltaire in his *Mémoires* referred to the Archbishop as an "homme opiniâtre, faisant le mal de tout son cœur par excès de zèle, un fou sérieux, un vrai saint dans le goût de Thomas de Cantorbéry,"[44] suggests that Beaumont's sincerity and integrity at least were not in doubt and that Rousseau's complimentary references to his character were not altogether unmerited. Whether he would have proceeded against *Emile* in any case even if the Parlement had not acted may be open to question. Voltaire evidently thought it was that body which had shown the Archbishop the way. Certainly, after the Parlement had condemned *Emile*, Beaumont, according to the beliefs of the times, could hardly have failed to condemn it also without appearing derelict in his duty. The action of the Parlement must then have been decisive.

[42] Moland, XXI, 11-12, n. 1.
[43] Cf. *Candide*, édition critique, by André Morize. Paris, 1913, 1931, p. 148, n. 1.
[44] Moland, I, 56.

Rousseau (p. 9; H. III, 61)

Petits & grands, tout s'en mêle; le dernier Cuistre vient trancher du capable; il n'y a pas un sot en petit collet, pas un chétif habitué de Paroisse qui, bravant à plaisir celui contre qui sont réunis leur Sénat & leur Evêque, ne veuille avoir la gloire de lui porter le dernier coup de pied. —

Tout cela, Monseigneur, forme un con<u>cours dont je suis le seul exemple:</u>

Voltaire
—
ne vois tu pas que tu te décrédites, quand tu dis que tout le monde est apres toy?

Voltaire's comment is obviously motivated by his hostility and has little merit even as a criticism of Rousseau's tactics in stressing such universal opposition. Certainly Rousseau was neither the first, nor likely to be the last, who, as Voltaire in his calmer moments well knew, might still be right though all the world came against him. The underlining of the phrase bringing out the supposed uniqueness of Rousseau's situation is understandable enough and more defensible. It was one of the latter's weaknesses to dwell too much upon his so-called individuality of life and misfortune and character. Perhaps, however, what we are inclined to call a weakness was really his strength. At any rate it was a distinguishing mark which he passed on to his successors, the Romantics. As the embodiment of the "man of nature" in contrast to the typical man of society in the eighteenth century, Rousseau was not wrong in feeling that he was different from most of his contemporaries. Nor was he wrong from the standpoint of his genius and his influence, however it may have affected his happiness, in emphasizing what set him apart from, rather than what made him like, his fellows. It would be too much, though, to expect Voltaire to know what only subsequent history has shown.

Rousseau (p. 10; H. III, 62)

Dix lignes seulement, & je couvre mes persécuteurs d'un ridicule ineffaçable. Que le public ne peut-il savoir deux anecdotes sans que je les dise! Que ne connoît-il ceux qui ont médité ma ruine, & ce qu'ils ont fait pour l'exécuter! Par quels méprisables insectes, par quels ténébreux moyens

Voltaire
quelle pitié! esce parce que tu n'as pas ecrit contre les jésuites que tu as

il verroit s'émouvoir les Puissances! quels
levains il verroit s'échauffer par leur pour-
riture & mettre le Parlement en fermenta-
tion! Par quelle risible cause il verroit les
Etats de l'Europe se liguer contre le fils
d'un horloger!

été condam
né a
geneve!

Rousseau suggests in a passage to be given presently that the
Archbishop became unconsciously the instrument of the Jansenists
in the warfare against the Jesuits and that his attack upon *Emile* was
one of the results of this larger struggle. Voltaire regards this explanation as preposterous. If, however, the condemnation of *Emile* at
Geneva was, as seems well-nigh certain from what has been given
above,[45] at least partly inspired by France, Voltaire's argument as
expressed in his marginal comment falls to the ground and leaves
the question open.

Rousseau at the beginning of the next paragraph referred to his
pen as "hardie à dire la vérité, mais *pure de toute* satire."[46] The last
phrase has been partly underlined, no doubt in irony at Rousseau's
disclaimer.

ROUSSEAU (pp. 10-11; H. III, 62)

VOLTAIRE

Une chose étonnante de cette espèce, &
que je puis dire, est de voir l'intrépide
Christophe de Beaumont, qui ne sait plier
sous aucune puissance ni faire aucune paix
avec les Jansénistes, devenir sans le savoir
leur satellite & l'instrument de leur ani-
mosité.

tu ments impudamment

Voltaire's contemptuous protest appears to be directed against
Rousseau's praise of the Archbishop's supposed courage and independence. Jean-Jacques throughout expressed admiration for Beaumont's character and said this fact was one of the chief reasons why
he thought it worth while to reply to his condemnation of *Emile*.[47]
As to the linking of the latter with the Jansenists, the Abbé Quesnel
commented from Paris that it was no less diverting "de voir ce
prélat devenu janséniste sans s'en douter."[48] Le Nieps wrote to

[45] Cf. above, p. 139.
[46] P. 10; H. III, 62.
[47] *Confessions*, Hachette, IX, 45.
[48] Rousseau, *Corr.*, IX, 255.

Rousseau on May 24: "On dit que le Prélat n'est fâché que de ce que vous avez dit que c'étoit les Jansénistes qui lui avoient fait rendre le mandement."[49] As a matter of fact, Rousseau had merely said that his adversary had played into Jansenist hands "sans le savoir," criticizing his judgment rather than his integrity, a charge, however, likely to be hardly less displeasing.

Rousseau (p. 11; H. III, 62)	Voltaire
Daignez, Monseigneur, jetter les yeux sur le sixième Tome de la nouvelle *Héloïse*, première édition; vous trouverez, dans la note de la page 138, la véritable source de tous mes malheurs.	tu crois donc quon a lu ton heloïse!

The popularity of Rousseau's *Nouvelle Héloïse*, destined to rival through the rest of the century that of *Candide*,[50] is evidently a very sore point with Voltaire, the hidden author of the malicious *Lettres sur la Nouvelle Héloïse* (1761) to which the Marquis de Ximenez, for reasons of his own, found it expedient to sign his name.[51] Voltaire's comment here is laughable in its petulance.

Rousseau (p. 12; H. III, 62)	Voltaire
Mon discours sur l'inégalité a couru votre Diocèse, & vous n'avez point donné de Mandement. Ma lettre à M. d'Alembert a couru *votre* Diocèse, & vous n'avez point donné de Mandement.	le diocese nen a rien su.

After insisting that all his previous books have expressed the same principles, Rousseau asks why the Archbishop did not protest and defend his flock from them before the appearance of *Emile*. Voltaire continues to deny Rousseau's popularity. By implication, however, he inadvertently suggests that, if the Archbishop acted against *Emile*, it must have been because the latter at any rate was likely to be widely read and hence dangerous.

Rousseau (p. 12; H. III, 63)   Voltaire
Pourquoi donc n'avez-vous rien dit alors?
Monseigneur, votre troupeau vous étoit-il

---

[49] *Ibid.*, 307.
[50] Cf. Daniel Mornet, *La pensée française au XVIIIe siècle* (Paris, 1929), p. 215, and, by the same author, "Les Imitations du 'Candide' de Voltaire," *Mélanges Lanson* (Paris, 1922), p. 299.
[51] Moland, XXIV, 165-66.

| moins cher? Me lisoit-il moins? Goûtoit- il moins mes Livres? | on na point tant gouté tes livres. |

Voltaire's viewpoint and taste are so fundamentally at variance with those of Rousseau that a sharp clash is inevitable. Instinctively Voltaire realized that Rousseau's vogue threatened his own. Hence his violent irritation at the latter's insistence upon the very real appeal of his works to large numbers of people.

Next Rousseau again charges that he was involved, as Lord Keith had suggested,[52] in the proscription of the Jesuits and that the tocsin was rung against him in protest at his alleged atheism and preaching of anarchy.

ROUSSEAU (p. 13; H. III, 63)	VOLTAIRE
Dans cette rage universelle, vous eûtes honte de garder le silence: vous aimâtes mieux faire un acte de cruauté que d'être accusé de manquer de zèle.	voila une plaisante cruauté de faire un mauvais mandement contre un mauvais roman.

In the midst of his prosperity and independence at Ferney, Voltaire took very lightly the campaign against Rousseau, but it was quite otherwise when he himself appeared in any way threatened. Perhaps his return homeless from the court of Frederick in 1753 presents the nearest parallel to Rousseau's situation at this time, a most imperfect parallel because of the sharp contrast between Voltaire's wealth and Rousseau's poverty, yet Voltaire's plaints in that situation were no less constant and on the whole were less dignified than Rousseau's. A little further on the latter explained clearly his attitude: "Je ne me plains donc pas que vous ayez donné un mandement contre mon livre, mais je me plains que vous l'ayez donné contre ma personne avec aussi peu d'honnêteté que de vérité."[53] At the end of the same paragraph, Rousseau once more expressed the admiration he had always felt for the personal character of the Archbishop.

ROUSSEAU (p. 14; H. III, 63)	VOLTAIRE
Et que vous avois-je donc fait, moi qui parlai toujours de vous avec tant d'estime; moi qui tant de fois admirai votre inébranlable fermeté.	il semble que l'archeveque ait été lami de jean jaques.

[52] See above, p. 137.
[53] Hachette, III, 63.

VOLTAIRE ON ROUSSEAU

Here, with sardonic humor, Voltaire's comment hits off rather well what seems excessive in Rousseau's expressions of admiration and respect for his adversary, entirely sincere as they probably were. In his *Confessions*, written much later, Jean-Jacques continued to speak in similar terms: "Un autre écrit m'affecta davantage, parce qu'il venoit d'un homme pour qui j'eus toujours de l'estime, et dont j'admirois la constance en plaignant son aveuglement. Je parle du mandement de l'archevêque de Paris contre moi."[54] Thus the passage in the *Letter to M. de Beaumont* and the passage in the *Confessions* entirely agree. Certainly they are both quite different in tone from the way in which Voltaire was accustomed to speak of his own enemies.

Having at length in these first pages of his Letter finished with preliminaries, Rousseau is now ready to explain in detail his position and endeavor to refute the Archbishop's strictures against his book and against his person.

ROUSSEAU (p. 15; H. III, 64)	VOLTAIRE
Mais quand on ne marche que la preuve à la main, quand on est forcé, par l'importance du sujet & par la qualité de l'adversaire à prendre une marche pésante & à suivre pied-à-pied toutes ses censures, pour chaque mot il faut des pages; & tandis qu'une courte satire amuse, une longue défense ennuie.	sophismes

Perhaps Voltaire was piqued because he himself was so accustomed to use the "courte satire" in preference to the "longue défense," certainly, as Rousseau said, likely to be less effective with the general public which prefers amusement to reasons. To thoughtful readers, however, Rousseau's carefully argued reply was but the more convincing.

In an important paragraph immediately following, Rousseau now emphasizes his idea of natural goodness as opposed to natural perversity and says that the former is the fundamental principle of all his works. He claims also to have shown how, in spite of this natural goodness, evil took its rise in the human heart.

[54] *Ibid.*, IX, 45.

ROUSSEAU (p. 16; H. III, 64)	VOLTAIRE
J'ai montré que tous les vices qu'on impute au cœur humain ne lui sont point naturels: j'ai dit la manière dont ils naissent.	tu n'as point fait voir cela.

Voltaire has put his finger on a weak place in Rousseau's explanation of the rise of evil in human character,[55] but the two men are not so completely divergent on this point as has often been thought. "L'homme n'est point né méchant; il le devient, comme il devient malade."[56] Who is the author of this remark? Rousseau? No; Voltaire in his *Dictionnaire philosophique*. While the viewpoint is more sporadic and less fundamental in the latter than the former, we may, however, perhaps conclude that Voltaire's comment attacks rather the manner of Rousseau's exposition than his actual position on this point.

Briefly Rousseau recapitulates his theory of the development of humanity and the three different phases of that development. In the first state man is an individual merely; in the second—and happiest —he begins to develop social relations and a code of morality; in the third, ambition and the clash of self-interest stifle the voice of conscience, and man's ruin is complete.

ROUSSEAU (pp. 17-18; H. III, 65)	VOLTAIRE
Quand enfin tous les intérêts particuliers agités s'entrechoquent, quand l'amour de soi mis en fermentation devient amour-propre, que l'opinion, rendant l'univers entier nécessaire à chaque homme, les rend tous ennemis nés les uns des autres, & fait que nul ne trouve son bien que dans le mal	et les hurons et les canadiens ne s'égorgent ils pas ne se mangent ils pas?

[55] That is to say: in the then embryonic state of the social sciences, Rousseau's explanation is incomplete and cursory, taking no account of evolution in the modern sense. His phraseology, taken apart from its context, is easily misleading. Nevertheless, rightly understood his explanation is suggestive in the highest degree and shows that the most fruitful method of improving human character in the mass is to improve human environment. Cf. M. Lanson's keen analysis in his *Histoire de la littérature française*, 12th ed., Paris, 1912, pp. 780-86, 791-98. See also the excellent, compact study of Rousseau's ideas by Ernest H. Wright, *The Meaning of Rousseau*, Oxford Press, London, 1929. Cf. my series of articles in RHL (1924-25) on "La bonté naturelle chez Rousseau." See also a refutation by Miss Jeannette Tresnon in PMLA (Dec., 1928), pp. 1010-25, and my reply, *ibid.* (Dec., 1929), pp. 1239-45.

[56] Moland, XX, 54. Cf. my study of the "Nature Doctrine of Voltaire," PMLA (Dec., 1925), pp. 852-62.

d'autrui; alors la conscience, plus foible que
les passions exaltées, est étouffée par elles.

Just as in his letter of 1755 replying to Rousseau's *Discours sur l'inégalité* Voltaire had ironically suggested that "les exemples de nos nations ont rendu les sauvages presque aussi méchants que nous,"[57] so now in more serious vein he opposes to Jean-Jacques' admiration for primitivism a more realistic picture of actual conditions.

But M. de Beaumont will have none of Rousseau's theories nor of his plan of education.

ROUSSEAU (p. 18; H. III, 65)
Là-dessus vous dites que mon plan d'éducation, "loin de s'accorder avec le Christianisme, n'est pas même propre à faire des Citoyens ni des hommes."

VOLTAIRE

sans doute. ton livre ne peut faire qu'un menuisier.

Thus Voltaire returns to his favorite charge against Rousseau's plan of education that it is adapted only to make a "garçon menuisier."[58]

The rest of Rousseau's sentence, however, is more to Voltaire's taste.

ROUSSEAU (p. 19; H. III, 65)
Et votre unique preuve est de m'opposer le péché originel.

VOLTAIRE

bon cela

For the first time in the case of the *Lettre à Beaumont*, Voltaire records approval. He joins Rousseau in opposition to the idea of Original Sin. A reaction against "le péché originel" and "la perversité naturelle" is the fundamental *raison d'être* of the opposite theory of "la bonté naturelle," which holds out for man a more hopeful future, independent of the doctrine of divine election and the arbitrary action of divine grace. Thus on this idea, so characteristic of the eighteenth century, Voltaire and Rousseau come together. In the *Dictionnaire philosophique* Voltaire later wrote: "On nous crie que la nature humaine est essentiellement perverse, que l'homme est né enfant du diable et méchant. Rien n'est plus malavisé . . . . Il serait bien plus raisonnable, bien plus beau de dire aux hommes: Vous êtes tous nés bons; voyez combien il serait affreux

[57] Moland, XXXVIII, 447. Cf. above, p. 12.
[58] See above, p. 81, n. 37.

de corrompre la pureté de votre être."⁵⁹ Certainly there are important divergences between the two men, but it is striking how near together they are here on the theory which is most closely associated with Rousseau and in connection with which he is too often made to stand in a unique position. The eighteenth century must have had urgent need of this theory that both Voltaire and Rousseau should have espoused it.

Rousseau continues his attack upon the doctrine of Original Sin.

Rousseau (p. 19; H. III, 65)	Voltaire
D'abord il s'en faut bien, selon moi, que cette doctrine du péché originel, sujette à des difficultés si terribles, ne soit contenue dans l'Ecriture ni si clairement ni si durement qu'il a plu au rhéteur Augustin & à nos Théologiens de la bâtir.	hardy et bon

The boldness of Jean-Jacques in attacking this fundamental doctrine of orthodoxy commands Voltaire's admiration as well as his approval. His marginal note reveals also that, prejudiced and unfair as his comments often are, he can nevertheless on occasion forget his general hostility when he does fully agree with Rousseau. This fact greatly increases the value of Voltaire's notes as generally dependable indications of his real opinions.

Rousseau (p. 19; H. III, 65-66)	Voltaire
Et le moyen de concevoir que Dieu crée tant d'âmes innocentes & pures, tout exprès pour les joindre à des corps coupables.	corps coupables bonne absurdité des téologiens.

Voltaire is again one with Rousseau in rejecting this outworn principle of theological metaphysics.

Rousseau (p. 19; H. III, 66)	Voltaire
Mais au fond que fait cette doctrine à l'Auteur d'*Emile?* Quoiqu'il ait cru son livre utile au <u>genre humain,</u> c'est à des Chrétiens qu'il l'a destiné.	ah mon ami! au genre humain a l'univers que tu es modeste.

The words *genre humain* have been underlined. Rousseau, if gifted with a sense of humor, might have made his expression more

⁵⁹ Moland, XX, 53-54. Cf. XIX, 381. For a more extended discussion, see my article, "The Nature Doctrine of Voltaire," PMLA. (Dec., 1925), pp. 858-62, where some of the characteristic differences between Voltaire and Rousseau on this question also come out.

tactful and more modest. As it is, however, he offers a ready mark for Voltaire's ironical comment.

Endeavoring now to meet M. de Beaumont on his own ground, Rousseau says that his book is intended primarily for Christians whose souls have been purified from Original Sin through the sacrament of baptism and restored to their primitive innocence.[60]

Rousseau (p. 20; H. III, 66)	Voltaire
Nous avons, direz-vous, contracté de nouvelles souillures: mais puisque nous avons commencé par en être délivrés, comment les avons-nous derechef contractées? Le sang du Christ n'est-il donc pas encore assez fort pour effacer entièrement la tache? ou bien seroit-elle un effet de la corruption de notre chair; comme si, même indépendamment du péché originel, Dieu nous eût créés corrompus, tout exprès pour avoir le plaisir de nous punir?	amerveilles. le peché originel traitté comme il faut.

Once launched into his argument, Rousseau is no mean antagonist. Voltaire had had occasion to feel his power in the famous *Lettre sur la Providence* written in refutation of *Le Poème sur le Désastre de Lisbonne* in 1756 and for one reason or another had shown no desire to reply in the forms of reasoned debate. Now, however, he is upon the side lines. He is fully in accord with this part of Rousseau's argument. He recognizes its cleverness and vigor and registers his enthusiastic applause.

Rousseau (p. 21; H. III, 66)	Voltaire
Je conçois que cette difficulté pressée pourroit devenir embarrassante: car que répondre à ceux qui me feroient voir que, relativement au genre humain, l'effet de la rédemption, faite à si haut prix, se réduit à peu près à rien?	bon
Le péché originel explique tout, excepté son principe, & c'est ce principe qu'il s'agit d'expliquer. (p. 22; H. III, 67)	bon

Voltaire obviously admires the mastery and the boldness with

[60] There is obviously a relationship between the Church doctrine of primitive innocence before the Fall and the eighteenth-century theory of primitive innocence before the degeneration caused by society.

which Rousseau presses home these arguments making the doctrine of Original Sin in its orthodox form untenable.

In a footnote Rousseau now turns to discuss the injustice of the severe punishment meted out to Adam for a very slight fault.

Rousseau (p. 23, n. 4; H. III, 67, n. 2)

Il y a de plus, un motif si naturel d'indulgence & de commisération dans la ruse du tentateur & dans la séduction de la femme, qu'à considérer dans toutes les circonstances le péché d'Adam, l'on n'y peut trouver qu'une faute des plus légères. Cependant, selon eux, quelle effroyable punition! Il est même impossible d'en concevoir une plus terrible; car quel châtiment eût pu porter Adam, pour les plus grands crimes, que d'être condamné, lui & toute sa race, à la mort en ce monde, & à passer l'éternité dans l'autre dévorés des feux de l'enfer? Est-ce là la peine imposée par le Dieu de miséricorde à un pauvre malheureux pour s'être laissé tromper? Que je hais la décourageante doctrine de nos durs Théologiens! si j'étois un moment tenté de l'admettre, c'est alors que je croirois blasphémer.

Voltaire

explication ridicule d'une histoire ridicule.

Rousseau and Voltaire are probably here substantially in agreement, for the former's story of the development of the human race from the state of nature would not accord with the narrative in Genesis. Jean-Jacques appears to accept the orthodox position merely for purposes of discussion and to show it to be inacceptable. The historian Voltaire, writing for himself alone in the privacy of his library, rejects the truth of the whole story of Adam. In the *Dictionnaire philosophique* he wrote: "Beaucoup de rabbins ont regardé la formation d'Adam et d'Eve, et leur aventure, comme une allégorie. Toutes les anciennes nations célèbres en ont imaginé de pareilles; et, par un concours singulier qui marque la faiblesse de notre nature, toutes ont voulu expliquer l'origine du mal moral et du mal physique par des idées à peu près semblables."[61] Both Rousseau and Voltaire evidently agreed in rejecting the theological implica-

[61] Moland, XVII, 58-59.

tions of Adam's supposed fall and condemnation. It is significant that Voltaire is here reading carefully enough to take cognizance of this long footnote in Rousseau's text.[62]

Rousseau returns now to his characteristic theory of how man became depraved. He says to the Archbishop: "Vous dites qu'il est méchant parce qu'il a été méchant; et moi je montre comment il a été méchant."[63]

ROUSSEAU (p. 27; H. III, 69)	VOLTAIRE
Je ne dis point qu'il ne faut pas réprimer le vice; mais je dis qu'il vaut mieux l'empêcher de naître. Je veux pourvoir à l'insuffisance des Loix, & vous m'alléguez l'insuffisance des Loix. Vous m'accusez d'établir les abus, parce qu'au lieu d'y remédier j'aime mieux qu'on les prévienne. Quoi! s'il étoit un moyen de vivre toujours en santé, faudroit-il donc le proscrire, de peur de rendre les médecins oisifs?	eh quel est ton moyen? oh le fou!

Rousseau is seeking, however stumblingly and embarrassed by the unscientific language of his time, a means of dealing constructively with the grave problem of human misconduct and crime. What he sees is that laws and punishments are not enough. They but lock the door when the stolen horse has gone. Only a more favorable environment, the elimination of all artificial inequality, the removal of motives for destructive rivalry and selfish ambition, can prevent the development of vice, which is better than merely repressing it. Impatient, however, of Rousseau's seemingly theoretical position and insistent upon practicalities, Voltaire breaks forth in demand for a concrete program calculated to bring about this ideal of complete social reform.

ROUSSEAU (p. 27; H. III, 69)	VOLTAIRE
J'ai prouvé que cette éducation, que vous appelez la plus saine, étoit la plus insensée.	tu n'as rien prouvé.

Rousseau has indeed given examples in *Emile* to illustrate some of the shortcomings of the too conventional, too abstract, and too entirely intellectual education of his day. His own position, however,

---
[62] Between pp. 24-25 is a marker with "Note marginale" written on it. Since no note is there, it is evidently misplaced.
[63] Hachette, III, 67-68.

LETTRE À BEAUMONT

is extreme in the opposite direction and Voltaire, a conservative in education, does not accept it.

ROUSSEAU (p. 28; H. III, 69)   VOLTAIRE
La jeunesse ne s'égare jamais d'elle-même; toutes ses erreurs lui viennent d'être mal conduite.   faux tres faux

This fundamental theory of Rousseau that environment is the decisive factor in influencing conduct is characteristic. It ignores the claims of heredity, itself a sort of predestination under another name. Rousseau's statement is extreme and categorical. Voltaire is no less categorical in denying it.

ROUSSEAU (pp. 28-29; H. III, 70)   VOLTAIRE
Je conviens qu'il est superflu de chercher de nouveaux plans d'Education, quand on est si content de celle qui existe; mais convenez aussi, Monseigneur, qu'en ceci vous n'êtes pas difficile. Si vous eussiez été aussi coulant en matière de doctrine, votre Diocèse eût été agité de moins de troubles; l'orage que vous avez excité, ne fût point retombé sur les jésuites; je n'en aurois point été écrasé par compagnie; vous fussiez   toy par compagnie?
resté plus tranquille, & moi aussi.

It has been already evident that Voltaire questions the theory of Rousseau, supported by the opinion of Lord Keith and by that of D'Alembert, to the effect that his condemnation was involved in the downfall of the Jesuits.[64]

ROUSSEAU (p. 30; H. III, 70)   VOLTAIRE
Je puis ajouter une observation qui devroit frapper tous les bons François, & vous-même comme tel; c'est que de tant de Rois   excellente idée
qu'a eus votre Nation, le meilleur est le seul que n'ont point élevé les Prêtres.

Once more Voltaire finds something to praise. He naturally welcomes this reference to Henri IV and seems to suggest by his note that this excellent line of attack upon the influence of the Church had not previously occurred to him. His words give the impression of complimenting Rousseau on his ingenuity.

[64] Cf. above, p. 137.

ROUSSEAU (p. 31; H. III, 71)

J'appelle éducation positive celle qui tend à former l'esprit avant l'âge & à donner à l'enfant la connoissance des devoirs de l'homme. J'appelle éducation négative celle qui tend à perfectionner les organes, instrumens de nos connoissances, avant de nous donner ces connoissances, & qui prépare à la raison par l'exercice des sens.

VOLTAIRE
positif négatif ridicule.

Voltaire's opinion of Rousseau's educational program, often too artificial and theoretical, is expressed with succinct force. That this program has elements of value, however, escapes the philosopher of Ferney.

Rousseau now discusses M. de Beaumont's objection that Rousseau's negative education will leave the child at ten without knowledge of the difference between good and evil, unable to understand that obedience to his father is good, disobedience bad. Rousseau maintains, however, that such confusion is exactly what will happen according to ordinary systems of education by which the child is instructed in arbitrary fashion without developing his judgment.

ROUSSEAU (p. 32; H. III, 71)

Bien loin de là, je soutiens qu'il sentira, au contraire, en quittant le jeu pour aller étudier sa leçon, qu'obéir à son père est un mal, & que lui désobéir est un bien, en volant quelque fruit défendu.

VOLTAIRE

sophisme

In his desire to get away from arbitrary authority in education and to develop self-determination in the child, Rousseau is led, perhaps by the exigencies of his position as an innovator, to overstate his case. Voltaire ranges himself with M. de Beaumont in favor of traditional opinion.[65]

Rousseau now says that, though he has in his two volumes demonstrated the truth of his position on this point, M. de Beaumont has endeavored to refute him in two lines of dogmatic statement. "Le prétendre," says the Archbishop, "c'est calomnier la nature humaine, en lui attribuant une stupidité qu'elle n'a point." But

[65] Cf. above, p. 80.

Rousseau replies that this is a moral ignorance, though not stupidity, which is constantly found in human nature in its undeveloped state.

ROUSSEAU (p. 33; H. III, 72)	VOLTAIRE
Attribuer cette ignorance à la nature humaine n'est donc pas la calomnier; & c'est vous qui l'avez calomniée en lui imputant une malignité qu'elle n'a point.	non avouons que l'homme est né avec des passions qui ont besoin de frein.

In clear-cut fashion and with no mingling of personalities, Voltaire takes his stand against Rousseau and in favor of discipline as an important element in education. Jean-Jacques would not have denied the necessity of discipline, but would have maintained that his system obtained it in other than the traditional ways. His position represents a reaction, however, against the arbitrary use of authority, a reaction more needed in eighteenth-century France than among us today. As a reaction, it represents a shift of emphasis in the direction of freedom, which has often resembled license and has been so interpreted by too many of Rousseau's successors. Nevertheless, the author of *Emile* does explain himself clearly on this point. Speaking of children, he says (and this has not been often quoted): "Accordez-leur, tant qu'il est possible, tout ce qui peut leur faire un plaisir réel; refusez-leur toujours ce qu'ils ne demandent que par fantaisie ou pour faire un acte d'autorité."[66]

Rousseau recognizes moreover the value in education of acquiring the habit of effort in the face of obstacles. "Parmi tant d'admirables méthodes pour abréger l'étude des sciences, nous aurions grand besoin que quelqu'un nous en donnât une pour les apprendre avec effort."[67] Thus Rousseau himself is often much more conservative than has been sometimes thought. Where he is, however, open to criticism is in saying thus in a few sentences scattered through his book the old that he still believes true, while expressing in many pages the new that is suggestive, stimulating, though often excessive. But it was the new that needed to be emphasized. Had Rousseau with balanced judgment set the pro against the con, he might have pleased modern scholars, but he would hardly have influenced his own or succeeding generations. Such is one of the grave shortcomings of average humanity. Its teachers must shout in order to win listeners.

[66] Hachette, II, 56, n.
[67] *Ibid.*, 147.

VOLTAIRE ON ROUSSEAU

Rousseau (p. 34; H. III, 72)   Voltaire
Vous dites: "Pour trouver la jeunesse plus docile aux leçons qu'il lui prépare, cet Auteur veut qu'elle soit dénuée de tout principe de Religion." La raison en est simple, c'est que je veux qu'elle ait une   sophisme
Religion, & que je ne lui veux rien apprendre dont son jugement ne soit en état de sentir la vérité.

Voltaire opposes Rousseau here, not of course because of the latter's opposition to orthodox religion, but probably because he thinks him insincere, or at least ill-advised, in urging another religion in its place. Jean-Jacques, however, defers his whole program of intellectual education, and with it of religion, in the formal sense at least, nearly to adult life. The reason he does this is simply because such had been the course of his own self-education. Since he was a man of genius, such a program in his case had been, in spite of grave shortcomings, astonishingly successful, though it could hardly be of general application. In the passage above, Rousseau is taking his stand against mere lip-service in religion and in favor of a simple, but vital belief, accepted not from habit, but from choice, and thoroughly linked with life and conduct.

Rousseau now insists, in opposition to M. de Beaumont, that it is impossible for a child to form other than anthropomorphic conceptions of God.

Rousseau (p. 35; H. III, 73)   Voltaire
J'en appelle de plus à l'expérience; j'exhorte chacun des lecteurs à consulter sa mémoire, & à se rappeler si, lorsqu'il a cru   tu as raison icy.
en Dieu étant enfant, il ne s'en est pas toujours fait quelque image.

As usual, Voltaire agrees with Rousseau in whatever constitutes an attack upon religious orthodoxy. The "icy" is interesting as an implication of Voltaire's feeling that his adversary is right but rarely.

Rousseau (p. 36; H. III, 73)   Voltaire
Une des commodités du Christianisme moderne[x] est de s'être fait un certain jargon   [x] et ancien
de mots sans idées, avec lesquels on satisfait à tout, hors à la raison.

LETTRE À BEAUMONT

A cross mark in the text and opposite Voltaire's note indicates the bearing of his comment. Thus he links early Christianity with later as equally coming under Rousseau's charge of consisting of words without ideas. For himself, he will have none of either.

ROUSSEAU (p. 37; H. III, 73)   VOLTAIRE
Ce passage que vous avez cru être dans la Profession de foi n'y est point, mais dans le corps même du Livre. Monseigneur, vous lisez bien légèrement.

monseign^r a tort.

Voltaire's agreement with Rousseau here is half ironical. He attaches little importance to the detail.

ROUSSEAU (p. 40; H. III, 75)   VOLTAIRE
Je dis qu'il faut avoir acquis quelque philosophie pour s'élever aux notions du vrai Dieu.

icy tu argumentes bien

As a deist and a member of the so-called philosophic party, Voltaire quite naturally welcomes Rousseau's insistence that only a person with a tincture of philosophy can form a conception of what God really is. The "icy" again appears to remind us of Voltaire's seeming surprise to find himself occasionally in accord with Jean-Jacques. At the same time it suggests his honesty in acknowledging this agreement.

ROUSSEAU (p. 41; H. III, 75)   VOLTAIRE
L'homme qui, privé du secours de ses semblables & sans cesse occupé de pourvoir à ses besoins, est réduit en toute chose à la seule marche de ses propres idées, fait un progrès bien lent de ce côté-là [du côté de la raison]; il vieillit & meurt avant d'être sorti de l'enfance de la raison. Pouvez-vous croire de bonne foi que d'un million d'hommes élevés de cette manière, il y en eût un seul qui vînt à penser à Dieu?

pourquoy donc as tu voulu les elever en brutes?

For one who has followed the course of these two minds, placed in juxtaposition with the same subject-matter, but only rarely in agreement, it is diverting to see how Rousseau appears here to have worked himself into something of a contradiction, which Voltaire is quick to seize upon.

156 VOLTAIRE ON ROUSSEAU

ROUSSEAU (p. 43; H. III, 76)

Aussi tel homme stupide & grossier, quoique simple & vrai, tel esprit sans erreur & sans vice, peut, par une ignorance involontaire, ne pas remonter à l'Auteur de son être, & ne pas concevoir ce que c'est que Dieu, sans que cette ignorance le rende punissable d'un défaut auquel son cœur n'a point consenti.

VOLTAIRE

oui, mais il ny a point de ces gens la parmi nous.

Voltaire considers this an entirely theoretical position so far as the France of his day is concerned, and hence of no value as argument.[68]

ROUSSEAU (pp. 45-46; H. III, 77)
(Quoted from *Emile*, H. II, 247)

Mais ce même monde est-il éternel, ou créé? Y a-t-il un principe unique des choses? Y en a-t-il deux ou plusieurs? et quelle est leur nature? Je n'en sais rien, et que m'importe? ... Je renonce à des questions oiseuses qui peuvent inquiéter mon amour-propre, mais qui sont inutiles à ma conduite & supérieures à ma raison.

VOLTAIRE

mais notre ami, l'unité de dieu n'est pas une question si oiseuse?

The word "oiseuses" has been underlined. In his *Lettres de Memmius à Cicéron* of 1771,[69] as in his play *Socrate* of 1759,[70] Voltaire took his stand in favor of the unity of God, thus indicating the importance he attached to the conception. It is surprising to find Rousseau more agnostic than Voltaire on this point. Perhaps the reason lies in a sort of mental inertia on the part of Rousseau in the face of metaphysical questions, though both he and Voltaire would have agreed on putting good conduct first as of primary importance and of more certainty.

ROUSSEAU (p. 46; H. III, 77)

On sait, j'en conviens, qu'il y a peu de Prêtres qui croyent en Dieu.ˣ

VOLTAIRE

ˣ trop fort.

Cross marks indicate the exact bearing of the comment. It is rather surprising to find Voltaire here on the side of moderation

---

[68] Between pp. 44-45 is a marker with the initials "N. M." (Note marginale), probably in Wagnière's hand. The marker has evidently been misplaced, for no note is to be found on these pages.
[69] Moland, XXVIII, 442-43.
[70] *Ibid.*, V, 388-89.

and defending the sincerity of belief of the priesthood. He probably felt that Rousseau was weakening his effect by exaggeration.

The Archbishop had attacked Rousseau's reference above in *Emile* to the unity of God as "une question oiseuse" and had quoted Tertullian to the effect that "la pluralité des dieux ... est une nullité de Dieu." Rousseau replied:

Rousseau (p. 47; H. III, 78)	Voltaire
Mais qui est-ce qui a dit qu'il y a plusieurs Dieux? Ah! Monseigneur, vous voudriez bien que j'eusse dit de pareilles folies, vous n'auriez sûrement pas pris la peine de faire un Mandement contre moi.	et pourquoy ny aurait il pas plusieurs dieux chacun dans son monde chacun eternel et puissant de sa nature?

Rousseau appears to be trying to squirm out of the unfortunate word "oiseuse" which he perhaps too thoughtlessly had let fall in *Emile*. On Voltaire's side, his comment, contrasting with that dealing with the unity of God on the preceding page of Rousseau's text, seems to suggest that he enjoys playing with both sides of the question and opposing Jean-Jacques as often as possible.

Rousseau has a footnote to the passage immediately preceding the one last cited.

Rousseau (p. 47, n; H. III, 78, n. 2)	Voltaire
Tertullien fait ici un sophisme très-familier aux pères de l'Eglise: il définit le mot *Dieu* selon les Chrétiens, & puis il accuse les payens de contradiction, parce que contre sa définition ils admettent plusieurs Dieux. Ce n'étoit pas la peine de m'imputer une erreur que je n'ai pas commise, uniquement pour citer si hors de propos un sophisme de Tertullien.	tertulien a tort et toy aussi. car ces pretendus payens admettaient un dieu supreme. les autres dieux etaient nos saints.

Voltaire's note is interesting, both for its attitude toward paganism as believing in a supreme God and its comparison of subordinate gods with Catholic saints. It shows too that he is reading carefully enough here to pay attention to footnotes. In fact, his comments follow thick and fast, hardly missing a page.

Rousseau states that there are two ways of conceiving of the origin of the universe. Either matter existed from all eternity or else it was created by a superior power. Both of these concepts offer philosophical difficulties and neither is comprehensible to human reason. The philosophers of all times, however, have with unanimity rejected the possibility of creation, except perhaps a small minority whose sincerity cannot be determined for the reason that free speaking on this question would have been dangerous to them.

Rousseau (pp. 48-49; H. III, 78-79)	Voltaire
Tant d'hommes & de philosophes, qui dans tous les tems ont médité sur ce sujet, ont tous unanimement rejetté la possibilité de la création, excepté peut-être un très-petit nombre qui paroissent avoir sincèrement soumis leur raison à l'autorité; sincérité que les motifs de leur intérêt, de leur sûreté, de leur repos, rendent fort suspecte, & dont il sera toujours impossible de s'assurer tant que l'on risquera quelque chose à parler vrai.	icy tu me parais avoir raison.

Again we find Voltaire and Rousseau in accord. As long as freedom of speech on religious questions does not exist, sincerity of belief, if the opinion expressed is in harmony with orthodoxy, cannot be determined. In the case of his "civic dogmas" at the end of the *Contrat social*, Rousseau had not been true to this principle and Voltaire had rightly taken sharp issue with him, as we have already seen.[71]

Rousseau (p. 49; H. III, 79)	Voltaire
Or l'idée de création, l'idée sous laquelle on conçoit que par un simple acte de volonté rien devient quelque chose, est, de toutes les idées qui ne sont pas clairement contradictoires, la moins compréhensible à l'esprit humain.	je suis de ton avis

Once more Voltaire and Rousseau are in agreement. Again it is an attack upon orthodoxy that brings them together.

Rousseau (p. 50; H. III, 79)	Voltaire
J'avoue bien que la création du monde étant clairement énoncée dans nos traductions de la *Genèse*, la rejetter positivement seroit à cet égard rejetter l'autorité.	point du tout

[71] Cf. above, p. 68.

LETTRE À BEAUMONT

Having hedged somewhat in regard to creation and allowed the Vicar to suspend judgment on the question, Rousseau again lays himself open to Voltaire's contradiction. The latter has underlined "clairement" to indicate the bearing of his comment. In the rest of the paragraph, however, Rousseau discusses the uncertainty of the exact meaning of the Hebrew word for "create" and essentially comes to the same position as Voltaire.

ROUSSEAU (p. 52; H. III, 80)
Quoiqu'il en soit, . . . sans soutenir les sentimens du Vicaire, je n'ai rien à faire ici qu'à montrer vos torts.

VOLTAIRE
larcheveque a tort comme etre pensant non comme pretre.

Voltaire obviously holds that for a priest straight thinking is impossible. He must support without question the cause in which he is enrolled.

Rousseau now criticizes M. de Beaumont again for taking him to task on the question of the unity of God which, he says, is supported by argument in *Emile*.

ROUSSEAU (p. 53; H. III, 80)
Vous avez tort de me qualifier pour cela d'Auteur téméraire, puisqu'où il n'y a point d'assertion, il n'y a point de témérité.[x]

VOLTAIRE
il y a des questions sur lesquelles le doute peut paraitre temeraire.

The great sceptic Voltaire realizes that to the orthodox doubt itself without positive denial may appear an unwarranted boldness. Perhaps his serious attitude on this point is the result of his conviction of the importance of belief in God, the same belief which he urged against D'Holbach's atheism. No doubt also his readiness to contradict Rousseau enters into the background of his comment.

Rousseau now proceeds to quote from the *Vicaire savoyard* in order to show that, while he believes firmly in God, he feels it completely impossible to reach positive conclusions regarding his nature.

ROUSSEAU (p. 55; H. III, 81)
Enfin plus je m'efforce de contempler son essence infinie, moins je la conçois; mais elle est, cela me suffit; moins je la conçois, plus je l'adore. Je m'humilie & lui dis: "Etre des êtres, je suis parce que tu es; c'est m'élever à ma source que de te méditer sans cesse. Le plus digne usage de

VOLTAIRE

ma raison est de s'anéantir devant toi: c'est
mon ravissement d'esprit, c'est le charme de
ma foiblesse de me sentir accablé de ta — très beau.
grandeur.

Whether Voltaire is ironic or serious here is hard to say. Certain parts of his works, such as the "Prière à Dieu" at the end of the *Traité sur la tolérance*,[72] the article *Dieu* of the *Dictionnaire philosophique*,[73] and others, are not altogether dissimilar in contrasting God's immensity with man's littleness, yet it is difficult to tell to what extent they are written for effect rather than as the expressions of a profound conviction. There is at any rate a possibility that Voltaire's comment here expresses enthusiastic approval.

Rousseau now says he is not an enemy of religion. He has merely proposed some of the difficulties in the way of religious belief on certain points. All human knowledge is open to various objections, even geometry.

ROUSSEAU (p. 56; H. III, 82)
Comme si toute connoissance humaine
n'avoit pas les siennes [ses difficultés];
comme si la Géométrie elle-même n'en
avoit pas, ou que les Géomètres se fissent
une loi de les taire pour ne pas nuire à
la certitude de leur art! — science

Voltaire drew a vertical line through the word *art* and amended it in the margin to *science*, thus putting geometry on a higher plane of certainty and exactness than Rousseau had done.

Rousseau now repeatedly and positively insists upon his religious faith.

ROUSSEAU (p. 56; H. III, 82)   VOLTAIRE
Je dirai ma religion, parce que j'en ai
une; & je la dirai hautement, parce que
j'ai le courage de la dire, & qu'il seroit à
désirer pour le bien des hommes que ce
fût celle du genre humain.

Monseigneur, je suis Chrétien, & sin-   comme il ment!
cèrement Chrétien, selon la doctrine de
l'Evangile.

[72] Moland, XXV, 107-08.
[73] *Ibid.*, XVIII, 376 ff.

LETTRE À BEAUMONT

Voltaire is entirely unable to see how Rousseau, rejecting so many of the beliefs of the Church, can sincerely claim to be a Christian nevertheless. Yet with Rousseau this claim is no pose as Voltaire thinks. As we have seen before,[74] Rousseau's position is of the essence of Protestant self-determination and independence of belief. In building a new and simplified creed of his own, he feels that he is simply reëstablishing true Christianity, the Christianity of Christ as distinguished from institutional and theological Christianity with which it has been confused. The same sharp divergence between the two men appears in the following passages.

ROUSSEAU (p. 57; H. III, 82)	VOLTAIRE
Il [Jésus-Christ] m'a dit par lui-même & par ses Apôtres que celui qui aime son frère a accompli La loi.	ainsi dit toute relligion.

Both Voltaire and Rousseau would equally insist upon the necessity of good conduct. The former, however, stresses the fact that the teachings of Jesus are to be found also in other religions and hence that Christianity is not uniquely important. Rousseau would probably have admitted the first part of the above statement, but would have continued to feel that the synthesis made by Christ, and especially the tone and spirit of his teaching, made a distinct contribution to what had gone before, and entitled Christianity therefore, stripped of its institutional and human excrescences, to the highest place.

ROUSSEAU (p. 58; H. III, 83)	VOLTAIRE
Pénétré de reconnoissance pour le digne Pasteur [M. de Montmollin] qui, résistant au torrent de l'exemple & jugeant dans la vérité, n'a point exclus de l'Eglise un défenseur de la cause de Dieu, je conserverai toute ma vie un tendre souvenir de sa charité vraiment Chrétienne.	tu es donc venu dans un desert flatter un predicant.

In his *Confessions* Rousseau narrates how he wrote to the pastor at Motiers-Travers, M. de Montmollin, declaring that he remained "toujours uni de cœur à l'Eglise protestante," that he would like to assist at the sacrament of the Lord's supper, but that he wanted

---

[74] Cf. above, p. 121.

no "explication particulière sur le dogme."[75] Expecting a refusal to receive him on such terms, Rousseau, to his surprise, was visited by the pastor and cordially invited to join in this worship with his congregation. Hence the friendliness and appreciation expressed by Rousseau in the above passage. As in previous instances, Voltaire can understand nothing of this spirit.

ROUSSEAU (pp. 58-59; H. III, 83)
Que si ma véracité les offense, & qu'ils [d'injustes prêtres] veuillent me retrancher de l'Eglise, je craindrai peu cette menace dont l'exécution n'est pas en leur pouvoir. Ils ne m'empêcheront pas d'être uni de cœur avec les <u>fidelles</u>.

VOLTAIRE

quels fideles?

Aussi longtems que je serai ce que je suis & que je penserai comme je pense, je parlerai comme je parle. Bien différent, je l'avoue, de vos <u>Chrétiens en effigie</u>, toujours prêts à croire ce qu'il faut croire ou à dire ce qu'il faut dire. (p. 59; H. III, 83)

Voltaire underlined without comment the words "Chrétiens en effigie," perhaps relishing the expressive phrase.

ROUSSEAU (pp. 59-60; H. III, 83)
Moi je pense, au contraire, que l'essentiel de la Religion consiste en pratique; que non-seulement il faut être homme de bien, miséricordieux, humain, charitable; mais que quiconque est vraiment tel en croit assez pour être sauvé.

VOLTAIRE

c'est etre juste et non cretien.

Again this important difference between Voltaire and Rousseau appears.

ROUSSEAU (p. 61; H. III, 84)
J'ai eu des amis sûrs & d'autres qui l'étoient moins; j'ai été environné d'espions, de malveillans, & le monde est plein de gens qui me haïssent à cause du mal qu'ils m'ont fait. Je les adjure tous, quels qu'ils puissent être, de déclarer au public ce qu'ils savent de ma croyance en matière de Religion.

VOLTAIRE

crois tu donc que diderot dalembert grimm iront te déceler?

[75] Hachette, IX, 44.

This passage expresses Rousseau's suspicion of a plot to persecute and defame him, a suspicion which saddened his later years. After the break with Diderot, D'Alembert, and Grimm, there is no question that they looked upon him without friendliness. It was this which gave color to his mad fears. Moreover, Jean-Jacques did undergo a very definite persecution from the governments of France, Geneva, and elsewhere. Voltaire himself was perhaps not without a hand in some of these hostile moves. Certainly he wrote against Rousseau in a style which was actually violent and not excused even by the bluntness of Rousseau's letter of rupture of June 17, 1760. Voltaire too was a bundle of irritable nerves. The whole question is complicated by too many ramifications for complete discussion here. At the basis of Rousseau's troubles was the fundamental difference of viewpoint between him on the one side, and his former friends of the philosophic party, along with the established powers of government, on the other. Not that the two latter groups were in accord, but for different reasons they were now bound to be aligned against Rousseau. His illness, his sensitive nature, and his brooding, aggravated by solitude and isolation, did the rest. Voltaire's comment, however, is doubtless correct in suggesting the element of exaggeration which, along with a certain basis of fact, accompanied Rousseau's fears.

Rousseau (p. 62; H. III, 84)	Voltaire
Je n'ai pas le bonheur de voir dans la révélation l'évidence qu'ils y trouvent; & si je me détermine pour elle, c'est parce que mon cœur m'y porte, qu'elle n'a rien que de consolant pour moi, & qu'à la rejetter les difficultés ne sont pas moindres; mais ce n'est pas parce que je la vois démontrée, car très-sûrement elle ne l'est pas à mes yeux. Je ne suis pas même assez instruit à beaucoup près pour qu'une démonstration qui demande un si profond savoir soit jamais à ma portée.	tu ne crois pas la révélation, et tu te dis cretien.

The same irreconcilable difference between the two men again crops up. Primarily it is a difference in definition of Christianity. Rousseau considers it as an unrealized ideal, expressed historically in Christ no doubt, but now to be reinterpreted by Jean-Jacques and accepted for himself. Voltaire identifies Christianity with its all too imperfect representative, the Church, and would have it frankly abandoned for simple justice and uprightness. Hence his inability to understand how Rousseau can admit his scepticism about revelation and yet still maintain himself to be a Christian.

Is it not strange, asks Rousseau, that he who frankly proposes his doubts is labeled a hypocrite, while those who with no better proofs nor better knowledge proclaim themselves firm believers are considered to speak in good faith?

ROUSSEAU (p. 63; H. III, 85)

Pourquoi serois-je un hypocrite? & que gagnerois-je à l'être? J'ai attaqué tous les intérêts particuliers, j'ai suscité contre moi tous les partis, je n'ai soutenu que la cause de Dieu & de l'humanité, & qui est-ce qui s'en soucie? Ce que j'en ai dit n'a pas même fait la moindre sensation, & pas une âme ne m'en a su gré.

VOLTAIRE

tu parles trop de toy, tu crois que l'univers est occupé de J. Jaques.

After being accused by M. de Beaumont of an "insigne mauvaise foi,"[76] after being referred to as "cet imposteur,"[77] and otherwise described in most unfavorable terms, it is not strange that the sensitive personality of Jean-Jacques Rousseau should defend his honesty of purpose and of character. Voltaire has indeed put his finger on a side of Rousseau that is open to criticism. His argument might be more effective, at least with readers of a judicial temperament, if more objective. With the public in general, however, it might perhaps have been less so. In any case Rousseau had definite provocation here, and to demand that he should not reply to such attacks upon his person would have been to demand the impossible in the case of a man of his temperament. Many another, less sensitive than himself, would have felt as he did.

ROUSSEAU (pp. 64-65; H. III, 85)

Monseigneur, si je suis un hypocrite, je suis un fou, puisque, pour ce que je demande aux hommes, c'est une grande folie de se mettre en frais de fausseté; si je suis

VOLTAIRE

tout cela me parait misérable

[76] Hachette, III, 54.
[77] Ibid.

un hypocrite, je suis un sot; car il faut
l'être beaucoup pour ne pas voir que le
chemin que j'ai pris ne mène qu'à des malheurs dans cette vie, & que quand j'y pour-
rois trouver quelque avantage, je n'en puis
profiter sans me démentir.

Mes ennemis auront beau faire avec leurs
injures; ils ne m'ôteront point l'honneur
d'être un homme véridique en toute chose,
d'être le seul Auteur de mon siècle & de
beaucoup d'autres qui ait écrit de bonne foi,
& qui n'ait dit que ce qu'il a cru. (p. 65;
H. III, 86)

quelle fatuité

Ils [les ennemis de Rousseau] pourront
un moment souiller ma réputation à force
de rumeurs & de calomnies: mais elle en
triomphera tôt ou tard; car, tandis qu'ils
varieront dans leurs imputations ridicules,
je resterai toujours le même, &, sans autre
art que ma franchise, j'ai de quoi les dé-
soler toujours. (pp. 65-66; H. III, 86)

quelle sottise!

It is true that Voltaire's censure of Rousseau's exaggerated self-complacency is in a measure just. Yet it is also true that to a considerable degree the latter did contrast with most of his contemporaries in saying what he thought and signing his name to it regardless of danger. Voltaire's conduct, as has been previously observed, proceeded from the quite different theory of expediency. Perhaps he was somewhat piqued by the element of truth in Rousseau's statement and of implied condemnation for his own practice. Perhaps it was only Rousseau's blunt self-assurance and complete lack of finesse and tact which shocked him. In any case Voltaire failed utterly to understand the value Rousseau put upon personal integrity in expressing his frank opinion upon dangerous subjects.

ROUSSEAU (p. 67; H. III, 86)

VOLTAIRE

Sitôt que je fus en état d'observer les
hommes, je les regardois faire, & je les écou-
tois parler; puis, voyant que leurs actions
ne ressembloient point à leurs discours, je
cherchai la raison de cette dissemblance, &
je trouvai qu'être & paroître étant pour eux
deux choses aussi différentes qu'agir &

pauvre homme crois tu
avoir inventé cela?

parler, cette deuxième différence étoit la cause de l'autre, & avoit elle-même une cause qui me restoit à chercher.

Rousseau's remark on human insincerity is indeed a commonplace of literature, but the important point is the keen impression made upon him by this sharp contrast between human speech and action. Instead of accepting cynically this characteristic of mankind, he continued to revolt against it and to seek its cause. For himself, he strove increasingly through his later years to put his own conduct in harmony with his words.

Rousseau (p. 67; H. III, 86)	Voltaire
Je la trouvai [la cause de l'insincérité des hommes] dans notre ordre social, qui, de tout point contraire à la nature que rien ne détruit, la tyrannise sans cesse, & lui fait sans cesse réclamer ses droits. Je suivis cette contradiction dans ses conséquences, & je vis qu'elle expliquoit seule tous les vices des hommes & tous les maux de la société. D'où je conclus qu'il n'étoit pas nécessaire de supposer l'homme méchant par sa nature, lorsqu'on pouvoit marquer l'origine & le progrès de sa méchanceté.	pitoiable l'amour propre rend l'homme méchant

In his Notes to the *Discours sur l'inégalité*, Rousseau had made a distinction between *l'amour de soi-même* and *l'amour-propre*.[78] The former was natural and good, the latter owed its origin only to society and was harmful. "L'amour de soi-même est un sentiment naturel qui porte tout animal à veiller à sa propre conservation, et qui, dirigé dans l'homme par la raison et modifié par la pitié, produit l'humanité et la vertu. L'amour-propre n'est qu'un sentiment relatif, factice, et né dans la société, qui porte chaque individu à faire plus de cas de soi que de tout autre, qui inspire aux hommes tous les maux qu'ils se font mutuellement, et qui est la véritable source de l'honneur."[79] Needless to say, Voltaire would not have recognized this distinction, which seems dogmatic and artificial. Rousseau assumes that social organization is not a *natural* development. Voltaire takes society for granted and considers *l'amour-propre* char-

[78] Hachette, I, 149.
[79] *Ibid.*

acteristic of human nature. He therefore puts the cause of evil upon man's unmastered selfishness, a much more conventional, but also more convincing, explanation than the one imagined by Rousseau. Nevertheless, one interesting question remains. Could not a different organization of society facilitate coöperation, instead of stimulating selfish individualistic rivalry? Might not good conduct be encouraged by society, instead of thwarted by the premium put upon wealth and display? Might not goodness under such circumstances become the rule rather than merely the exceptional achievement of a few noble spirits? It is with these questions that Rousseau, in spite of his confusing language,[80] is really concerned. The answer lies with the historian of the future.

Rousseau (p. 68; H. III, 87)	Voltaire
J'ai cherché la vérité dans les Livres; je n'y ai trouvé que le mensonge & l'erreur. J'ai consulté les Auteurs; je n'ai trouvé que des Charlatans qui se font un jeu de tromper les hommes.	tu penses donc etre le seul? et les anglais?

In this interesting note, Voltaire not only takes Rousseau to task for implying that there was anything unique about his experience in finding books untrustworthy; he also suggests that the English in general are an exception in this respect and scrupulous in their search for truth. Brief as it is, this note emphasizes strikingly Voltaire's admiration for English thought. On January 16, 1760, he had written to George Keith in the latter's own language: "I am confident no body in the world looks with a greater veneration on y^r good philosophers, on the crowd of y^r good authors; and I am these thirty years the disciple of y^r way of thinking."[81] That this was no mere compliment intended for an English friend is shown by his writing to Mme du Deffand the preceding year: "Que j'aime la hardiesse anglaise! que j'aime les gens qui disent ce qu'ils pensent!"[82]

Rousseau (p. 69; H. III, 87)	Voltaire
Les hommes ne doivent point être instruits à demi. S'ils doivent rester dans	

---

[80] Largely imposed upon him by his age and needing retranslation into modern terms.
[81] Moland, XL, 284.
[82] *Ibid.*, 193.

l'erreur, que ne les laissiez-vous dans l'igno-   déclamation
rance? A quoi bon tant d'écoles & d'uni-
versités pour ne leur apprendre rien de ce
qui leur importe à savoir?
Si des hommes sans passions instruisoient
des hommes sans préjugés, nos connoissances   bien plus etendues et plus
resteroient <u>plus bornées,</u> mais plus sûres.   sures.
(p. 70; H. III, 88)

After having brushed aside with a favorite criticism, "déclamation," Rousseau's extreme and over-generalized sally against contemporary education, Voltaire underlined the words "plus bornées" and modified in interesting fashion Rousseau's sentence to show that he agreed with his ideal of education given by men without passions and without prejudices, but did not think that the knowledge so gained would be more limited. Quite the contrary, in his opinion: it would not only be sounder, but more extensive as well. In reality, however, the difference here between Rousseau and the admirer of "le sage Locke," between Jean-Jacques and the author of *Le Philosophe ignorant*, is purely verbal. Rousseau means merely that men educated under such circumstances would know less that was not true. Their really sound knowledge would be more extensive just as Voltaire said.

ROUSSEAU (p. 71; H. III, 88)   VOLTAIRE
Ne faisons pas surtout comme votre M.   ce maraut de joli méritait
Joly de Fleuri, qui, pour établir son Jan-   une plus severe reprimande.
sénisme, veut déraciner toute loi naturelle
& toute obligation qui lie entre eux les humains; de sorte que selon lui le Chrétien &
l'Infidèle qui contractent entre eux, ne sont
tenus à rien du tout l'un envers l'autre,
puisqu'il n'y a point de loi commune à
tous les deux.

Omer Joly de Fleury was an enemy of the *philosophes*, the author, as Advocate General, of proceedings against the *Encyclopédie*, against Helvétius' *De l'Esprit*, Rousseau's *Emile*, and other radical works. He was often the butt of Voltaire's caustic wit and it is not strange that the latter was dissatisfied with Rousseau's mild reprimand. Nevertheless, in his letter to D'Argental previously cited, Voltaire wrote with glee: "J'oubliais de vous dire que Jean-Jacques, dans son épître, prouve à Omer qu'il est un sot, en quoi je suis entièrement de son avis."[83] It is amusing to see how vivid and personal Voltaire is even when writing only for himself in the privacy of his library. Words do not come colorless from his pen. He writes with *blacker ink* than his contemporaries, as M. Jusserand said.[84] Voltaire's instinctive contempt comes hot from his pen in the scornful reference to "ce maraut de joli."

Rousseau now argues that the most humane and sociable religion should be the best, provided it is true that man is made to live in society. The glory of God must lie in the welfare of man.

ROUSSEAU (p. 72; H. III, 89)	VOLTAIRE
Mais ce sentiment, tout probable qu'il est, est sujet à de grandes difficultés, par l'historique & les faits qui le contrarient. Les Juifs étoient les ennemis nés de tous les autres Peuples, & ils commencèrent leur établissement par détruire sept nations, selon l'ordre exprès qu'ils en avoient reçu: Tous les Chrétiens ont eu des guerres de Religion, & la guerre est nuisible aux hommes.	tu rends les juifs et les cretiens abominables ose donc netre pas cretien.
Tous les partis ont tourmenté leurs frères, tous ont offert à Dieu des sacrifices de sang humain. Quelle que soit la source de ces contradictions, elles existent; est-ce un crime de vouloir les ôter? (p. 74; H. III, 89)	et tu peux avoir la bonté de te dire cretien?

Truly M. de Beaumont had run afoul of a rude antagonist. Rousseau is incisive and vigorous in his indictment. Voltaire of course agrees with him here, as he had previously, in the negative side of his attack. The marginal comments indicate, however, as before, that Voltaire wants Rousseau to break definitely with the traditions of the past and abandon the very name of Christian as too inescapably allied with the abuses mentioned. Jean-Jacques on the other hand regards these abuses as not inherent and not representative of the true spirit of Christianity which he seeks to restore.

Rousseau now says that charity and love for one's neighbor do not produce murder. The cause of persecutions does not lie in

[83] Moland, XLII, 460.
[84] J. J. Jusserand, *Shakespeare en France sous l'ancien régime,* Paris, 1898, pp. 145, 169.

zeal for the salvation of men, but rather in *amour-propre* and pride. The less reasonable a cult is, the more one is inclined to seek to establish it by force. To the partisans of such a cult, reason becomes the greatest of crimes.

ROUSSEAU (p. 74; H. III, 89-90)   VOLTAIRE
Ainsi l'intolérance & l'inconséquence ont
la même source. Il faut sans cesse intimider,   excellent
effrayer les hommes. Si vous les livrez un
moment à leur raison, vous êtes perdus.

Thus Voltaire, in the midst of many passages to which he objected, suddenly came upon this condemnation of intolerance and praised it without reserve. The execution of Jean Calas and Voltaire's *Traité sur la tolérance*, published in November of this same year 1763, must at that time have been much in his mind and made Rousseau's words particularly welcome.

ROUSSEAU (p. 75; H. III, 90)   VOLTAIRE
Celui qui aime la paix ne doit point recourir à des livres, c'est le moyen de ne
rien finir. Les livres sont des sources de disputes intarissables; parcourez l'histoire des
Peuples: ceux qui n'ont point de livres[x] ne   [x] ouy mais ils sont soumis
disputent point.   au grand lama

An X mark indicates the bearing of Voltaire's note. Thus quickly in his comment does he dispose of Rousseau's characteristic hostility to books and seeming praise for ignorance. Voltaire sees in ignorance only the certainty of servitude. What Rousseau appears really to be saying, however, in his often inaccurate and excessive phraseology, is that man should argue only from the facts of life and disregard the claims to authority of theologians. The next passage expresses this thought more clearly.

ROUSSEAU (p. 75; H. III, 90)   VOLTAIRE
N'argumentez point sur des argumens &
ne vous fondez point sur des discours. Le
langage humain n'est pas assez clair. Dieu
lui-même, s'il daignoit nous parler dans nos   hardy
langues, ne nous diroit rien sur quoi l'on
ne pût disputer.

Rousseau perceives that even the idea of revelation presupposes the use of human language for communicating to men the divine thoughts and thus leaves room for all kinds of arguments and disputes. Voltaire, with a keen sense of what is novel and bold in the realm of ideas, appreciates at once Rousseau's insight and courage.

Rousseau (p. 75; H. III, 90)	Voltaire
Supposons qu'un particulier vienne à minuit nous crier qu'il est jour; on se moquera de lui: mais laissez à ce particulier le tems & les moyens de se faire une secte, tôt ou tard ses partisans viendront à bout de nous prouver qu'il disoit vrai.	répété de fontanelle.

In his *Confessions* Rousseau tells us that Fontenelle's *Pluralité des mondes* and his *Dialogues des morts* came early into his hands.[85] Years later in Paris Rousseau bore a letter of introduction to him from the Abbé de Mably[86] and took pleasure in visiting him.[87] So there would be nothing strange if Jean-Jacques had repeated here from Fontenelle this phrase recognized by Voltaire. I have not, however, been able to locate it.

Rousseau (p. 76; H. III, 90)	Voltaire
La plupart des cultes nouveaux s'établissent par le fanatisme, & se maintiennent par l'hypocrisie.ˣ	et par la sottise
Assurément il y a loin de l'esprit du <u>Deutéronome</u> à l'esprit du *Talmud* & de la *Misnah*, & de l'esprit de l'Evangile aux querelles sur la Constitution! (p. 79; H. III, 92)	pas si loin

Thus Voltaire shows his hostility toward religious cults in general and toward Christianity in particular. In the *Bible enfin expliquée* of 1776,[88] Voltaire sufficiently indicates his contempt for Deuteronomy. Likewise in commenting upon the Gospels Voltaire says in the same work: "Tout l'Ancien Testament se conforme à l'ignorance et à la grossièreté du peuple pour lequel il fut fait. . . . L'auteur sacré suit en tout les préjugés vulgaires; il ne prétend point enseigner la philosophie. Il en est de même de Jésus."[89] Voltaire excels in

---

[85] Hachette, VIII, 4.
[86] *Ibid.*, 197.
[87] *Ibid.*, 197, 202. Cf. also 206; II, 317; XII, 302-03.
[88] Moland, XXX, 114-20.
[89] *Ibid.*, 309-10.

destructive criticism; Rousseau tends to emphasize respect and admiration for Christ and his teachings, while to some extent passing over or pushing aside rationalistic problems raised by the sacred books.

ROUSSEAU (pp. 79-80; H. III, 92)
Ils [les théologiens] nous font sentir avec leur modestie ordinaire que les Auteurs Sacrés avoient grand besoin de leur secours pour se faire entendre, & que le Saint-Esprit n'eût pas su s'expliquer clairement sans eux.

VOLTAIRE
ils font comme toy, ils trouvent le st. esprit fort inintelligible

Voltaire's comment speaks for itself. Rousseau now says that, when orthodoxy takes precedence over good conduct, religion becomes useless to society.

ROUSSEAU (p. 80; H. III, 92)
Quand la religion en est là, quel bien fait-elle à la société? de quel avantage est-elle aux hommes? Elle ne sert qu'à exciter entre eux des dissensions, des troubles, des guerres de toute espèce; à les faire s'entre-égorger pour des Logogryphes: Il vaudroit mieux alors n'avoir point de Religion que d'en avoir une si mal entendue.

VOLTAIRE

très vrai.

So again Voltaire indicates his agreement with Rousseau, but, as usual, it is on the negative side of the latter's position, when he says that it would be better to have no religion at all than to have one which puts doctrine before uprightness.

ROUSSEAU (pp. 80-81; H. III, 92)
Supposons que, las des querelles qui le déchirent [le genre humain], il s'assemble pour les terminer & convenir d'une Religion commune à tous les Peuples: Chacun commencera, cela est sûr, par proposer la sienne comme la seule vraye, la seule raisonnable & démontrée, la seule agréable à Dieu & utile aux hommes.

VOLTAIRE

fort bon

Once more the two are in agreement. Rousseau now says that, after the assembly has for some time argued futilely, some one will hit upon the sensible idea of excluding all the theologians. Then in the search for a common basis of understanding they will perceive that utility to man, and not pleasure to God, must be the test determining which is the best religion, for this is the only test of which men can judge. It is to be assumed also that God himself takes pleasure in that which is most useful to his creatures.

ROUSSEAU (p. 82; H. III, 93)
Cherchons d'abord s'il y a quelque affinité naturelle entre nous, si nous sommes quelque chose les uns aux autres.

VOLTAIRE
cela est tiré de Zadig.

The rest of this passage in Rousseau continues in dialogue form between Jews, Christians, and Turks in order to show that all agree as to man's common origin and his worship of what is essentially the same God. It is true, as Voltaire indicates, that Chapter XII of *Zadig*[90] offered Rousseau a model of a similar dialogue used for an exactly similar purpose. It is quite possible, therefore, that Rousseau had it more or less consciously in mind while writing his *Lettre à M. de Beaumont*, but there is no similarity in wording nor in characters to indicate imitation of anything but the general idea and the use of the dialogue form, both of which were so much in the spirit of the eighteenth century that they might have been arrived at by Rousseau independently of Voltaire.

ROUSSEAU (p. 83; H. III, 93)
En procédant ainsi d'interrogations en interrogations, sur la Providence divine, sur l'économie de la vie-à-venir, & sur toutes les questions essentielles au bon ordre du genre humain, ces mêmes hommes ayant obtenu de tous des réponses presque uniformes, leur diront: (On se souviendra que les Théologiens n'y sont plus.) "Mes amis, de quoi vous tourmentez-vous? Vous voilà tous d'accord sur ce qui vous importe; quand vous différerez de sentiment sur le reste, j'y vois peu d'inconvénient. Formez de ce petit nombre d'articles une Religion universelle, qui soit, pour ainsi dire, la Religion humaine & sociale que tout homme vivant en société soit obligé d'admettre.

VOLTAIRE

tu adheres formellement a la pure et sainte relligion du deisme et tu feins d'etre cretien!

[90] *Ibid.*, XXI, 61-64. Cf. the critical edition by G. Ascoli, Paris, 1929, I, 55-59. This Chapter XII is one of the chapters added in 1748. See Moland, XXI, p. ix.

Rousseau, as has been said previously,[91] does not *feign* to be a Christian; he considers rather that he is giving the essentials of Christianity and omitting the unessential or the harmful. He is reinterpreting, not abandoning. It is interesting to note Voltaire's reference to deism as "la pure et sainte religion." This statement in the privacy of his own notes indicates his great esteem for this simplified deistic religion in which little of the dogma and creed of the Church remains. At the end of Rousseau's passage is his pronouncement in favor of a minimum code of religious articles which must be accepted by all members of organized society. This is the position which, as we have seen,[92] he had already taken in the *Contrat social*. There Voltaire had censured it severely as an unwarranted censorship upon belief. Here, perhaps because it is less emphasized and less completely developed, he passes over it without notice.

Rousseau now argues that respect should be accorded to the founders of all religions. Their attribution to themselves of divine inspiration cannot be judged true or false by majority vote, "les preuves n'étant pas également à sa portée."

Rousseau (p. 84; H. III, 94)	Voltaire
Mais quand cela ne seroit pas, il ne faut point les traiter si <u>légèrement d'imposteurs.</u>	oh ils sont ou fourbes ou fanatiques. tu oublies ton sisteme.

In making this comment, Voltaire doubtless had in mind a passage which he had annotated a few pages back. Rousseau had said: "La plupart des cultes nouveaux s'établissent par le fanatisme, & se maintiennent par l'hypocrisie."[93] Voltaire takes special pleasure in finding Jean-Jacques guilty of such a contradiction and in throwing it back at him.

Rousseau (p. 85; H. III, 94)	Voltaire
Socrate a cru avoir un esprit familier, & l'on n'a point osé l'accuser pour cela d'être un fourbe.	sil la cru il extravaguait. Sil nelapas cru il trompait.

Voltaire's comment gives an interesting illustration of the clear-cut definiteness with which his mind worked. This very clarity, how-

[91] Cf. above, pp. 121, 161.
[92] Cf. above, p. 68.
[93] Cf. above, p. 171.

ever, prevented him from entering easily into the spirit of men of more primitive times, and particularly into that of religious mystics, to whom no questions presented themselves in such a coolly analytical manner. Rousseau, with his occasional contradictions which represent often emphasis upon different aspects of the truth, with his frequent lack of strict clarity and close reasoning, with his warm enthusiasms, comes nearer to understanding how the founder of a religious sect really felt. He was himself, in spite of his strong mingling of eighteenth-century rationalism, very much of a religious leader. Voltaire's keen intellectual analysis is eminently fitted to give a rationalistic evaluation of almost any question. It is not adapted to understand sympathetically the viewpoint of earlier ages or peoples in whom philosophical reason played little or no part. This is the reason why the principle of relativity, beginning to be potent in eighteenth-century thought, had little influence upon Voltaire, particularly in the field of religion.

ROUSSEAU (p. 85; H. III, 94)	VOLTAIRE
La forme du culte est la police des Religions & non leur essence, & c'est au Souverain qu'il appartient de régler la police dans son pays.	prends garde la police est contre toy.

In this mainly personal remark Voltaire warns Rousseau of the danger to him of conceding entire police authority to the sovereign at the very time when this authority is being used against him. At the same time the remark may easily have a wider application.

ROUSSEAU (p. 86; H. III, 94)	VOLTAIRE
Je crois qu'un homme de bien, dans quelque Religion qu'il vive de bonne foi, peut être sauvé. Mais je ne crois pas pour cela qu'on puisse légitimement introduire en un pays des Religions étrangères sans la permission du Souverain; car si ce n'est pas directement désobéir à Dieu, c'est désobéir aux Loix; & qui désobéit aux Loix, désobéit à Dieu.	tu te prens de tes armes car tu desobeis en ecrivant contre nos superstitions.

This remark of a tendency similar to the one immediately preceding also resembles one made on the *Contrat social:* "tuo te gladio jugulas."[94] Whether motivated by the Biblical principle, "Render

[94] Cf. above, p. 51.

therefore unto Cæsar the things which are Cæsar's,"[95] or led by a certain inner conservatism which balked at complete religious freedom, Rousseau here clearly lays himself open to Voltaire's thrust.

ROUSSEAU (p. 87; H. III, 95)   VOLTAIRE
Je conviens sans détour qu'à sa naissance la Religion réformée n'avoit pas droit de s'établir en France malgré les loix: Mais lorsque, transmise des Pères aux enfans, cette Religion fut devenue celle d'une partie de la Nation Française, & que le Prince eut solennellement traité avec cette partie par l'Edit de Nantes; cet Edit devint un Contrat inviolable, qui ne pouvoit plus être annulé que du commun consentement des deux parties, & depuis ce tems l'exercice de la Religion Protestante est, selon moi, légitime en France.

si elle n'a pas eu ce droit d'abord, elle ne l'a jamais eu

As in the case of the "civic dogmas" imposed at the end of the *Contrat social*, Rousseau here adopts what seems an unsound position in regard to the introduction of new religious beliefs into a country. Voltaire's mind goes straight to the heart of the question. If Protestantism was not entitled at the beginning to existence in France, it could not legally acquire such a right later. Rousseau sees the importance of tradition and the species of contract implied by the Edict of Nantes. Fundamentally, however, his position abandons real freedom of thought and toleration. Voltaire on the other hand is for such freedom without restriction and from the beginning. "Tout dogme est ridicule, funeste," he had written on the margins of the *Contrat social*. "Toutte [*sic*] contrainte sur le dogme est abominable. Ordonner de croire est absurde. Bornez-vous à ordonner de bien vivre."[96]

Rousseau now imagines a speech addressed to the judges by a Parsee condemned to death for marrying a Mohammedan. He charges them with barbarous customs.

ROUSSEAU (p. 92; H. III, 97)   VOLTAIRE
Vous mangez <u>les animaux</u> & vous massacrez les humains.   les mages en mangeaient.

[95] Matthew, XXII, 21.
[96] Cf. above, p. 68.

In 1774 Voltaire quoted Porphyry on abstinence from flesh eating: "C'est en vain que Porphyre propose pour modèles les brachmanes et les mages persans de la première classe, qui avaient en horreur la coutume d'engloutir dans nos entrailles les entrailles des autres créatures; il n'est suivi aujourd'hui que par les Pères de la Trappe."[97] Since the Parsees, though resident in India, were Persian in origin and Zoroastrians in religion, this passage appears to nullify Voltaire's marginal comment against Rousseau, at least as far as the "mages de la première classe" were concerned.

Rousseau continues his defense against the charges of blasphemy, impiety, scandal, and danger to the human race.

Rousseau (p. 94; H. III, 98)	Voltaire
Est-ce apprendre au peuple à ne rien croire que le rappeller à la <u>véritable foi</u> qu'il oublie?	c'est à dire a nulle foy.

Again Voltaire holds that Rousseau's *faith* is not real religious faith. It is, in the opinion of the former, no faith at all.

Rousseau (p. 95; H. III, 98)	Voltaire
Maintenant, hommes cruels, vos décrets, vos bûchers, vos mandemens, vos journaux le troublent [le peuple] & l'abusent sur mon compte. Il me croit un monstre sur la foi de vos clameurs, mais vos clameurs cesseront enfin; mes écrits resteront malgré vous pour votre honte.	voyla une plaisante accolade de buchers et de journaux.

Rousseau's tone throughout his *Lettre à M. de Beaumont*, quite naturally in view of his situation, is serious, even tragic. In fact, humor is a trait most conspicuously lacking in all of his work. Voltaire, at his ease in Ferney, relatively safe from the persecution to which Rousseau was subject, felt the element of the ridiculous in bracketing *bûchers* with *journaux* of which Jean-Jacques was totally unconscious.

At this point Rousseau discusses an objection made in *Emile* to the intervention of men between God and himself. The Archbishop,

[97] Moland, XX, 576. Lévesque de Burigny's translation, *Traité de Porphyre touchant l'abstinence de la chair des animaux*, avec la vie de Plotin par ce philosophe, et une dissertation sur les génies, Paris, 1747, in-8, was in Voltaire's private library and is now preserved at Leningrad. Cf. G. R. Havens and Norman L. Torrey, "Voltaire's Books: A Selected List," *Modern Philology*, XXVII (August, 1929), p. 6.

M. de Beaumont, had said that human testimony is all that permits us to know of any historical event. With this Rousseau agrees, but insists that knowledge of historical events is not necessary for salvation. In the case of what it is needful for man to know, God should speak to him directly.

ROUSSEAU (p. 101; H. III, 101)	VOLTAIRE
Est-il simple, est-il naturel que Dieu ait été chercher Moïse pour parler à Jean-Jacques Rousseau?	et plus bas tu dis que tu es cretien pour avoir lu l'écriture c'est donc moyse et jesu qui ont parlé a jean jacques.

Presumably Voltaire in his comment is referring to the long passage a few pages below[98] quoted from *Emile* and dealing with the "majesté des Ecritures" and "la sainteté de l'Evangile." To this passage Rousseau adds in refutation of M. de Beaumont: " 'Que d'hommes entre Dieu et lui!' Pas un seul. L'Evangile est la pièce qui décide, & cette pièce est entre mes mains. De quelque manière qu'elle y soit venue & quelque auteur qui l'ait écrite, j'y reconnois l'esprit divin, cela est immédiat autant qu'il peut l'être; il n'y a point d'hommes entre cette preuve & moi: & dans le sens où il y en auroit, l'historique de ce saint livre, de ses auteurs, du tems où il a été composé, etc., rentre dans les discussions de critique où la preuve morale est admise."[99] Thus Rousseau has refuted in advance Voltaire's comment. Jean-Jacques accepts the testimony of Moses or Jesus or other characters of the Bible, not because it is the testimony of Moses or Jesus, not on the authority of the Church, not on any authority outside of himself. He accepts the Bible strictly on its moral and ethical appeal to his own conscience. Thus he maintains his complete independence. Moreover, since he regards conscience as divinely inspired,[100] this appeal of the Bible to his own conscience brings God and himself in direct relation without intermediary, just as he had said.

M. de Beaumont had charged Rousseau's incredulity to self-interest. Most effectively he replied:

[98] Hachette, III, 104-106.
[99] *Ibid.*, 106.
[100] *Ibid.*, II, 262 *(Emile)*: "Conscience! conscience! instinct divin, immortelle et céleste voix."

LETTRE À BEAUMONT 179

ROUSSEAU (p. 104; H. III, 102-03) VOLTAIRE
Monseigneur, si jamais elle me procure
un Evêché de cent mille Livres de rente, plaisanterie nest pas raison.
vous pourrez parler de l'intérêt de mon
incrédulité.

Rousseau was entirely justified in turning M. de Beaumont's *ad hominem* argument back against him. His retort is convincing. In any case he has already given plenty of other reasons. Voltaire's criticism here is entirely captious.

Expressing now his enthusiastic admiration and respect for Christ, Rousseau writes as follows:

ROUSSEAU (p. 109; H. III, 105) VOLTAIRE
<u>Quelle élévation</u> dans ses maximes! dans les paraboles de la
moutarde et de l'usure
et du souper.

Voltaire has underlined "élévation" to show the bearing of his comment. In his reference to the parables of the mustard seed,[101] the talents,[102] and the marriage feast with the guests who refused to come,[103] he appears to be scornful of the homeliness of the illustrations used. His classical mind seems unable to recognize merit in these plain, simple stories of everyday life. It may be too that he objects to the treatment in the parables of the servant who refused to increase his talent and the guest without the wedding garment, but their allegorical application and Jesus' idea that such conclusions are among the inevitabilities of moral life are clear enough. In his manner of living, in his whole experience, in his sympathies, Rousseau is far closer to the common people than the aristocratic M. de Voltaire.

ROUSSEAU (p. 111; H. III, 105) VOLTAIRE
Oui, si la vie et la mort de Socrate sont quesce que la mort d'un
d'un sage, la vie & la <u>mort de Jésus</u> sont dieu esce par ce quil sua
d'un Dieu. sang et eau? on ne sait ce
que tu veux, tu ne le scais
pas toy meme.

Evidently this statement of Rousseau particularly irritated Voltaire, for twice before he commented in the same spirit when he

---
[101] Matthew, XIII, 31-32; Mark, IV, 30-32; Luke, XIII, 18-19.
[102] Matthew, XXV, 14-30; Luke, XIX, 11-27.
[103] Matthew, XXII, 1-13; Luke, XIV, 16-24.

ran upon it in his two copies of *Emile*. In the Leningrad copy he wrote opposite this passage: "Quelle extravagante absurdité! As-tu vu mourir des dieux, pauvre fou!"[104] In the *Emile* now at Geneva he commented in the same sentence used at the beginning of the marginal note just cited from the *Lettre à M. de Beaumont*: "Qu'est-ce que la mort d'un Dieu!"[105] Nevertheless, in spite of his hostility to Rousseau's attribution of divinity to Christ on such rhetorical grounds, Voltaire evidently found the comparison with Socrates useful, for he employed it three times within the next five or six years: first, in the *Traité sur la tolérance* composed during this very same year 1763, where the reference to the bloody sweat[106] almost certainly indicates influence of his own marginal comment, as well as of the Bible; second, in the *Homélie sur l'interprétation du Nouveau Testament* of 1767;[107] and finally, in the *Profession de foi des théistes* of 1768.[108] In each case, however, there is this important difference between Voltaire and Rousseau, that while the latter stresses the superiority of Christ, the former emphasizes the similarity between him and Socrates. Thus the total effect in Voltaire is entirely different from that of Rousseau. However, Masson has pointed out that Rousseau's own expressions in regard to the death of Christ varied significantly between the first and the final version of the *Vicaire savoyard*. In the first draft he had written in a most Voltairean spirit: "Laissez-moi de grâce aller voir ce merveilleux pays, où les vierges accouchent, où les dieux naissent comme des hommes, mangent, souffrent et meurent."[109] The explanation of the seeming contradiction on the part of Rousseau lies, as Masson has also indicated,[110] in the fact that the application of the epithet "divine" to Christ is to be taken simply in the sense of the highest moral supremacy, and is not to be endowed with the supernatural connotations against which Voltaire protests. In fact, then, the two contemporaries appear to be in essential accord in their rationalistic attitude. The difference lies in Rousseau's spirit of reverence and respect

[104] Cf. above, p. 118.
[105] Cf. above, *ibid.*
[106] Moland, XXV, 87.
[107] *Ibid.*, XXVI, 353.
[108] *Ibid.*, XXVII, 69.
[109] Pierre-Maurice Masson, *op. cit.*, 411, n. 2, 413, 384-85, n. 1 (not p. 172, as indicated).
[110] *Ibid*, 413, n.

toward the character and teaching of Christ, a spirit which, however, Voltaire himself shares on occasion.[111] Voltaire's marginal criticism remained fresh in his mind and was repeated in a letter to the Abbé d'Olivet in 1767: "Un charlatan est parvenu jusqu'à dire, dans je ne sais quelles lettres, en parlant de l'angoisse et de la passion de Jésus-Christ, que si Socrate mourut en sage, *Jésus-Christ mourut en Dieu:* comme s'il y avait des dieux accoutumés à la mort; comme si on savait comment ils meurent; comme si une sueur de sang était le caractère de la mort de Dieu; enfin comme si c'était Dieu qui fût mort."[112]

Voltaire now passes over the next ten pages without comment, until he notes with characteristic approval Rousseau's attack upon transubstantiation.

Rousseau (p. 121; H. III, 110)	Voltaire
Vous conviendrez bien, je pense, qu'une de ces vérités éternelles qui servent d'élémens à la raison est que la partie est moindre que le tout, & c'est pour avoir affirmé le contraire que l'Inspiré vous paroît tenir un discours plein d'ineptie. Or selon votre doctrine de la transsubstantiation, lorsque Jésus fit la dernière Cène avec ses disciples & qu'ayant rompu le pain il donna son corps à chacun d'eux, il est clair qu'il tint son corps entier dans sa main, et, s'il mangea lui-même du pain consacré, comme il put le faire, il mit sa tête dans sa bouche.	on a trouvé cette plaisanterie mauvaise, elle me parait fort bonne.

Evidently Voltaire liked this pleasantry against one of his pet abominations, the doctrine of transubstantiation, better than the one quoted a few pages back against the "cent mille livres de rente" of the Archbishop,[113] and in his comment defended it against contemporary criticism. In a letter to Helvétius as early as May 1, 1763, Voltaire remarked apropos of this passage: "Jean-Jacques dit, à mon gré, une chose bien plaisante, quoique géométrique, dans sa *Lettre à Christophe*, pour prouver que, dans notre secte, la partie est plus grande que le tout. Il suppose que notre sauveur Jésus-Christ communie avec ses apôtres: En ce cas, dit-il, il est clair que Jésus mit

---
[111] Moland, XX, 342-48.
[112] *Ibid.*, XLV, 13. Cited by Masson, p. 411, n. 2.
[113] Cf. above, pp. 178-79.

sa tête dans sa bouche. Il y a par-ci par-là de bons traits dans ce Jean-Jacques."[114]

Voltaire now passes over the next six pages without stopping. At this point Rousseau says that the Bible is so infused with love of virtue and hatred of vice that it would deserve admiration and respect even if it were not to be regarded as true.

Rousseau (p. 127; H. III, 113)	Voltaire
Eh! quand il n'y auroit pas un mot de vérité dans cet ouvrage, on en devroit honorer & chérir les rêveries, comme les chimères les plus douces qui puissent flatter & nourrir le cœur d'un homme de bien.	une [?]

This note I have been unable to read, but it is clear that Voltaire would be unlikely to approve of Rousseau's thought in this passage.[115]

Rousseau (p. 127; H. III, 113)	Voltaire
Oui, je ne crains point de le dire; s'il existoit en Europe un seul gouvernement vraiment éclairé, un gouvernement dont les vues fussent vraiment utiles & saines, il eût rendu des honneurs publics à l'Auteur d'*Emile*, il lui eût élevé des statues. Je connoissois trop les hommes pour attendre d'eux de la reconnoissance; je ne les connoissois pas assez, je l'avoue, pour en attendre ce qu'ils ont fait.	rien de plus modeste.

Voltaire's comment resembles his "que tu es modeste!" in the early part of the *Lettre à M. de Beaumont*.[116] In his letter to D'Argental of April 25, Voltaire wrote of Rousseau: "Il persiste toujours à dire qu'il fallait lui élever des statues au lieu de le brûler,"[117] thus showing that he had already perused this latter part of Jean-Jacques' reply. While Rousseau was never distinguished for modesty and obviously lacked tact, there was doubtless back of this passage the sincere feeling that his object in *Emile* had been to benefit the cause of real religion and of humanity in general. Hence his resentment at being attacked for questions of doctrine which he

[114] Moland, XLII, 463-64.
[115] This note and the one immediately preceding are in blacker, unfaded ink as compared with the others, but this is probably an accident without consequence.
[116] Cf. above, p. 147.
[117] Moland, XLII, 460. Cf. above, p. 132.

regarded as of no importance and of no real bearing upon conduct. Voltaire, however, again found Rousseau's self-eulogy extremely vulnerable.

The latter now quotes from M. de Beaumont's *Mandement* and makes a parenthetical comment which Voltaire also attacks.

ROUSSEAU (p. 129; H. III, 114)	VOLTAIRE
Du sein de l'erreur ... il s'est élevé (pas fort haut) un homme plein du langage de la philosophie.	tu crois modestement que cela veut dire élévation cela ne veut dire que hardiesse. insurrexit

It seems hardly likely that Rousseau was, as Voltaire thought, the dupe of M. de Beaumont's phrasing, but rather that he merely took advantage of the form of expression for his parenthetical pleasantry.

In a brief running criticism M. de Beaumont had referred to Rousseau's previous works, among them, the *Nouvelle Héloïse*. Jean-Jacques continues his parenthetical comments.

ROUSSEAU (pp. 130-31; H. III, 114)	VOLTAIRE
Dans une autre production plus récente il avoit insinué le poison de la volupté. (Eh! que ne puis-je aux horreurs de la débauche substituer le charme de la volupté! Mais rassurez-vous, Monseigneur; vos Prêtres sont à l'épreuve de l'*Héloïse*; ils ont pour préservatif l'*Aloïsia*.)	injure grossiere et injuste.

This is the last of Voltaire's comments. Six paragraphs later the *Lettre à Beaumont* comes to an end. We have seen that in his letter to D'Argental of April 25, 1763, which has been cited above,[118] Voltaire had already commented upon this reference to Chorier's licentious novel: "Il [Rousseau] assure que si on trouve quelques traits voluptueux dans son *Héloïse*, il y en a davantage dans l'*Aloïsia*, que tous les prêtres ont à Paris dans leurs bibliothèques."[119] This would seem pretty definitely to date this marginal comment and probably most of the others[120] as contemporary with Voltaire's first reading of

[118] Cf. above, p. 132.
[119] Moland, XLII, 460.
[120] Note the previous comments on transubstantiation and on Rousseau's thinking he deserved statues in his honor, both of which were reflected in letters of late April and early May. Cf. above, pp. 132, 181-82.

the *Lettre à Beaumont* at the end of March or early in April, 1763.[121] According to Rousseau's friend, Moultou, this attack upon the uprightness of the priesthood was condemned even by Protestant friends of Rousseau at Geneva. "Un seul trait leur déplaît [à M. Jallabert et à M. Mussard], et s'il était possible de faire un carton, je crois que vous feriez bien de suivre leur avis, c'est l'endroit où vous dites que *les prêtres ont pour préservatif l'Aloïsia*. Cela est un peu trop fort, ils craignent que cela ne blesse à Genève même. Nous ne sommes pas, ou ne devons pas être les champions des prêtres mais quand les choses se traitent avec passion, et que l'on agit par esprit de parti, on prend occasion de tout pour clabauder. S'il était possible de changer cela, je crois que vous feriez bien de faire un carton. On empêcherait que le livre ne se publiât ici, jusqu'à l'arrivée du carton."[122] The final sentence confirms one's previous impression that the Letter to Beaumont did not go on sale until April,[123] for Moultou's counsel dates from March 30 and indicates that there was still time to delay publication. The passage from Moultou shows also that Voltaire was far from being alone in considering extreme this attack upon the priesthood. In spite of his own numerous excoriations of the representatives of the Church, on at least two occasions elsewhere he did express his esteem for an upright, non-persecuting priesthood more concerned with inculcating virtue than with maintaining a creed."[124] Even though these passages might be regarded as representing what Voltaire thought ought to be rather than what actually existed, his marginal comment indicates clearly that he believed Rousseau's attack both unjust and in bad taste. Probably also he found an additional reason to oppose it in its very excessive character, which would tend to decrease the effectiveness of the *Lettre à Beaumont* taken as a whole. For there is no doubt from what we have seen that Voltaire would have liked to see effective many parts of Rousseau's reply to the Archbishop. "Oh! si quelqu'un pouvait rendre aux hommes le service de leur montrer les mêmes vérités, dépouillées de tout ce qui les défigure et les avilit chez cet écrivain, que je le bénirais!"[125] was his comment to Helvétius.

[121] Cf. above, p. 130.
[122] Rousseau, *Corr.*, IX, 205.
[123] Cf. above, p. 131.
[124] Moland, XVIII, 379; XX, 273.
[125] *Ibid.*, XLII, 447. Cited above, pp. 131-32.

In all, Voltaire made on the *Lettre à M. de Beaumont* one hundred and seven marginal comments. In spite of the fact that Rousseau's reply to the Archbishop is only 131 pages long in the original edition and only 59 pages long in the modern closely printed Hachette edition, this number of comments is over one third greater than those on *Emile*, which has the next largest number. Thus Voltaire almost averaged a comment upon every page. Hostile as so many of these comments were, their frequency is evidence of great interest. Voltaire could not neglect Rousseau. He had to reckon with him and he had to express his own attitude.

The large number of notes dealing with personalities shows that by this time the feud between Voltaire and Jean-Jacques had grown still more bitter. The frequent use of *tu* or *toy* emphasizes Voltaire's familiarity and contempt. Nevertheless, if such personalities are more picturesque than honorable to their author, he still does not withhold his approbation when he thinks it deserved. When Rousseau attacks the doctrine of original sin, Voltaire writes in the margin: "bon cela"[126] or again: "hardy et bon."[127] When Jean-Jacques praises Henri IV as the best king France has had and the only one not brought up by priests, the author of the *Henriade* writes enthusiastically in the margin: "excellente idée."[128] Likewise when Rousseau says that one must have acquired some philosophy in order to attain to a true conception of God, Voltaire comments in approval: "icy tu argumentes bien."[129] The author of *Emile* says that the idea of creation out of nothing is one of the least intelligible to the human mind and Voltaire agrees: "je suis de ton avis."[130] Other similar examples could be mentioned. Although in this work also there are a large number of cases where Voltaire shows himself critical or hostile or even unfair, there are at the same time more cases than formerly where he finds himself in entire agreement with Rousseau and frankly admits it. This seeming paradox is doubtless due to the accord brought about in many instances by their mutual opposition to the archbishop and his doctrines.

Among the important instances where Voltaire disagrees with

[126] See above, p. 146.
[127] See above, p. 147.
[128] See above, p. 151.
[129] See above, p. 155.
[130] See above, p. 158.

Rousseau must be counted those in which he takes his adversary to task on account of still claiming for himself the name of Christian. Rousseau says: "l'essentiel de la Religion consiste en pratique."[131] Voltaire comments: "c'est être juste et non crétien." When Jean-Jacques admits that he does not consider divine revelation has been proved, the master of Ferney notes in the margin: "tu ne crois pas la révélation, et tu te dis crétien."[132] Rousseau attacks the Old Testament Jews for their destruction of the natives of Canaan and criticizes the Christians for their wars of religion. Voltaire comments: "tu rends les juifs et les crétiens abominables; ose donc n'être pas crétien."[133] In religion Voltaire would break completely with the past, would abandon the very name of Christian as too indissolubly bound up with a system of which he thoroughly disapproves, and would limit himself strictly to natural religion or simple deism. Rousseau with a Protestant's individualism felt justified in keeping the old name while reïnterpreting it according to his own ideas. While Voltaire's attitude is more clear-cut and logical, Rousseau's is probably nearer to the method by which human ideas and institutions generally evolve. *Natura non facit saltus.* So monarchy, democracy, liberty, and other general terms remain, while acquiring in each age a somewhat different meaning in actual practice. Thus progress becomes possible, while breaking less painfully, and perhaps less dangerously, with the traditions of the past.

[131] See above, p. 162.
[132] See above, p. 163.
[133] See above, p. 169.

CONCLUSION

There was a time when *Dialogues des morts* were in fashion. So, like Lucian, Fontenelle and a little later Fénelon brought together the illustrious dead and endeavored to make them speak in character. Some such dialogue we have just witnessed between Rousseau and Voltaire. It has been, however, a real, and not a fictitious dialogue and much more extensive than the *jeux d'esprit* of an author's imagination. Its chief limitation is that Rousseau was given no opportunity for rebuttal. No doubt he would often have had effective parries for Voltaire's thrusts. The author of the *Lettre sur la Providence*, the *rude jouteur* who replied to M. de Beaumont, the writer of the *Lettres de la montagne*, was no mean antagonist in debate. If Rousseau could have replied, Voltaire would have had a more difficult rôle than that which he actually played here, scribbling his marginal notes in the privacy of his study or propped up at his ease in bed.[1]

In this dispute, we have tried, modestly, to be the arbiter between these two illustrious antagonists, to score the hits and the misses, to weigh justly and without bias the pros and cons of opinion. From the vantage point of the twentieth century, any of us may perceive some things hidden from the greatest of the eighteenth. Yet it is perhaps more surprising, except to those who realize the slow march of ideas, to see how many of the important questions raised by Voltaire and Rousseau still press urgently upon us for their final solution. Many of the questions discussed are burning issues of the present day. It is this which gives the greatest interest to their debate.

As early as 1755, before the open break in their personal relations,[2] Voltaire, as the notes on the *Discours sur l'inégalité* clearly show, was already strongly hostile to the essentials of Rousseau's po-

---

[1] Cf. Dom Chaudon, *Historical and Critical Memoirs of the Life and Writings of M. de Voltaire*, from the French, London, 1786, p. 271.

[2] Voltaire's witty letter of acknowledgment of the *Discours* in 1755, though ironical, was still courteous in form, and from the general tone of Rousseau's *Lettre sur la Providence* of the following year he evidently so considered it. In Voltaire's brief letter of Sept. 12, 1756, the latter even half-apologized for his "mauvaises plaisanteries." Moland, XXXIX, 109.

sition on primitivism.[3] From the first to the last of his marginal comments, their author frequently took his adversary to task with an impulsiveness and even violence characteristic of his temperament. It is often highly diverting to follow the play of his picturesque invective. The notes on the *Lettre à M. de Beaumont* in particular offer a fascinating evocation of this aspect of Voltaire, while at the same time illuminating his thought. Almost they seem to bring before us in the flesh the philosopher of Ferney. Yet he could be mild at times, even in disagreement. He could register frank accord, or occasionally outspoken praise. Unfair often, sometimes illogical or unscientific in his prejudice, bitterly personal in many instances, Voltaire's criticisms of detail tend to ignore the general spirit of Rousseau's discussion. Moreover, it is natural in making marginal comments to note readily points of disagreement and to pass over in silence many things to which no exception is taken. In any event, it is obvious that no one should consider this exposition of Voltaire's notes and the passages to which they refer as doing full justice to Rousseau's ideas. More even than most authors the latter must suffer from taking isolated passages from his text and giving them thereby inevitably a disproportionate emphasis. Frequently, however, as we have seen, Rousseau appears obscure, over-theoretical, or involved in his wording, justifying many of Voltaire's criticisms. It should now be possible to admire what is admirable in the work of both, to evaluate their ideas, without prolonging a century and a half later their quarrels.

Agreed in their opposition to slavery, conquest, despotism, war, intolerance (except for Rousseau's unfortunate "civic dogmas"), hostile to the doctrine of original sin, and in general to most of the creed and orthodox theology of the church, the two differ sharply on primitivism, the social effects of wealth, and particularly on the emotional and mystical side of religion. The details of their contrasting attitudes have been given in the concluding summaries at the end of each chapter.

Opposed to each other in so many respects during their lifetime, Voltaire and Rousseau have been now in curious fashion inseparably united after their death. On the pages of the same volumes in the

---

[3] The date of composition of *Timon* (Moland, XXIII, 483-84), published in 1756, remains uncertain. It expresses similar satire of Rousseau's primitivism.

CONCLUSION

Leningrad library, their ideas repose together. By a strange turn of fate these volumes are to be found in Russia, where Voltaire's attacks on the church and Rousseau's war upon private property find their most potent and thorough-going expression thus far in history. How much each may have contributed to this modern evolution it is impossible to say with accuracy. Through many intermediaries, in Russia and out, these two men have influenced modern tendencies. Yet neither would wholly have approved of what is now going on in the cities and villages of the Soviet Union. Neither would have completely sanctioned the French Revolution which, so much nearer their own time, they helped to set in motion. As one reads tranquilly before a table in the library at Leningrad, from outside comes something of the noise and bustle of the busy life in the streets below, toiling, struggling, to build a civilization on a new basis, untried on such a scale before. Little they know, these hurrying people, of Voltaire and Rousseau, yet some of the most characteristic ideas of these great Frenchmen are here in Russia affecting profoundly the whole course of daily life. One wonders what Catherine the Great would think now. Would she again have ordered Grimm to purchase for her the Voltaire library? Would she again have engaged Wagnière to arrange on her bookshelves this literary dynamite which, after helping tear down the ancient order in France, has contributed to the even more complete uprooting of the old Russia for which she stood? In any case, the Voltaire library with its interesting marginalia has been preserved. Its contents are not matter for academic discussion alone. We may now witness something of the powerful impact of eighteenth-century ideas upon these very days in which we live.

APPENDIX

Other Volumes in the Voltaire Library by, or about, Rousseau

J.-J. Rousseau, Citoyen de Genève, à M^r. D'Alembert, sur son Article Genève dans le VIIme Vol. de L'Encyclopédie et particulièrement sur le projet d'établir un Théâtre de Comédie en cette Ville. A Amsterdam, chez Marc Michel Rey, 1758. (Call-number 5-115.)

P. 7, footnote, end of page; Hachette, I, 184, n: "Tout homme, de quelque Religion qu'il soit, qui dit croire à de pareils misteres, en impose donc, ou ne sait ce qu'il dit." (Red cross mark in the margin.)

P. 11; H. 186: "Je ne vois naître qu'avec effroi toute occasion pour eux de se rabaisser jusqu'à n'être plus que des Gens d'Eglise." (Cross mark.)

P. 12, note; H. 186, n. 2: "De deux célèbres Historiens, tous deux Philosophes, tous deux chers à M. d'Alembert," . . . (Cross mark.)

P. 15; H. 187: "La nature même a dicté la réponse de ce Barbare à qui l'on vantoit les magnificences du Cirque & des Jeux établis à Rome." (Cross mark.)

P. 18; H. 189: "Il n'y a que la raison qui ne soit bonne à rien sur la Scène." (Cross mark.)

P. 21; H. 190: "C'est, tout au-contraire, que cette Pièce favorise leur tour d'esprit, qui est d'aimer & rechercher les idées neuves & singulières. Or il n'y en a point de plus neuves pour eux que celles de la nature." (Cross mark.)

P. 48; H. 199: "Non . . . je le soutiens, & j'en atteste l'effroi des Lecteurs, les massacres des gladiateurs n'étoient pas si [barbares]" . . . (Cross mark.)

P. 57; H. 202: "Les uns, parce qu'ils sont méchans.
 Et les autres, pour être aux méchans complaisans."
(Cross mark.)

P. 72; H. 207: "On a peine à quitter cette admirable Pièce, quand on a commencé de s'en occuper." (Cross mark.)

P. 77; H. 209: "Il peut y avoir dans le monde quelques femmes dignes d'être écoutées d'un honnete-homme." (Cross mark.)

P. 78; H. 209: "C'est ainsi que, sur la foi d'un modele imaginaire, sur un air modeste & touchant, sur une douceur contrefaite." (Cross mark.)

P. 80; H. 210: "Chés nous, au-contraire, la femme la plus estimée est celle qui fait le plus de bruit; de qui l'on parle le plus." (Cross mark.)

P. 91; H. 213: "Qu'après avoir mieux consulté son cœur, Titus ne voulant ni enfreindre les loix de Rome, ni vendre le bonheur à l'ambition, vienne, avec des maximes opposées, . . ." (Cross mark.)

P. 98; H. 216: "Ceux de mes compatriotes qui ne désapprouvent pas les spectacles en eux-mêmes ont donc tort.   Outre ces effets du Théâtre, relatifs aux choses représentées, . . ."
(Cross mark.)

P. 102; H. 217: "Les habitans [à Paris], plongés dans une stupide inaction n'y font que végéter, ou tracasser & se brouiller ensemble." (Cross mark.)

P. 103; H. 218: "& peu sensible aux louanges, s'il se connoît, il ne s'assigne point sa place & jouit de lui-même sans s'apprécier." (Two cross marks.)

P. 104; H. 218: "Ces maisons, à distances aussi égales que les fortunes des propriétaires, offrent à la fois aux nombreux habitans de cette montagne le recueillement de la retraite & les douceurs de la société." (Cross mark.)

P. 119; H. 223: "Premièrement, que la force n'ayant aucun pouvoir sur les esprits, il falloit écarter avec le plus grand soin tout vestige de violence . . ." (Cross mark.)

P. 126, n; H. 225, n: "Les Militaires ne se battent plus que pour passe-droits, ou pour n'être pas forcés de quitter le service." (Cross mark.)

P. 129; H. 226: "Que le Tribunal n'eût point statué sur des bagatelles, mais qu'il n'eût jamais rien fait à demi; que le Roi même y eût été cité, quand il jetta sa canne par la fenêtre, 'de peur, dit-il, de frapper un gentilhomme!'" (Cross mark.)

The upper corner of this page is turned down. Except for the marking over in ink of the 2 of p. 208, there is no further indication of this volume's having been used. Perhaps this edition was not read with care beyond p. 129, which is about half way through the *Lettre à D'Alembert*.

Lettres sur la Nouvelle Héloïse ou Aloïsia de J.-J. Rousseau, 1761. Lettres à Monsieur de Voltaire. (Contained in: *Recueil de diverses pièces*, 5-122.)

Pp. 20-21. Troisième Lettre. A blank marker. P. 20 begins: "Il est étrange, Monsieur, que Jean-Jacques ne sache pas que personne ne mange de pain bis à Paris, . . ." P. 21 ends: "étant devenu si à la mode parmi nous, & nous faisant l'honneur d'être . . ." (Cf. Moland, XXIV, 175-76.)

La Nouvelle Héloïse Dévoilée. A Bruxelles et se trouve à Paris chez Antoine Boudet, Imprimeur du Roi, rue Saint Jacques. 1775. (Contained in: *Pot-pourri*, 11-137.) (No markers, notes, nor marginalia.)

Le Vicaire Savoyard, Tiré du Livre Intitulé *Emile*, de J.-J. Rousseau. (Contained in: *Pot-pourri*, 11-121.)

Pp. 10-11, 14-15, uncut.

Ibid. (Contained in: *Pot-pourri*, 11-134.) No markers, notes, nor marginalia.

APPENDIX 193

Jean-Jacques Rousseau, citoyen de Genève, à Christophe de Beaumont. A Amsterdam, chez Marc Michel Rey, 1763 (*Œuvres de J. J. Rousseau,* Tome 3, Seconde Partie) (Contained in: *Recueil de diverses pièces,* 5-122.)

P. 59; H. III, 83: "Bien différent, je l'avoue, de vos Chrétiens en effigie, toujours prêts à croire ce qu'il faut croire, ou à dire ce qu'il faut dire pour leur intérêt ou pour leur repos, . . ." This passage is marked in the margin with a horizontal line opposite the first words. There is also a blank marker between the pages. See above, Chapter V, p. 162 of this study for another indication of Voltaire's interest in this particular passage.

Pp. 62-63: Blank marker. P. 62 begins: "avoir une, s'accordent au moins s'ils peuvent entre eux. Les uns ne trouvent dans mes Livres qu'un Sistême d'athéisme," (Hachette, III, 84). P. 63 ends: "j'aurois ôté tout d'un coup à ses Ministres le moyen de me harceller." (Hachette, III, 85.) In his other copy of this work, Voltaire commented upon two passages falling within these pages. See above, pp. 163-64.

Pp. 64-65: Blank marker. P. 64 begins: "sans cesse, & de me faire endurer toutes leurs petites tirannies;" (Hachette, III, 85.) P. 65 ends: "& qui n'ait dit que ce qu'il a cru: ils pourront un moment souiller" (Hachette, III, 86.) Two passages on these pages drew Voltaire's comments elsewhere. See above, pp. 164-65.

Pp. 112-13: Blank marker. P. 112 begins: "preuve négative qui vous fait dire on croiroit, au lieu d'on croit." (Hachette, III, 106.) P. 113 ends: "si frappans, si parfaitement inimitables, que l'inventeur en se-[roit]" . . . (Hachette, III, 107.) While nothing has been marked here, or in the other edition, there is evidently much that might interest Voltaire in these pages where the debate between Rousseau and the Archbishop presents attack and riposte in increasingly rapid succession.

Pp. 120-21: Blank marker. P. 120 begins: "mien. Là-dessus vous me taxez d'une insigne mauvaise foi," (Hachette, III, 109.) P. 121 ends: "mais pour ne pas rester muet" . . . (Hachette, III, 110.) In his other copy, Voltaire commented interestingly on a passage on p. 121. See above, p. 181.

Pp. 126-27: Blank marker. P. 126 begins: "& le sort de l'Auteur en seroit un autre encore plus frappant." (Hachette, III, 112.) P. 127 ends: "Charité chrétienne, que vous avez" . . . (Hachette, III, 113.) Two passages on these pages drew Voltaire's comments in his other copy of Rousseau's Letter. See above, p. 182.

Dialogues de Village: Lettre à Monsieur^{xxx} Rélative à J. J. Rousseau, avec la Réfutation de ce Libelle, Par le Professeur de Montmollin, 1765. (Contained in the same volume as the preceding *Lettre à Beaumont,* 5-122.)

Pp. 32-33: Tiny blank marker. P. 32 begins: "comunié de la façon de M. de V^{xxx} m'amusera fort aussi." P. 33 ends: "porté garant que l'excommunication seroit prononcée contre M. Rousseau, aussi, l'oficier du"...

(Same Volume: *Réfutation du Libelle Précédent, par M. le Professeur de Montmollin.*)

Pp. 90-91: Blank marker. P. 90 begins: "ocasion il a exalté la Religion naturelle, come étant le fondement de la révélée,"... P. 91 ends: "Que loin de jetter"...

Pp. 148-49: Blank marker. P. 148 begins: "Septieme Lettre." P. 149 ends: "S'il ne le fait pas, quelle"...

(Same Volume: *Information présentée au Public par le Professeur de Montmollin.* 1765.)

Seconde Lettre relative à M. J. J. Rousseau adressée à Mylord Comte de Wemyss. 1765. (In same volume as the preceding.)

Pp. 20-21: Blank marker. P. 20 begins: "[châte-]lain repartit, que le Diacre avoit très prudemment"... P. 21 ends: "& que l'Arrêt de premier Avril ne lioit les mains à son égard qu'au seul Con-[sistoire]"...

Pieces Justificatives Transcrites sur les originaux. (In same volume as the preceding.)

Pp. 118-199: Badly torn marker. On it is written: "comme quoi Jean j. fondait en larmes à la communion." P. 118 begins: "je vous l'avoue, fut un des plus doux de ma vie." P. 119 ends: "je l'ai toujours trouvé si soigneux d'éviter toute discussion sur la doc-[trine,]"... Voltaire's comment on the marker is ironical, as might be expected in this connection.

Pp. 194-95: Blank marker. P. 194 begins: "autorité est toute subordonnée à celle de la Seigneurie." P. 195 ends: "mais j'ignorois qu'elle convînt à un Pasteur, à un"....

Troisieme Lettre relative à M. J. J. Rousseau, du 19 Septembre, servant de postscriptum à celle du 31 août, 1765. (At the end of the same volume.)

Lettre de J. J. Rousseau de Genève, qui contient sa renonciation à la Société Civile, & ses derniers adieux aux Hommes, adressée au seul Ami qui lui reste dans le monde. (Contained in *Pot-pourri,* 1-200.)

Pp. 8-9: Blank marker. P. 8 begins: "c'est ouvrir 1 boete de Pandore sur vos têtes,"... P. 9 ends: "pour un moment, que ces Décrets émanés d'une force illicite"...

Lettres écrites de la Campagne. (In the same volume.) (Letters 1, 2, 3, 5 appear here, Letter 4 is missing.) At the top of the title-page Voltaire has written: "lettres sur les petites tracasseries de Geneve 1763."

P. 3. "mais la chose jugée est, & doit être regardée comme la vérité même, parce qu'il faut que les affaires finissent, que pour les faire finir, il faut une autorité qui prononce en dernier ressort;"   VOLTAIRE et les calas!

APPENDIX

Deep in his struggle to rehabilitate the Calas, Voltaire feels too sceptical about courts of justice to accord them infallibility, or to be willing to accept their mistakes with equanimity. In this case, Voltaire's comment is directed against Rousseau's adversary, J.-B. Tronchin, the author of the *Lettres écrites de la campagne,* 1763.

Lettres écrites de la Montagne. Par J. J. Rousseau. Première Partie. A Amsterdam, chez Marc Michel Rey, 1764. (Contained in *Pot-pourri*, 11-132.)

Pp. 16-17: Marker. P. 16 begins: "Livre pernicieux. Des principes établis, la chaîne d'un raisonnement suivi, des conséquences deduites manifestent l'intention de l'Auteur," . . . (Hachette, III, 122.) P. 17 ends: "Mais pour le flétrir, pour" . . . (Hachette, III, 122.)

Pp. 60-61: Marker. P. 60 begins: "Livre scandaleux, téméraire, impie, dont la morale est d'enrichir le riche & de dépouiller le pauvre," . . . (Hachette, III, 133.) P. 61 ends: "verra que c'est ainsi que tous m'ont traité." (Hachette, III, 134.)

Pp. 78-79: Marker. P. 78 begins: "[ils se se-]roient tous unis avec moi qui n'attaquois que leurs adversaires." (Hachette, III, 138.) P. 79 ends: "alors par de telles décisions ces assemblées." . . . (Hachette, III, 139.)

Pp. 136-137: Marker. On it is written: "rousseau fait des miracles à Venise." This evidently refers to the footnote k on p. 136: "J'ai vu a Venise en 1743 une manière de sorts assez nouvelle. . . . Le magicien qui faisoit ces sorts . . . s'appeloit J. J. Rousseau." (Hachette, III, 154, n. 1.)

Pp. 290-91: Marker. P. 290 begins: "Puissances pour autoriser le mal qu'elles ignorent . . ." (Hachette, III, 194-95.) P. 291 ends: "Eh! plût-à-Dieu que je n'en eusse pas plus à Genève." (Hachette, III, 195.)

Pp. 296-97: Marker. P. 296 begins: "que [sic] un mépris révoltant pour ce qu'ils respectent & par conséquent pour eux." (Hachette, III, 196.) P. 297 ends: "n'y a-t-il que des plaisanteries dans ces Livres-là? Moi-même, . . ." (Hachette, III, 197.) This passage contains an interesting reference to Voltaire.

Seconde Partie.

Pp. 76-77: Marker. P. 76 begins: "dépouiller les Citoyens & Bourgeois de leurs droits." (Hachette, III, 227.) P. 77 ends: "Je ne connois de volonté vraiment . . ." (Hachette, III, 227.)

The markers, except the one containing the comment in connection with p. 136, are scraps of printed paper taken from an article: "Mémoires de [ ]bbé de Montg [ ]."

Pot-pourri (9-44) (No marginalia nor notes.)

1. *Exposé Succinct de la Contestation qui s'est élevée entre M. Hume et M. Rousseau, avec les Pieces Justificatives.* A Londres, 1766.

2. *Examen de Deux Ouvrages, Intitulés Emile & le Contrat Social, qu'on attribuë à M^r. Rousseau.*

3. *Notes sur la Lettre de Monsieur de Voltaire à Monsieur Hume par Mr L....*

Œuvres de J. J. Rousseau de Genève. Nouv. Ed. Tome I. A Amsterdam chez Marc-Michel Rey, 1769. *Discours qui a remporté le prix à l'Académie de Dijon, en l'Année* 1750. (5-106)

Ibid., Tome II, 1769. *Discours sur l'Origine et les Fondemens de l'Inégalité parmi les Hommes.* (5-106)

Ibid., Tome III, 1769. *J. J. Rousseau à M^r D'Alembert sur son Article Genève et Particuliérement sur le Projet d'établir un Théâtre de Comedie.* Quatrieme Edition, A Amsterdam, chez Marc Michel Rey, 1769. (5-106).

Ibid., Tome IV. *Julie ou la Nouvelle Heloïse,* Par J. J. Rousseau, Tome Premier. Pp. 382-83 uncut. (5-106)

Ibid., Tome VII. *Julie ou la Nouvelle Heloïse,* ... Tome III. Pp. 142-43, 206-07, 302-03, 352-53, 366-67, uncut. (5-106)

Ibid., Tome VIII. *Emile, ou de l'Education,* par Jean Jaques Rousseau, Citoyen de Genève, Tome III. A Amsterdam, chez Jean Néaulme, Libraire, 1762. (5-106)

Ibid., Tome IX. *Jean Jaques Rousseau, Citoyen de Genève, à Christophe de Beaumont.* A Amsterdam, chez Marc Michel Rey, 1769. *Lettres écrites de la Montagne,* par J. J. Rousseau, en Deux Parties. A Amsterdam, chez Marc Michel Rey, 1764. Pp. 78-79, 94-95, 110-11, 126-27, 142-43, uncut. (5-106)

From this set of Rousseau's Works, Vols. V and VI (part of *La Nouvelle Héloïse*) are missing, though the catalogue lists nine volumes. The books offer no evidence of having been used by Voltaire. Some pages are still uncut. There are no comments. The pages appear whiter than those of used books. Voltaire read and annotated earlier editions.

BIBLIOGRAPHY

Ascoli. See Voltaire.

Bayle, Pierre, *Dictionnaire historique et critique*, Rotterdam, 1697. 4 vols. fol.

The Bible, King James version.

Bouvier, Bernard, "Notes inédites sur la 'Profession de foi du Vicaire sayoyard,'" *Annales de la Société Jean-Jacques Rousseau*, I (1905), pp. 272-84.

Chaudon, Dom, *Historical and Critical Memoirs of the Life and Writings of M. de Voltaire*, from the French. London, 1786.

Diderot, Denis, *Œuvres*, Assézat-Tourneux edition. Paris, Garnier, 1875-77. 20 vols.

Ducros, Louis, J.-J. *Rousseau: de Genève à l'Hermitage (1712-1757)*. Paris, 1908. (Referred to for convenience as Vol. I.)

..............., *J.-J. Rousseau: de Montmorency au Val de Travers (1757-1765)*. Paris, 1917. (Referred to as Vol. II.)

..............., *J.-J. Rousseau: de l'Ile de Saint-Pierre à Ermenonville (1765-1778)*. Paris, 1918. (Referred to as Vol. III.)

Dufour, Théophile, *Recherches bibliographiques sur Jean-Jacques Rousseau*. Paris, 1925. 2 vols.

Encyclopædia Britannica, 11th edition, New York, 1911.

Grimm, Diderot, etc., *Correspondance littéraire*, ed. by Maurice Tourneux. Paris, Garnier, 1877-82. 16 vols.

Havens, George R., "La théorie de la bonté naturelle de l'homme chez J.-J. Rousseau," *Revue d'Histoire littéraire de la France*, XXXI (1924), pp. 629-42; XXXII (1925), pp. 34-37, 212-25.

..............., "The Nature Doctrine of Voltaire, "*Publications of the Modern Language Association of America*, XL (Dec. 1925), pp. 852-62.

.... and Norman L. Torrey, "The Private Library of Voltaire at Leningrad," *ibid.*, XLIII (Dec., 1928), pp. 990-1009.

.... and Norman L. Torrey, "Voltaire's Books: A Selected List," *Modern Philology*, XXVII (August, 1929), pp. 1-22.

.... and Norman L. Torrey, "Voltaire's Library," *The Fortnightly Review*, Sept. 2, 1929, pp. 397-405.

..............., "Rousseau's Doctrine of Goodness according to Nature," *Publications of the Modern Language Association of America*, XLIV (Dec., 1929), pp. 1239-45.

..............., "A Corrected Reading of One of Voltaire's Notes on Rousseau's *Emile*," *Modern Language Notes*, XLVII (Jan., 1932), pp. 20-21.

..................., "Voltaire's Note on *Emile* Once More," *Ibid.*, (May, 1932), p. 325.
..................., "Voltaire's Marginal Comments on Rousseau," *The South Atlantic Quarterly*, Duke University Press, XXXI (Oct., 1932), pp. 408-16.
..................., Voltaire, *Candide*, edited with Introduction, Notes, and Vocabulary. New York, Holt. (To appear in 1933 or 1934.)
Isham, Ralph H., *The Private Papers of James Boswell*, Vol. IV, New York, 1929.
Jusserand, J. J., *Shakespeare en France sous l'ancien régime*. Paris, 1898.
Lanson, Gustave, *Histoire de la littérature française*, 12th ed., Paris, 1912.
.... See Voltaire.
Le Goff, Marcel, *Anatole France à La Béchellerie*. Paris, 1924.
Littré, E., *Dictionnaire de la langue française*. Paris, 1881-82. 5 vols. fol.
Longchamp and Wagnière, *Mémoires sur Voltaire et sur ses ouvrages*. Paris, 1826. 2 vols.
Masson. See Rousseau.
Maugras. See Perey.
Montesquieu, *Œuvres complètes*, Laboulaye ed. Paris, Garnier, 1875-79. 7 vols.
Morize. See Voltaire.
Mornet, Daniel, *Les Sciences de la nature en France, au XVIIIe siècle*. Paris, 1911.
..................., "Les Imitations du 'Candide' de Voltaire," *Mélanges Lanson*. Paris, 1922, pp. 298-303.
..................., *La pensée française au XVIIIe siècle*, 2nd ed. Paris, 1929.
Perey, Lucien, and Gaston Maugras, *La Vie intime de Voltaire aux Délices et à Ferney*. Paris, 1885.
Prévost, Abbé, *Le Pour et Contre*, 1733-40. 20 vols.
Rousseau, Jean-Jacques, *Discours sur l'origine et les fondemens de l'inégalité parmi les hommes*. Amsterdam, Rey, 1755.
..................., *Extrait du Projet de Paix perpétuelle de M. l'abbé de Saint-Pierre*. [Paris], 1761.
..................., *Du Contrat social, ou Principes du droit politique*. Amsterdam, Rey, 1762.
..................., *Emile, ou de l'éducation*. Néaulme, Amsterdam [Duchesne, Paris], 1762. 4 vols.
..................., *La "Profession de foi du Vicaire savoyard,"* édition critique par Pierre-Maurice Masson. Paris, 1914.
..................., *A Christophe de Beaumont*. *Œuvres*, tome III, 2e Partie.

Amsterdam, Marc-Michel Rey, 1763. 134 pp. (followed by 45 pp., *Mandement*, Paris, 1762.)

―――――――, *Correspondance générale*, éd. par Théophile Dufour et Pierre-Paul Plan. Paris, Colin. 1924 ff. 18 vols. thus far published.

―――――――, *Œuvres complètes*, Hachette ed., 1885-1905. 13 vols.

Sedaine, *Le Philosophe sans le savoir*, Critical Edition by T. E. Oliver, University of Illinois Press, 1913.

Steel, Richard, *The Conscious Lovers*. (In *The Complete Plays of Richard Steele*, ed. by G. A. Aitken, London and New York, 1899.)

Torrey. See Havens.

Tresnon, Jeannette, "The Paradox of Rousseau," *Publications of the Modern Language Association of America*, XLIII (Dec., 1928), pp. 1010-25.

Voltaire, *Candide*, édition critique par André Morize. Paris, 1913 and 1931.

―――――――, *Lettres philosophiques*, édition critique par Gustave Lanson. 2nd ed., Paris, 1915-17. 2 vols.

―――――――, *Zadig*, édition critique par Georges Ascoli. Paris, 1929. 2 vols.

―――――――, *Œuvres complètes*, Moland ed. Paris, Garnier, 1877-85. 52 vols.

Wagnière. See Longchamp.

Wright, Ernest Hunter, *The Meaning of Rousseau*. Oxford University Press, London, 1929.